0 kilometers   400

0 miles   400

FLORENCE, AREZZO AND CASENTINO

CHIANTI AND SIENA

MONTALCINO AND THE SIENESE CRETE

MAREMMA AND MONTE AMIATA

GROSSETO

SIENA

AREZZO

FLORENCE

PRATO

See pages 20–47

FLORENCE, AREZZO AND CASENTINO

See pages 96–123

CHIANTI AND SIENA

See pages 124–151

MONTALCINO AND THE SIENESE CRETE

A TASTE OF TUSCANY

A Taste of
Tuscany

edited by
Guido Stecchi

DORLING KINDERSLEY
LONDON • NEW YORK • MUNICH
MELBOURNE • DELHI
www.dk.com

◁ **A Tuscan farmhouse in the countryside near Pienza**

A DORLING KINDERSLEY BOOK

www.dk.com

Produced by Fabio Ratti
Editoria Libraria e Multimediale
Milan, Italy

TEXT Guido Stecchi, Maria Cristina Beretta, Marco Scapagnini
EDITORS Diana Georgiacodis, Laura Recordati,
Federica Romagnoli
DESIGNERS Massimo Costa, Carlotta Maderna
MAPS AND ILLUSTRATIONS Massimo Costa, Carlotta Maderna,
Alberto Ipsilanti, Daniela Veluti, Oriana Bianchetti,
Roberto Capra

Dorling Kindersley Ltd
EDITORS Felicity Jackson, Fiona Wild
PROOFREADER Stewart Wild DTP DESIGNER Jason Little
PRODUCTION Marie Ingledew
SENIOR PUBLISHING MANAGER Louise Bostock Lang

ENGLISH TRANSLATION Richard Sadleir

Reproduced by Colourscan, Singapore
Printed and bound in Italy by Graphicom

First published in Italy in 2000 by Arnoldo Mondadori Editore
S.p.A., Milan and Fabio Ratti Editoria S.r.l., Milan as Guida
Gourmet Toscana

First published in Great Britain in 2001 by
Dorling Kindersley Ltd,
80 Strand, London WC2R 0RL

A CIP CATALOGUE RECORD IS AVAILABLE FROM THE BRITISH LIBRARY

ISBN 0 7513 3542 8

The photographs and information in this book are intended to
help the reader select produce, particularly mushrooms, in a
market, and are not intended as a guide to picking wild produce.
If you are in any doubt about the edibility of any species,
do not cook or eat it.

**The information in every
DK Eyewitness Guide is checked annually**.
Every effort has been made to ensure that this book is as
up-to-date as possible at the time of going to press. Some
details, however, such as telephone numbers, opening hours,
prices and travel information are liable to change. The publishers
cannot accept responsibility for any consequences arising from
the use of this book, nor for any material on third party websites,
and cannot guarantee that any website address in this book will
be a suitable source of travel information.
We value the views and suggestions of our readers very highly.
Please write to: Senior Publishing Manager, DK Travel Guides,
Dorling Kindersley, 80 Strand, London WC2R 0RL.

CONTENTS

HOW TO USE THIS GUIDE 6

TUSCANY
THROUGHOUT THE YEAR 8

WINES 10

OLIVE GROWING
IN TUSCANY 12

FISH AND SEAFOOD 14

PORCINI MUSHROOMS 16

TRUFFLES 18

FLORENCE, AREZZO
AND CASENTINO
20

WINES 24

SALUMI 27

EXTRA VIRGIN OLIVE OIL 30

CHIANINA BEEF 32

TRADITIONAL PRODUCE 34

WILD PRODUCE 36

PLACES OF INTEREST 38

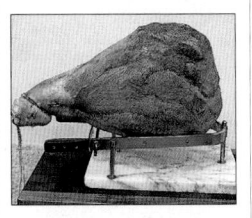

LUNIGIANA,
GARFAGNANA
AND VERSILIA
48

WINES 52

FISH AND SEAFOOD 54

GAME BIRDS *58*

TRADITIONAL PRODUCE *60*

WILD PRODUCE *64*

PLACES OF INTEREST *66*

PISA AND LIVORNO
74

FISH *78*

WINES *80*

TRADITIONAL PRODUCE *83*

WILD PRODUCE *86*

PLACES OF INTEREST *88*

CHIANTI AND SIENA
96

WINES *100*

CINTA SENESE PORK *104*

SIENESE FRUIT CAKES *106*

TRADITIONAL PRODUCE *108*

WILD PRODUCE *110*

PLACES OF INTEREST *112*

MONTALCINO AND THE SIENESE CRETE
124

WINES OF MONTALCINO *128*

OTHER WINES FROM SOUTH OF SIENA *130*

PECORINO FROM THE SIENESE CRETE *132*

HONEY *134*

TRADITIONAL PRODUCE *136*

WILD PRODUCE *138*

PLACES OF INTEREST *140*

MAREMMA AND MONTE AMIATA
152

WINES *156*

WILD GAME *158*

TRADITIONAL PRODUCE *160*

WILD PRODUCE *162*

PLACES OF INTEREST *164*

TRAVELLERS' NEEDS
170

RESTAURANTS *172*

ACCOMMODATION *192*

PRACTICAL INFORMATION *196*

GENERAL INDEX *202*

PHRASE BOOK *207*

How to Use this Guide

This guide uncovers the best of Tuscany's food and wine for visitors to the region. Tuscany has been divided into six areas or zones (see the map inside the front cover). There is a brief description of places of gastronomic interest: shops, wineries, vineyards and estates, and restaurants with local character. To make it easy for travellers to find them, there is a map and a *Places of Interest* section for each of the areas. There is practical information about the most important *Traditional* *Produce*, such as wine, cheese and *salumi* (cured meats), all clearly illustrated. *Wild Produce* with its descriptions of truffles and mushrooms, herbs and wild fruits will encourage excursions into meadows and woods to search for them (or at least to keep an eye open for them in the markets). The delights of the local cuisine are highlighted in a selection of traditional dishes from each area, and the region's restaurants are assessed for quality, atmosphere, traditional dishes, good service and value for money.

A TASTE OF TUSCANY AREA BY AREA

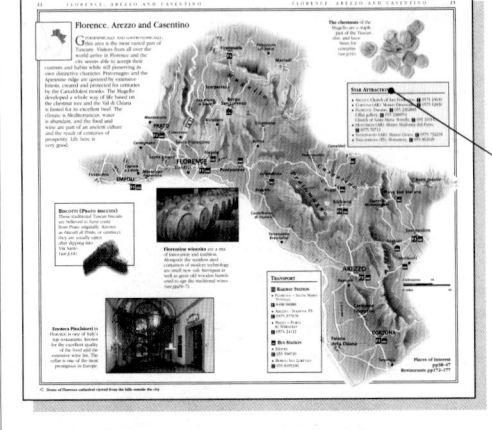

The guide has divided Tuscany into six areas, each of which covers a geographical area based on the local produce and the gastronomic traditions.

The title page *for each area illustrates one of the most important local products.*

Star Attractions *indicates important artistic and cultural sights no visitor should miss.*

The map illustrates the area dealt with in the chapter and illustrates the region's most important produce and places.

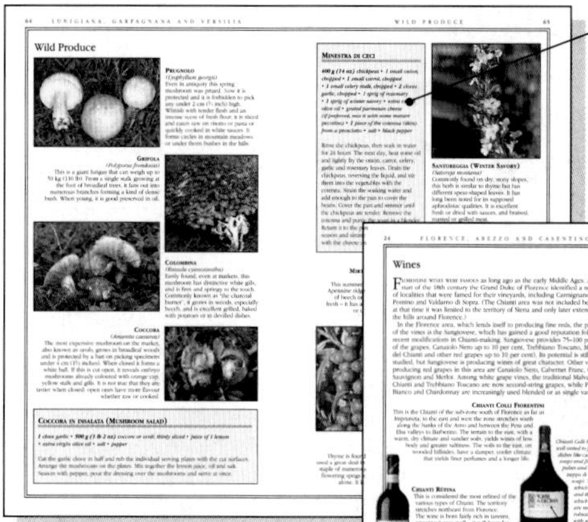

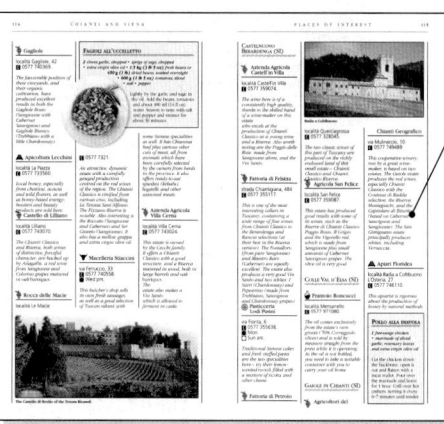

*In the traditional **recipes**, quantities are for six people unless otherwise stated.*

*There are descriptions of **traditional produce**, such as wine, salumi, olive oil and cheese.*

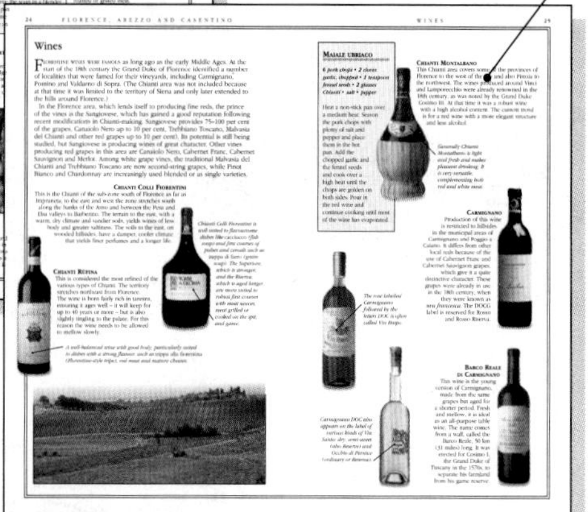

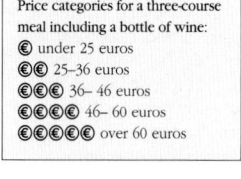

Wild produce traditionally picked by local people in Tuscany includes truffles, mushrooms, herbs and various wild fruits.

Each entry for a place of interest gives the address, phone number, opening and closing days. It is advisable to telephone before calling at a farm, vineyard or agriturismo.

Places of interest are marked with a symbol (see inside back cover for key to symbols) to indicate the kind of produce available and they are listed in alphabetical order by place.

Each restaurant entry gives the address, telephone number and weekly closing day.

Price categories for a three-course meal including a bottle of wine:
€ under 25 euros
€€ 25–36 euros
€€€ 36–46 euros
€€€€ 46–60 euros
€€€€€ over 60 euros

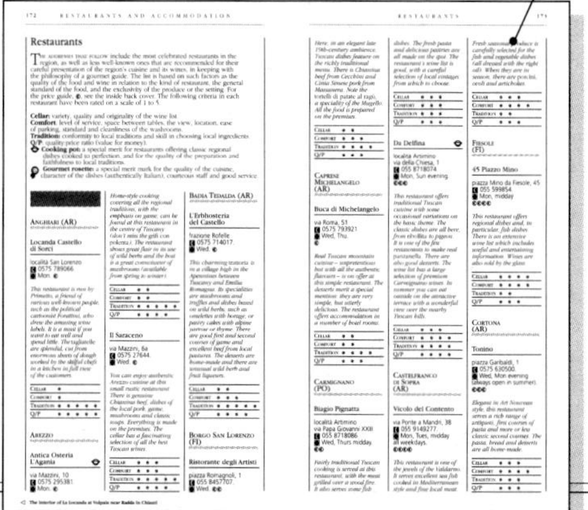

The restaurant entries assess quality, comfort, traditional food, service and value for money.

Tuscany Throughout the Year

SPRING

TUSCAN SPRING can come as early as March, especially along the coast. In the hedgerows and thickets, you can find the young, tender wild shoots known locally as "asparagus", such as butcher's broom or even the sweet young tips of wild hops. Waste ground is studded with borage flowers – one of the most valuable of wild herbs – looking like little blue stars. Coastal pine woods and the inland woods on hills and mountains conceal magnificent morel mushrooms, while richly scented St George's mushrooms form circles round sloe-trees which are sprinkled with white blossom. Specially trained hounds nose out white truffles under the pine woods that stretch along the coast from Cecina to Argentario.

Spring is when Tuscan extra virgin olive oil reaches peak quality, shedding the bitter, pungent taste it has when newly pressed. This is the ideal time to visit the olive groves and presses to buy oil. Northwest Tuscany has some of the finest chocolate confectioners in Italy – Europe even – and spring is the perfect time to sample their wares in the form of chocolate eggs, the traditional Easter gift. Another Tuscan springtime tradition is the Easter lamb or kid: those raised in the Garfagnana or the Casentino are particularly famous. This is also a good time to sample some of the seafood specialities: local mullet and swordfish cooked Livorno-style, cuttlefish in sauce, and grilled eels from Orbetello are tasty in April.

SUMMER

SUMMER IS THE time for wandering through Tuscany's mountain woods or exploring the coast, but this time of year is a mixed blessing for gourmets. In June the coast offers a wealth of wonderful fish, but July and August bring hordes of holiday-makers from the towns and there is not enough fish caught in the local seas to go round. Then there is the breeding period when fishing is banned and only a fortunate few are able to buy from the small boats exempt from the ban. Shellfish are at their finest in the summer, but make sure you buy from reputable sources.

For those who prefer not to risk the seafood, the hinterland compensates with an abundance of flavourful vegetables: taste the *bruschetta* (bread rubbed with garlic, toasted and topped with ripe tomato) or *panzanella* (moist bread seasoned with oil, vinegar and herbs). In June and early July the small artichokes on sale are perfect for preserving in oil. Peaches, yellow in Tuscany, white on Elba, are especially good if bought at orchards where they are allowed to ripen on the tree. Summer brings thyme, oregano and other herbs that colour and scent the dry meadows, while the woods on the Apennine ridges provide juicy bilberries, raspberries and wild strawberries. In the mountains there are mushrooms, but the season is short. Generally, high summer is too dry for them and you have to wait until late September, when they are plentiful.

AUTUMN

FOR GOURMETS this is Tuscany's prime season. At San Miniato, Volterra, the Sienese Crete, around Arezzo and many other small villages, the white truffles are ripening. In the Garfagnana and the Casentino there are very fine porcini (cep mushrooms), while other parts of Tuscany have an abundance of different mushrooms, which sometimes linger until after Christmas. They include numerous varieties that are essential to the peasant dishes of the region – sauces with fresh pasta and thick seasonal soups like *acquacotta* (tomatoes, mushrooms, vegetables, eggs and bread). This is the season for sweet chestnuts, a staple of the cuisine of areas like the Lunigiana, Amiata and the Mugello, and for the renowned wild boar of Maremma, which adorns tables in both homes and restaurants. Game birds are traditional throughout the region, with wood-pigeons a particular favourite.

At Chiusi, and above all Torre del Lago, this is the season for the famed local dish of coot cooked *alla Puccini* and wild duck. Game dishes go well with Brunello and the region's other fine red wines. In the autumn the ban on fishing is lifted and this is the time to eat the young squid and mullet, skilfully prepared by the chefs of Viareggio or San Vincenzo, plus the larger fish passing through local waters at this time, especially the amberjack *(ricciola)*.

WINTER

IN MEDITERRANEAN REGIONS like Tuscany, outdoor life continues through the mild winter months, and both the local cuisine and the natural setting are tempting for the gourmet tourist. Nature is still active: there are lots of evergreen herbs, all kinds of

tasty mushrooms and fruits there for the picking in the woods, hedgerows and meadows. The typical Tuscan meal, with a choice of meats roasted on a spit over the fire, and the rustic cooking found in farmhouses and simple *trattorie* all over the region, serving up traditional thick soups and full-bodied red wines, seem designed to warm up the diners gathered convivially around a large table.

The first mild days are traditionally enjoyed among the crowds at the famous carnival of Viareggio in February. This is the chance to sample the excellent local shellfish, especially scampi and mantis shrimps. Nature is particularly generous in certain localities dotted across Tuscany where the valuable black truffle is found. Not far from the sea there are market gardens producing early artichokes, and black cabbage, an important ingredient in *ribollita* (vegetable soup). This is the time when the pig is killed, after an autumn spent grazing in the woods on the chestnuts and acorns, giving its flesh a rich flavour. Now, home-made *salumi* (preserved meats) begin their long slow curing, lasting up to two years for a *prosciutto crudo*.

Wines

TUSCANY IS ONE OF ITALY'S prime wine regions, producing great red wines. The
rather folksy image of Chianti in its straw-lined flask has given way in recent
years to designer bottles of fine wine that rival the best French reds. This is not
the result of some invention of modern marketing but the rightful success of a
deep-rooted local tradition, as illustrated by the ancient farmhouses that stand
amid the vines. The changeover from a patrician, but antiquated, management
of the estates to a bold modern business approach is recent.

Despite the miracles worked by technology, Tuscany will never become a
region of great white wines because the French vines planted here produce
wines lacking in local character, and the traditional Trebbiano and Malvasia
vines are limited by the soil. There are three exceptions: Vernaccia di San
Gimignano, Montecarlo, and the whites of the islands, all of which show great
potential. Dessert wines also show great promise – if the Vin Santo (Tuscany's
traditional "holy wine") lacks the noble flavour of the great French dessert
wines, here too the Tuscans are learning to exploit the potential of their yeasts to
obtain outstanding wines made from grapes that have been semi-dried on racks.

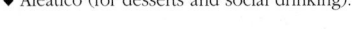

A CHOICE SELECTION OF TUSCAN WINES

To accompany the full range of the typical cuisine of the region
you need a choice selection of Tuscan wines, which should
include the following:

♦ Vermentino from the Luni hills, Apuan Alps or hills of Lucca
(a light summer aperitif).

♦ Vernaccia di San Gimignano, aged (as a general table wine and as
an accompaniment to white meats).

♦ Montecarlo Bianco (good with seafood).

♦ Young Vernaccia di San Gimignano (with fish, summery first courses, savoury toast).

♦ Young Chianti (with *cacciucco* – Livornese fish soup; for dining al fresco; with
salumi – cured meats; and with *crostini* and *bruschetta* – savoury toasts).

♦ Chianti, medium-aged reds of Montalcino and Montepulciano, Morellino of Sansano
(traditional first courses, main courses with white meat).

♦ Chianti Classico or Rufina, Brunello di Montalcino, Vino Nobile di Montepulciano,
(roasted or stewed red meat).

♦ Brunello di Montalcino cru, fully aged, Sassicaia (well-aged *pecorino* cheese).

♦ Vin Santo (*cantucci* biscuits).

♦ Ansedonia Passito or Moscadello (various desserts).

♦ Aleatico (for desserts and social drinking).

THE RIGHT GLASS

The shape of a wine glass is designed to reduce contact between the hand holding the glass and the wine itself. Its form reduces possible interference from any odours or the heat of the hand. The glass should be held by the stem, between the goblet that holds the wine and the foot of the glass. Modern designers produce wine glasses that are both beautiful and practical. Wine glasses should be perfectly transparent so you can appreciate the wine's colour and also check its state of health (for example, too few bubbles or too large bubbles in a spumante *metodo classico*, or an orangey colour in a young red wine, which is a symptom of early ageing). The best glasses are made of crystal.

BALLOON
This glass is perfect for fine wines of a great age such as Brunello, as its distinctive rounded form slowly releases the complex subtle elements of the bouquet. (Serve at 16–20°C/60–68°F.)

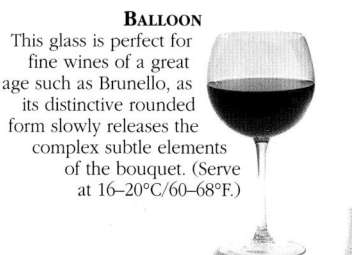

FLUTE
The elongated shape of the flute holds the subtle aromas of spumanti *metodo classico* or charmat, dry, very dry or semi-dry. (Serve at 6–8°C/43–46°F.)

RED WINE GOBLET
Serve medium-aged wines such as Chianti Classico in this glass, which is wider than an ordinary wine glass, to gather the bouquet more fully. (Serve at 14–16°C/57–60°F.)

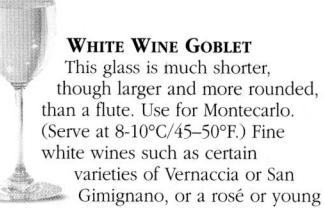

WHITE WINE GOBLET
This glass is much shorter, though larger and more rounded, than a flute. Use for Montecarlo. (Serve at 8-10°C/45–50°F.) Fine white wines such as certain varieties of Vernaccia or San Gimignano, or a rosé or young red – a Novello or Chianti, are better served cooled rather than chilled. (Serve at 10–14°C/50–57°F.)

DESSERT WINE GOBLET
For Vin Santo and similar dessert wines, this small, narrow-mouthed glass concentrates the bouquet. (Serve at 14–16°C/57–60°F.)

SPARKLING WINE GOBLET
The flared mouth of this glass allows the intense bouquet of sweet and aromatic spumanti (sparkling wine) to disperse without overwhelming the nose. (Serve at 6–8°C/43–46°F.)

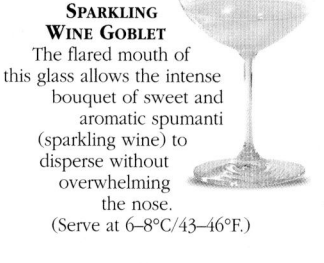

DECANTER
The purpose of a decanter, usually used for an aged red wine, is to awaken the dormant bouquet of the wine. Pouring it into a decanter oxygenates the wine and also allows any sediment to be left in the bottom of the wine bottle. In ceremonial decanting, the colour of the wine is viewed against a lighted candle and the wine is then poured straight from the decanter.

Olive Growing in Tuscany

Tuscany is a famous olive-growing region and the olive groves on the wooded hillsides are a characteristic feature of the Tuscan landscape, though some areas are more favourable than others. Olive groves are usually quite small, so the local crop is not large but produces very fine olive oil. The traditional business skills of the region and the expertise of olive growers have played an important role in the success of Italian olive oil world-wide, providing a model for other olive oil producers.

Olive growing in Italy goes all the way back to the Etruscans of the 6th century BC and it was further developed by the Romans. With the fall of the Roman empire the vast organization for growing and marketing olives fell into disarray. Monasteries were the first to tend the great olive groves again before the medieval city states started to foster olive growing once more. The trade in olive oil grew in economic importance until it became a formidable instrument of political power in the 14th century. Today, olive oil remains an essential ingredient of Tuscan cuisine, a vital flavouring in cooked dishes and salads.

THE ORIGINS OF OLIVE GROWING

The Medici (a powerful political family in the 15th, 16th and 17th centuries) fostered the growing of olives. They gave wooded hillsides to the municipalities on condition they were leased cheaply for planting olive groves and vineyards. Growing olives became one of the main economic resources of the region, resulting in the distinctive Tuscan landscape of today.

THE FLAVOUR OF TUSCAN OLIVE OIL

Tuscany produces some of the finest olive oils in Italy and, although they vary in much the same way that wines do, generally they have a strong aromatic scent. Tuscan olives are harvested well before they ripen, to produce oils richer in anti-oxidants and other nutritious substances. The early harvesting, combined with the soil, climate and the local olive varieties, results in peppery, slightly bitter oils with a rich colour.

OLIVE OIL

The quality of Italy's olive oil is guaranteed by strict legislation. Olives are picked, mostly by hand, and crushed to produce oil and a watery liquid, which are then separated. This oil is the first cold-pressed virgin olive oil – "virgin" because it is pure, not having been heated or processed. Virgin olive oil varies in flavour and quality and is graded according to the level of acidity; lower is better. The best quality is extra virgin olive oil which has an acidity of less than 1%. Olive oils are usually blended so the flavour is constant.

OLIVE VARIETIES

With its long olive-producing history and the diversity of soil and climate within the region, Tuscany has developed numerous cultivated varieties (cultivars) of the olive tree, including 106 that have been classified, some of which are of great importance. In addition to the varieties described below, other important ones include **Pendolino**, a type which is widespread, hardy and produces abundant oil of reasonable quality; **Maurino**, a variety typical of the area between Monte Albano and Lucchesia, with a medium-sized tree bearing fruits that ripen early and produce fine oil; **Santa Caterina**, a large vigorous tree that produces bright green olives that are usually harvested in September for immediate eating. Other common varieties are **Coroiolo**, **Crapitea**, **Lavagnino**, **Leccarpa**, **Manzanilla**, **Nebbio**, **Oglialoa**, **Passola**, **Piangente**, **Ravece**, **San Francesco** and **Taggiasca**.

MORAIOLO

This variety originated in Tuscany but is widely grown in other parts of Italy, especially Umbria, and in other Mediterranean countries. It has a good resistance to wind but not to intense, prolonged cold. It produces an abundance of olives, which ripen over a medium-long period of time, and have a good oil yield. The oil is very fine, without marked aromatic notes but with excellent texture and a distinctly bitter and pungent flavour.

CORREGGIOLO

A self-pollinator similar to Frantoio, this variety's fruit ripens late and over a fairly long period. The trees are fairly vigorous, with drooping branches and the fruits borne on thin, supple canes. The olive yield is high and consistent, producing an oil that is particularly aromatic, full-bodied and flavoursome.

MAREMMANA

A vigorous plant with large, intensely green, spear-shaped leaves. It produces a good oil with rather muted bitter notes.

LECCINO

Grown in nearly all olive-producing regions both in Italy and world-wide, this variety is well-known for its resistance to inclement weather, cold and disease. A consistent high-yielding variety, the olives ripen early and uniformly. Its oil is not particularly aromatic.

FRANTOIO

A Tuscan original, this variety has spread throughout Italy and nearly all olive-growing areas of the world, a testimony to its consistently high yields and the notable quality of its oil, which is fine, aromatic and flavoursome. The variety is not resistant to bad weather and is very sensitive to cold.

Fish and Seafood

UNLIKE THE LIGURIAN COAST, the Tuscan coastline is not studded with little fishing harbours, but its larger ports, notably Viareggio and Livorno, provide fine fish. The waters of Gorgona and other islands, the shallows of Vada and the Formiche of Grosseto offer an excellent range of fish, including scampi and crayfish, delivered live to the counters of the fish shops. The lagoon of Orbetello, with its modern fish farms, is particularly productive, but this is not always reflected in the restaurants. Inland there are not that many restaurants specializing in fish cuisine, although fish is commonly eaten on a Friday thoughout Tuscany. The best fish restaurants are found mainly along the coast.

RICCIOLA SERIOLA DUMERILI (AMBERJACK)

Amberjack, which grow to a large size, are found in schools in deep water around rocky headlands and steep cliffs. They abound in the Tuscan archipelago and are prized for their firm, flavoursome white flesh. They are usually eaten as fish steaks or grilled whole.

PESCE SPADA (SWORDFISH)

The white close-grained flesh of this fish is delicious provided it is not overcooked and it remains moist. Swordfish is found particularly in the port of Livorno, usually sold as steaks.

CALAMARETTI (YOUNG SQUID)

The fry of squid are one of the delicacies of Tuscan cuisine. They need only a few seconds' cooking by steaming or tossing in a pan with vegetables. Their delicate flavour provides great scope for many delicious dishes.

CALAMARO (SQUID)

The squid is the most prized and costly of cephalopods (soft-bodied shellfish). Its sweet flesh is delicious cut into rings and fried. It is also very good poached, stuffed and baked or served cold in a mixed *antipasto di mare*, or seafood salad.

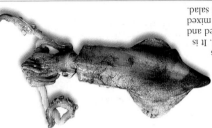

SPARNOCCHIA OR MAZZANCOLIA (MANTIS SHRIMP)

The mantis shrimp is common in Tuscan waters, especially around the island of Gorgona. It is popular for grilling, steaming and is also an ingredient in more expensive versions of *cacciucco* (fish soup). Mantis shrimps are sold live at the market at Viareggio – always avoid those sold headless.

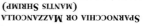

SARDINA

A common and very economical fish, the sardine makes good eating and is very nourishing. It is ideal fried, grilled, made into fish cakes or preserved in oil.

PAGRO (PORGY)

This is a white fish typical of the Tyrrhenian coast and is highly prized in Tuscany, especially when it is baked. Sea bream (called *pagelli* in Italian, *paraghi* in the Tuscan dialect) is similar but has a flatter snout and pinkish markings. Larger specimens are called *occhialone* or *fragolino*.

MISTO DI SCOGLIO (MIXED SEA FISH)

The fish referred to as *misto di scoglio* include small bream, wrasse, young scorpion fish and rainbow wrasse, gurnard, sea perch and hake. Delicious but too small to grill or fry on their own, they are essential for an authentic *cacciucco* and a variety of other fish soups.

VONGOLA VERACE OR ARSELLA NERO (CLAMS)

This very common shellfish is usually cooked but may be served raw like oysters. Though somewhat expensive, clams are found in numerous modern Tuscan seafood dishes as well as the traditional *cacciucco* (fish soup). Called *vongole veraci* or *arselle* in Italian, in Viareggio they are known as *nicchi*.

Porcini Mushrooms

T USCAN CUISINE REGULARLY FEATURES *porcini* mushrooms, which are also known as ceps, from the French *cèpe*. *Porcini* are distinguished from other *Boletus* mushrooms – a family which has tiny tubes under the cap instead of gills – by four features: strong smell, sweet taste, a net-like pattern covering the stalk and by the white flesh, which does not discolour when cut. They are found all over the region, fresh, dried or preserved in oil, in homes and all types of restaurant, from the humblest *trattoria* to the grandest *ristorante*. Dishes featuring *porcini* do not vary greatly, and the mushrooms are eaten in quite simple ways, in *risotto*, or in *ravioli* for example. In certain areas of Tuscany, including Lunigiana, Garfagnana, and Casentino, you can find the world's finest examples of *porcini*, judged on aroma, flavour and texture. In other areas, such as Monte Amiata, the Maremma Grossetana, Colline Metallifere, the hinterland of Livorno, the Mediterranean scrublands and the woods of Siena and Arezzo, the quality is not as high but they are more abundant.

PORCINI D'AUTUNNO
(*Boletus edulis*)
The autumn *porcini* shuns the heat, so in summer it is found only in the mountains and in the depths of woods; in autumn it appears on hillsides, but prefers cool areas. The mushroom's stalk is usually white and the cap appears in various shades of brown, sometimes almost white under beech trees, and is slimy in wet weather. The most flavoursome examples are found growing under chestnut trees, the firmest examples among fir and beech trees; those in oak woods are much less prized.

PORCINO DEL FREDDO
(*Boletus pinicola*)
This species grows between May and November but rarely during the hottest months. It is found under chestnut, beech, pine or fir trees, especially with bilberries or heather. It has unusual red colouring and is the largest of all the *porcini*. It is best suited to preserving in oil because it is generally very hardy, not particularly aromatic, and the colour is very striking.

FIORONE OR PORCINO D'ESTATE
(*Boletus reticulatus*)
This summer *porcini* starts growing in May and is rarely found after September. It grows throughout the region at all altitudes but only in grassy glades and in sunny areas. This is the most richly scented and flavoursome of the *porcini* but it is vulnerable to parasites. The cap is velvety and slightly cracked, the stalk is beige with a raised net-like pattern and the flesh has a very light texture.

DRIED PORCINI

Porcini secchi, or dried *porcini*, are even more common throughout Tuscany than fresh ones. The local varieties are prized over those from other regions, although the latter have flooded the market. If possible, buy unpackaged dried mushrooms directly from the pickers or at small shops in areas where they are found locally. Store them either in the freezer or at least place them there from time to time to kill the eggs of potential parasites.

PORCINI IN OIL

Jars of *porcini* preserved in oil are a feature of the region's farmhouses and traditional *trattorie*. In keeping with tradition, the oil is usually extra virgin olive oil. Jars should be stored in a cool dark place and kept no later than the spring after the season of picking.

MORECCIO OR PORCINO NERO
(Boletus aereus)

This black *porcini* mushroom is commonest along the coast and on warm hillsides. It grows almost exclusively in autumn, usually under holm-oaks, deciduous oaks and chestnut trees. It has a dark brown cap marbled with ochre and an ochre-coloured stalk. It is full-flavoured and aromatic when picked but the scent and taste soon fade. The flesh remains snowy white when dried, making it ideal for keeping in this way.

Truffles

Tuscany is one huge truffle patch with many areas producing black truffles and even the prized white variety. Numerous fairs and festivals celebrate this wonderful gift of nature, especially in the areas that are lucky enough to produce white truffles, such as the Sienese Crete and San Miniato. Truffles are seasonal but, fortunately, Tuscany has a truffle for every month of the year, so there are always fresh ones available. Always buy truffles in season when they are very fresh and clearly identifiable. Be wary of various speciality foods described as "truffle flavoured" *(al tartufo)*: in reality, they may be perfumed with a synthetic aroma. The high prices these truffles command and the strong international demand for them have led to some cases of fraud. The commonest type of swindle is to import flavourless truffles from abroad, bought cheaply (sometimes less than 50 eurocents per kilo), and then artificially perfume them with a synthetic aroma. Tasteless unripe truffles are sometimes gathered – seriously damaging the truffle patches – and these are likewise flavoured artificially.

TARTUFO BIANCO PREGIATO
(Tuber magnatum)
The white truffle is actually a light hazel colour if found growing under oak, almost whitish if under poplar or willow, or with reddish tones if under linden (lime) trees. It is identifiable by its strong and distinctive aroma and fine, densely veined flesh – marked veining is the first sign of proper ripeness. It ripens from October to December and by law it can only be gathered in these three months. Its flavour is best appreciated when added raw to hot dishes. Areas where it is found are San Miniato, the Sienese Crete, Volterra, and there are some small patches near Arezzo.

BIANCHETTO OR MARZOLO
(Tuber borchii)
The perfume of this March truffle is strong and very garlicky but it lasts only a few hours after picking and then begins to fade. It adds an excellent flavour to soups. Picking is permitted from 15 January to 20 April. It is found in many parts of Tuscany, and is abundant in the coastal pine woods.

The March truffle differs from the prized white truffle by the coarse loose veining and domed shape.

TUBER MACROSPORUM
This truffle occasionally turns up among batches of summer black truffles. It is often mistakenly sold at the same price even though it is far more highly prized because its perfume is almost identical to that of the white truffle. Sadly, it is very rare. Harvesting is permitted from September to December.

The wrinkled grey surface of this truffle has dark reddish tints.

The flesh is grey with fine reddish veins, which are often not evident because they darken on contact with the air.

SCORZONE
(*Tuber aestivum*)

The summer black truffle is the most common truffle in Tuscany, found all over the region. It is excellent when fresh, though not as good as the black truffle (*see below*), but it usually costs about one-tenth of the price of the white truffle. Its flavour is heightened in stuffings and in baked dishes. Harvesting is allowed from May to December.

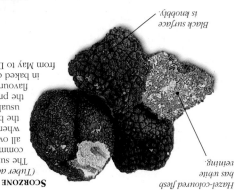

Black surface is knobbly.

Surface is rough but not knobbly.

Hazel-coloured flesh has white veining.

TARTUFO NERO PREGIATO
(*Tuber melanosporum*)

The prized black truffle is usually found in oak woods where the sun can penetrate. This is the *diamant noir* (black diamond) of the French; in Italy it is also called *nero di Norcia* (black truffle of Norcia). It has a delicious scent of ripening fruit with a whiff of garlic. It has an extraordinary capacity to blend with other foods and it will enhance the flavour of hot sauces and stuffings, terrines and pâtés. It is at its best from 15 November to 15 March and costs about half as much as the white truffle. It grows in scattered patches across the region.

Flesh is black with fine white, translucent veining.

Greyish flesh with sparse, thick veins.

TARTUFO D'INVERNO
(*Tuber brumale*)

Hazel trees rather than oak are preferred by the winter black truffle, though it is sometimes found together with the prized black truffle. At the market (and in the kitchen) it is rather less valuable than the summer black and the prized black (its perfume is less delicate and persistent), but its gastronomic uses are the same. Harvesting is permitted from 15 November to 15 March.

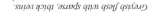

Black grainy surface.

OTHER TRUFFLES

There are various small truffles that are very similar to the March truffle. These can be distinguished only with a microscope but they ripen at different times from the March truffle. These include the *Tuber puberulum*, *Tuber dryophilum* and *Tuber maculatum*. While the law does not allow their sale, the law is not enforced. A black truffle called *Tuber mesentericum* is sometimes found in the Tuscany region. Unfortunately it has an unpleasant smell of carbolic acid and is not worth buying.

FLORENCE, AREZZO AND CASENTINO

Florence, Arezzo and Casentino

GEOGRAPHICALLY AND GASTRONOMICALLY, this area is the most varied part of Tuscany. Visitors from all over the world arrive in Florence and the city seems able to accept their customs and habits while still preserving its own distinctive character. Pratomagno and the Apennine ridge are covered by extensive forests, created and protected for centuries by the Camaldolesi monks. The Mugello developed a whole way of life based on the chestnut tree and the Val di Chiana is famed for its excellent beef. The climate is Mediterranean, water is abundant, and the food and wine are part of an ancient culture and the result of centuries of prosperity. Life here is very good.

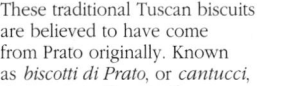

Firenzuo
FS

Scarperia

San Pietro
a Sieve
Borgo
San Lore

Montemurlo
Bivigliano

PRATO
FS

Calenzano

Carmignano
Sesto Fiorentino

Lastra a Signa
Fiesole

Capraia
a Limite
FLORENCE
Arno

Scandicci
FS
Pontassie

Fucecchio

Montelupo
Fiorentino

EMPOLI
FS

BISCOTTI (PRATO BISCUITS)
These traditional Tuscan biscuits are believed to have come from Prato originally. Known as *biscotti di Prato*, or *cantucci*, they are usually eaten after dipping into Vin Santo *(see p34)*.

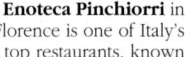

Florentine wineries are a mix of innovation and tradition. Alongside the stainless steel containers of modern technology are small new oak *barriques* as well as great old wooden barrels used to age the traditional wines *(see pp24–7)*.

Enoteca Pinchiorri in Florence is one of Italy's top restaurants, known for the excellent quality of the food and the extensive wine list. The cellar is one of the most prestigious in Europe.

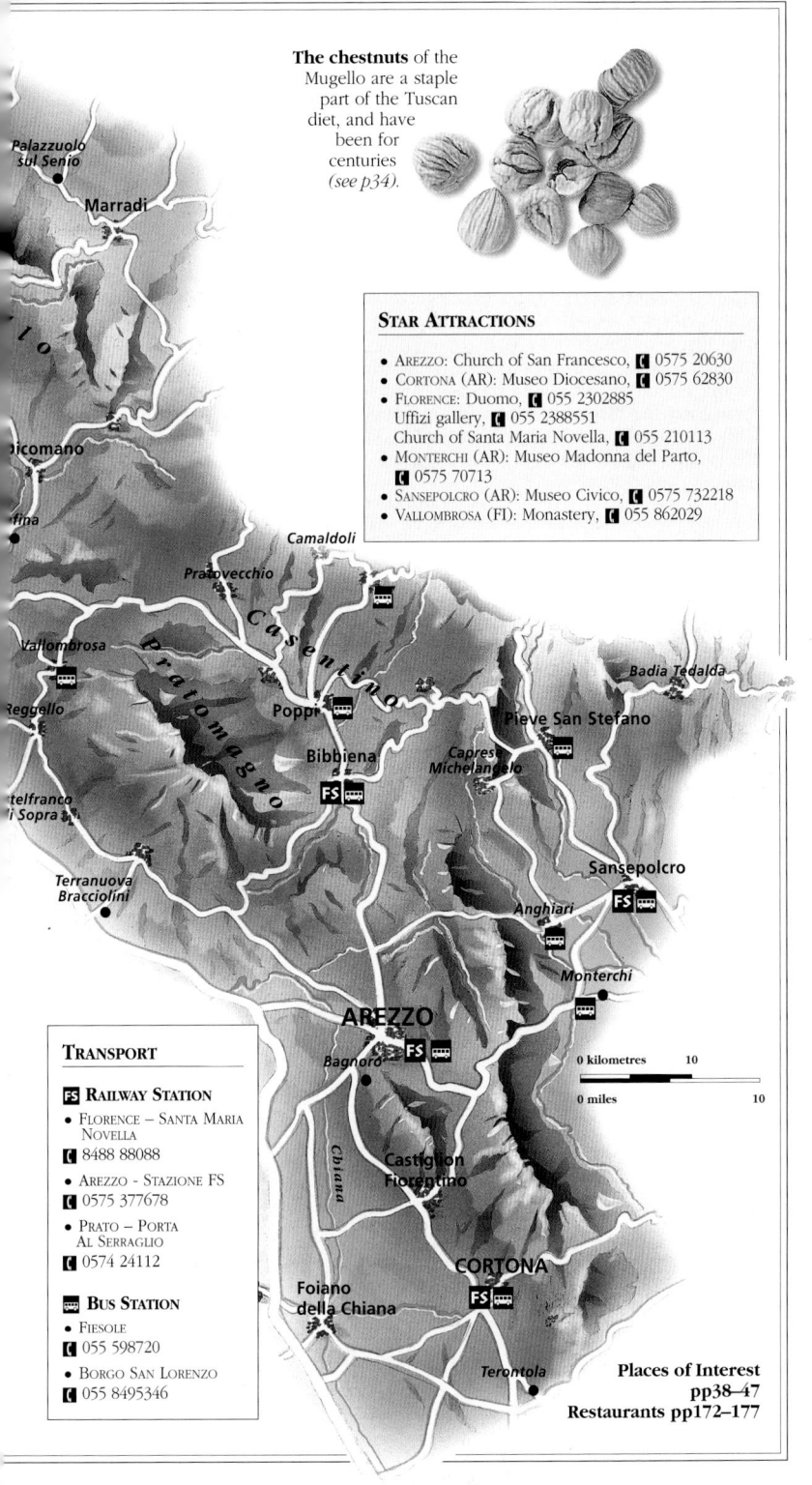

The chestnuts of the Mugello are a staple part of the Tuscan diet, and have been for centuries *(see p34).*

STAR ATTRACTIONS

- AREZZO: Church of San Francesco, ℂ 0575 20630
- CORTONA (AR): Museo Diocesano, ℂ 0575 62830
- FLORENCE: Duomo, ℂ 055 2302885
  Uffizi gallery, ℂ 055 2388551
  Church of Santa Maria Novella, ℂ 055 210113
- MONTERCHI (AR): Museo Madonna del Parto,
  ℂ 0575 70713
- SANSEPOLCRO (AR): Museo Civico, ℂ 0575 732218
- VALLOMBROSA (FI): Monastery, ℂ 055 862029

TRANSPORT

FS RAILWAY STATION

- FLORENCE – SANTA MARIA NOVELLA
  ℂ 8488 88088
- AREZZO - STAZIONE FS
  ℂ 0575 377678
- PRATO – PORTA AL SERRAGLIO
  ℂ 0574 24112

BUS STATION

- FIESOLE
  ℂ 055 598720
- BORGO SAN LORENZO
  ℂ 055 8495346

Places of Interest
pp38–47
Restaurants pp172–177

0 kilometres   10

0 miles   10

Wines

FLORENTINE WINES WERE FAMOUS as long ago as the early Middle Ages. At the start of the 18th century the Grand Duke of Florence identified a number of localities that were famed for their vineyards, including Carmignano, Pomino and Valdarno di Sopra. (The Chianti area was not included because at that time it was limited to the territory of Siena and only later extended to the hills around Florence.)

In the Florence area, which lends itself to producing fine reds, the prince of the vines is the Sangiovese, which has gained a good reputation following recent modifications in Chianti-making. Sangiovese provides 75–100 per cent of the grapes, Canaiolo Nero up to 10 per cent, Trebbiano Toscano, Malvasia del Chianti and other red grapes up to 10 per cent. Its potential is still being studied, but Sangiovese is producing wines of great character. Other vines producing red grapes in this area are Canaiolo Nero, Cabernet Franc, Cabernet Sauvignon and Merlot. Among white grape vines, the traditional Malvasia del Chianti and Trebbiano Toscano are now second-string grapes, while Pinot Bianco and Chardonnay are increasingly used blended or as single varieties.

CHIANTI COLLI FIORENTINI

This is the Chianti of the sub-zone south of Florence as far as Impruneta; to the east and west the zone stretches south along the banks of the Arno and between the Pesa and Elsa valleys to Barberino. The terrain to the east, with a warm, dry climate and sandier soils, yields wines of less body and greater saltiness. The soils to the east, on wooded hillsides, have a damper, cooler climate that yields finer perfumes and a longer life.

Chianti Colli Fiorentini is well suited to flavoursome dishes like caciucco (fish soup) and first courses of pulses and cereals such as zuppa di farro (grain soup). The Superiore, which is stronger, and the Riserva, which is aged longer, are more suited to robust first courses with meat sauces, meat grilled or cooked on the spit, and game.

CHIANTI RÚFINA

This is considered the most refined of the various types of Chianti. The territory stretches northeast from Florence. The wine is born fairly rich in tannins, ensuring it ages well – it will keep for up to 40 years or more – but is also slightly tingling to the palate. For this reason the wine needs to be allowed to mellow slowly.

A well-balanced wine with good body, particularly suited to dishes with a strong flavour, such as trippa alla fiorentina (Florentine-style tripe), red meat and mature cheeses.

MAIALE UBRIACO

6 pork chops • 2 cloves garlic, chopped • 1 teaspoon fennel seeds • 2 glasses Chianti • salt • pepper

Heat a non-stick pan over a medium heat. Season the pork chops with plenty of salt and pepper and place them in the hot pan. Add the chopped garlic and the fennel seeds and cook over a high heat until the chops are golden on both sides. Pour in the red wine and continue cooking until most of the wine has evaporated.

CHIANTI MONTALBANO

This Chianti area covers some of the provinces of Florence to the west of the city and also Pistoia to the northwest. The wines produced around Vinci and Lamporecchio were already renowned in the 18th century, as was noted by the Grand Duke Cosimo III. At that time it was a robust wine with a high alcohol content. The current trend is for a red wine with a more elegant structure and less alcohol.

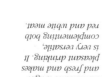

Generally Chianti Montalbano is light and fresh and makes pleasant drinking. It is very versatile, complementing both red and white meat.

CARMIGNANO

Production of this wine is restricted to hillsides in the municipal areas of Carmignano and Poggio a Caiano. It differs from other local reds because of the use of Cabernet Franc and Cabernet Sauvignon grapes, which give it a quite distinctive character. These grapes were already in use in the 18th century, when they were known as *uva francesca*. The DOCG label is reserved for Rosso and Rosso Riserva.

BARCO REALE DI CARMIGNANO

This wine is the young version of Carmignano, made from the same grapes but aged for a shorter period. Fresh and mellow, it is ideal as an all-purpose table wine. The name comes from a wall, called the Barco Reale, 50 km (31 miles) long. It was erected for Cosimo I, the Grand Duke of Tuscany in the 1570s, to separate his farmland from his game reserve.

Carmignano DOC also appears on the label of various kinds of Vin Santo: dry, semi-sweet (also Reserve) and Occhio di Pernice (ordinary or Reserva).

The rosé labelled Carmignano followed by the letters DOC is often called Vin Ruspo.

WINE TYPE	GOOD VINTAGES	GOOD PRODUCERS
Red Wine		
Chianti Rufina	97, 95, 90.	Frescobaldi di Firenze, Fattoria di Basciano a Rufina
Super Tuscans (see p130)	98, 97, 95, 90	Antinori di Firenze, D'Alessandro di Cortona, Frescobaldi di Firenze, Ruffino di Pontassieve

WINE TYPE	GOOD VINTAGES	GOOD PRODUCERS
Red Wine		
Carmignano	97, 95, 90	Tenuta Capezzana di Carmignano
Chianti	97, 90	Antinori di Firenze

POMINO

The zone of production for Pomino wine is very small and forms part of the municipal territory of Rùfina. A feature is the presence of French vines, introduced in the early 19th century, which found a suitable microclimate in the high altitudes (500–800 m/1600–2400 feet) above sea level. White wine is produced from Pinot Bianco and Chardonnay grapes and red from Sangiovese, Canaiolo, Cabernet Franc and Cabernet Sauvignon grapes.

A Reserve red is also produced and the Pomino range is completed with a white and a red Vin Santo, both especially good wines.

BIANCO VERGINE VALDICHIANA

This white wine is produced either still, lightly sparkling or fully sparkling in eight communes of the province of Arezzo and roughly half the province of Siena. It goes well with delicate *antipasti*, soups, vegetable dishes and unsalted fish.

The basic grape is Trebbiano Toscano, comprising at least 60 per cent, blended with other white grapes, especially Malvasia.

CHIANTI COLLI ARETINI

Chianti from the Colli Aretini is lighter-bodied and has a lower alcohol content than other Tuscan Chianti. Chianti Colli Aretini is ideal for general use as a table wine and is also well suited to first courses with meat sauces and also to pork and veal dishes, even those with well-seasoned sauces.

Salumi

TUSCANY HAS a quite different approach to *salumi* (cured meats) from the rest of Italy, preferring a dry, highly seasoned product with plenty of pepper (often whole black peppercorns), made for eating with the unsalted local bread. These preserved meat products reflect a taste developed over many centuries. In Tuscany, pigs were not fed on swill, scraps and cereals but raised wild, free to graze and root about in the woods where they ate acorns, sweet chestnuts, truffles and other tubers, which in turn made their flesh firm and flavoursome and naturally produced hams and salami with these tasty qualities. Because of the warm Tuscan climate, the meat products were then salted abundantly to ensure they kept well.

TUSCAN SALAMI

This salami (cured sausage) is eaten uncooked. It is made of minced lean pork and lardons of hard fat chopped with a knife. It has a firm texture and is extremely tasty, with a marked flavour of black pepper.

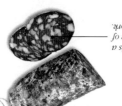

Filling is a mixture of beef and pork.

Natural casing.

Pure pork filling.

SPALLA (SHOULDER)

Shoulder of pork is often cured to produce ham, but not on all estates since it may also be used for salami. This is "poor man's *prosciutto* (cured ham)", the fare of people who work on the land. Compared with the leg, the shoulder tastes more salty, peppery and fatty. It must be stored in cool, dry conditions.

RIGATINO

In Tuscany this *pancetta* (cured pork belly) is always rather dry and well seasoned. Sometimes chilli is added to give it a spicy flavour.

GUANCIALE (Pig's Cheek)

The cheek of the pig is salted, seasoned with pepper and matured. *Guanciale* is very tasty but is usually used as a flavouring ingredient in other dishes rather than eaten on its own.

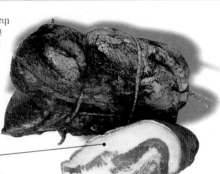

Thick layers of fat are streaked with lean meat.

SBRICIOLONA OR FINOCCHIONA

These salamis are flavoured with fennel seed and, frequently, with plenty of garlic as well.

This medium-sized type of salami is usually less garlicky. It is often found at small traditional delicatessens.

Traditionally Florentine salami with fennel (finocchiona) is a fairly large size.

Meat is finely minced for a soft texture.

ZUPPA DI FAGIOLI CON I PIEDUCCI

1 pig's trotter • 500 g (1 lb 2 oz) dried zolfini beans

Soak the pig's trotter in cold water for 48 hours to remove the salt. After 24 hours, add the beans to soak with the trotter. The next day, drain the meat and beans and put them in an earthenware pot or large saucepan. Cover with water, bring to the boil, then cover and simmer over a low heat for 2 hours. Remove some of the beans with a slotted spoon and mash them. Break up the trotter meat and return it to the pot with the mashed beans. Reheat. Serve the soup with *bruschetta* rubbed with garlic and drizzled with olive oil, or use it as stock for soups made with grains or cabbage.

PIEDUCCI (Pig's Trotters)

Pig's trotters are seasoned with salt, vinegar, garlic and rosemary, then dried. They are used to flavour soups.

SALSICCIA

This classic sausage is made from different cuts of pork, finely minced, seasoned with salt, pepper and a little garlic and stuffed into thin natural casing. Sausages are best eaten straight from the grill. Cured sausage, which may contain spices, liver, fennel or red wine, can be sliced and eaten on *crostini* (toasted Tuscan bread).

SOPPRESSATA OR COPPA (PIG'S HEAD SAUSAGE)

This sausage is prepared using all parts of the pig's head. The head is boiled with herbs and spices, chopped coarsely and flavoured with garlic and pepper. Parsley and chilli may also be added.

This sausage has a firm, gelatinous, spongy texture.

TUSCAN PROSCIUTTO CRUDO (CURED HAM)

Cheaper hams are saltier and smell mainly of pepper. A fine *prosciutto crudo* has a delicate aroma, and, while it is more salty than classic Parma ham and San Daniele from the Veneto, it is not excessively so. The texture is firm and it has a definite, lingering meaty flavour, spiced with pepper. The quality depends on the ingredients and the skill of the producer, and no two hams taste exactly the same.

Tuscan prosciutto crudo should be sliced very thinly.

OTHER PORK SPECIALITIES WORTH TRYING

Sanguinaccio or **buristo** (blood sausage) is made of pork blood and cartilage and may come in a sausage shape such as *buristo di Cinta (see p104)* or in a large piece such as the *buristo* of Montalcino. Other cured meats made from lean cuts of pork – fillet, loin or the collar – are common. **Capocollo** (cured neck of pork) is similar to the *coppa* from Lombardy and Emilia-Romagna, but is much drier and more peppery. Some producers flavour small spicy salamis by adding chilli to them. **Lardo** (lard), flavoured mainly with rosemary, is another very popular delicacy in Tuscany.

Extra Virgin Olive Oil

FLORENCE IS RINGED with olive groves and all the lower ridges of the Valdarno and its tributaries are dotted with olive trees. The types of oil produced in the area differ greatly, not so much through tradition – because nearly everywhere the tendency is to harvest early and produce fruity oils – but because of differences in soil and the choice of different varieties of olive tree. Most olive-growing estates in the region are small or medium-size and the majority aim for high quality. Nearly all the estates combine olive oil production with making wine or, in areas unsuited to vineyards, with other types of agriculture such as grain or vegetables.

RÙFINA OLIVE OIL
This oil is produced in an area north of Florence comprising the communes of Rùfina, Dicomano and Londa. The oil is fruity with a marked scent of herbs, strong, quite full-bodied and flavoursome. Selvapiana olive oil is one of the best in the area.

OIL FROM PRATOMAGNO
This oil is produced in the territory east of Florence in the bend of the upper Valdarno lying between the provinces of Florence and Arezzo. The territory includes the communes of Reggello (FI), Castelfranco di Sopra and Loro Ciuffenna (AR). The oil is very similar to that of the Colli Fiorentini, but generally less intense.

OIL FROM THE COLLI FIORENTINI
Inland south of Florence is the area that produces this oil. The territory covers Bagno a Ripoli, Fiesole, Scandicci, Impruneta, Incisa and San Casciano, stretching as far as Poggibonsi and San Gimignano. The oil is medium-bodied with a full, smooth, fruity flavour which has a vegetable aftertaste and some slightly bitter, pungent notes.

LAUDEMIO OLIVE OIL

This was originally the finest oil – the one that the share cropper was required to reserve for the landowner – it was referred to as "the master's oil". Today Laudemio is a brand name given to the produce of a consortium of estates all of whom use the same bottle design. The denomination does not represent a traditional area or specific properties of quality, and the regulations are vague about some essential factors. They cover a very broad area of membership (central Tuscany), best-by dates, harvesting by 15 December (normal for Tuscany, unusual weather apart), and rather vaguely defined production techniques. In other words, the quality from different estates may vary.

The olive tree breaks the monotony of great fields of grain.

OIL FROM THE COLLI ARETINI

Produced in the territory south of Arezzo, covering various communes including Castiglione Fiorentino and Cortona, this is a medium-bodied fruity oil, fresh and aromatic. Body and fluidity is average. It has a harmonious taste with slightly bitter and pungent notes and a hint of artichoke.

OIL FROM MONTE ALBANO

East of Lucca, between the province of Pistoia and the northern part of the province of Florence, is the area producing this olive oil, especially at Vinci, Carmignano, Artimino and Montelupo Fiorentino. The oil is generally medium-light and fruity with herbal scents and a balanced flavour. This flavour varies in intensity from season to season.

PUTTANAIO

3–4 tablespoons virgin olive oil • 3 onions, sliced • 2 sprigs rosemary • 3 cloves garlic, chopped • 2 stalks celery, crushed • 3 potatoes, diced • 800 g (1 lb 12 oz) green peppers, seeded and diced • 3 aubergines, diced • 2 carrots, diced • 2 courgettes, diced • 8 kg (18 lb) ripe tomatoes, chopped • 3 tablespoons chopped fresh basil, thyme and parsley • salt

Heat the oil in a large pan, add the onions, rosemary and garlic; fry until soft. Add the diced vegetables and tomatoes. Season and simmer until the vegetables are cooked. Garnish with the chopped herbs before serving the soup.

Chianina Beef

THE CELEBRATED DISH Bistecca alla Fiorentina (Florentine T-bone steak), traditionally cooked over hot wood embers, is best when made with beef from pedigree Chianina cattle, which is generally rated as of superior quality. Chianina cattle are traditionally reared in the Val di Chiana, particularly around Cortona. The distinctive, white-coated breed – one of the oldest breeds in existence – only produces high quality meat if it has been raised in exactly the right conditions, however. While other breeds of cattle are rarely temperamental, Chianina cattle are unusually sensitive and their state of wellbeing influences the quality of the meat – if the animal is nervy, the meat is tough. The Chianina cow flourishes when looked after by the same person. It objects to sharing its stall with other cattle, and the calf has to be raised alongside its mother. There is debate as to whether the quality of beef is better when the cattle graze freely out of doors or when they are kept in a stall and fed on a mixture of fresh grass and hay.

For Chianina beef to be first-rate, the animal should be mature – this means over 16–18 months old – and it should have grown to over 800 kilos (1760 lb), yielding 500 kilos (1100 lb) of meat.

BISTECCA ALLA FIORENTINA
This is a T-bone steak (rib steak with the fillet steak still attached). Its total weight varies from 500 g–1 kg (1 lb 2 oz–2 lb 4 oz) and it is usually sliced thickly, up to about 5 cm (2 inches).

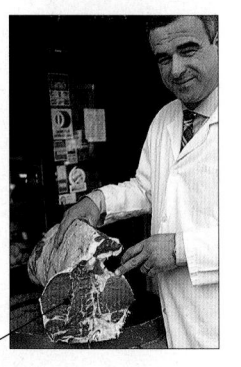

An essential feature of Chianina beef is the very firm flesh which is tender but never dry, despite the small amount of surface fat and marbling. The flavour is quite distinctive.

BISTECCA ALLA FIORENTINA

1 T-bone steak, about 1 kg (2 lb 4 oz) in weight and including the fillet steak, rib and under-rib • extra virgin olive oil • salt • pepper

Heat the grill or light the barbecue. Sprinkle both sides of the steak with pepper and lay it on the grill, keeping it some distance from the embers, if cooking on a barbecue. Cook for 5 minutes, then turn over and season the cooked side with salt. Cook the second side for 5 minutes (or longer, if preferred) and season with salt. Remove from the grill and brush with olive oil (season the oil with garlic and herbs, if liked).

BISTECCA (CHOP)
This is the ordinary rib steak without the fillet. It is often used as part of a plate of assorted roast meats for a typical Tuscan meal.

For the thickness to be just right for perfect cooking, there has to be both the rib and the under-rib.

OTHER CHIANINA CUTS

Because the Chianina breed is mainly associated with the T-bone steak, other cuts tend to be neglected. However, the superiority of Chianina beef is obvious in all cuts, from forequarter to rump. In Tuscany it is particularly important to use Chianina beef for traditional dishes, recipes devised for that type of very tender beef. For *stracotto alla fiorentina* (Florentine braised beef), for example, the best cuts, in addition to **polzo**, are **scannello** (sirloin) and **cappello del prete**; for *scottiglia* ask for **reale**.

NOCE (RUMP)

This lean part of the leg is used for escalopes, breaded cutlets and small steaks.

This lean cut is very popular because it is easy to cook.

SPICCHIO DI PETTO (MIDDLE BRISKET)

This is called *biancostato* in the rest of Italy and is typically used for making boiled beef. It is also used for *scottiglia* (stew) after removing part of the fat.

The layers of lean beef alternating with fat and bone make a tasty broth when boiled.

GIRELLO (TOPSIDE)

This lean cut is good for roasting and for cutlets.

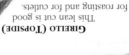

This small fat-free joint is suitable for machine slicing for carpaccio (steak sliced very thin and eaten raw).

POLZO

This is the cut under the shoulder, good for *stracotto* (braising), boiling and, above all, *scottiglia* (stew).

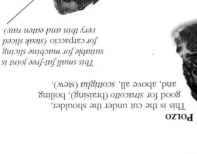

Traditional Produce

A DEEP-SEATED LOVE of tradition ensures the continuing popularity of all kinds of local produce. A traditional meal in this region will never stray far from a long-standing pattern: *crostini (see p36), prosciutto (see p29), pappardelle* (a type of ribbon pasta) with hare, and mixed roast meats. The mild Tuscan climate and the exacting demands of producers and consumers mean that you can still find free-range chickens, *salumi (see p27)* made with local ingredients, local varieties of vegetables, traditional cakes and freshly baked breads.

CHESTNUTS

The quality of a chestnut is determined by the size and the number of nuts in a single husk. Chestnut trees may produce fruit with a single large nut in each husk or several small ones. The larger varieties with a single nut are much prized by confectioners for their fine flavour and also for their appearance because the inside shell does not press into the kernel. Larger nuts are also easier to work with.

CHESTNUT FLOUR

A staple in mountain areas since ancient times, chestnut flour *(farina di castagne)* is the basic ingredient of *castagnaccio* (chestnut cake). The flour becomes stale quite quickly so it should not be stored for too long.

ZOLFINI BEANS FROM PRATOMAGNO

These small, pale yellowish beans, which are now quite rare, are exclusive to Pratomagno. The thin-skinned beans have a smooth texture and a good flavour. They are easily digested and particularly rich in iron and fibre.

Small zolfini beans are a pale yellow colour.

These sweet almond biscuits are traditionally eaten after dinner dipped in sweet Vin Santo.

ZUCCOTTO

This cream and sponge-cake dessert is a Florentine speciality, now seen all over Italy. A mould of sponge is filled with whipped cream, confectioner's custard and chocolate. The chilled *zuccotto* is turned out to serve.

BISCOTTINI DI PRATO

These almond biscuits, which come from Prato, are also called *cantuccini*. They are made from flour, eggs, sugar, almonds and pine nuts. The dough is shaped into a long loaf and baked, then it is sliced and baked again until the slices are crunchy.

SUGO DI PECORA

1 kg (2 lb 4 oz) boned shoulder or leg of mutton, trimmed of excess fat and cubed • olive oil for frying • 2 onions, chopped • 3 cloves garlic, finely chopped • 1–2 sprigs of rosemary • 1 sprig of sage • 200 g (7 oz) minced lean mutton • 100 g (3½ oz) chopped prosciutto crudo • the zest of ½ a lemon • pinch of freshly grated nutmeg • 1 tablespoon tomato paste diluted in a little warm water • 500 g (1 lb 2 oz) tomatoes, peeled • salt • pepper

MUTTON
Pecora (mutton), which is meat from the adult sheep, is widely eaten in the Campi Bisenzio area. Shepherds used to move their flocks seasonally and customarily paid their way in kind. They handed over the weaker sheep exhausted by travelling the Passo dei Pecorai before they made their descent to marshy plains that were difficult for sheep to cross.

Heat a frying pan, add the cubed mutton and fry for 1–2 minutes to seal the meat. Heat a little oil in a saucepan, add the onions, garlic, rosemary and sage and fry until softened. Add the minced mutton and ham, stirring well. Add the cubed mutton, nutmeg, lemon zest and diluted tomato paste. Cook over a moderate heat until the water has evaporated. Add the tomatoes and season. Cook over a low heat for about 1 hour, until the meat is tender, adding extra hot water, if necessary. Serve the mutton sauce with pasta.

PANE SCIOCCO (UNSALTED BREAD)
When it comes to bread, Tuscans are great traditionalists. The large loaves, elongated or rounded, above all unsalted, have a fairly heavy texture well suited for making the popular *crostoni* (toasted bread), for mopping up sauces or as a base for soups.

GEMMA D'ABETO
The monks of Monte Senario produce this aromatic liqueur from herbs and fir cone seeds.

VALDARNO COCKERELS
These free-range cockerels with yellow legs and a bright red crest are typical of certain villages in the Valdarno. They have firm, flavoursome flesh and are especially delicious in casseroles.

WHAT TO SAMPLE
Cantucci all'anice are sweet crunchy biscuits flavoured with aniseed. They are usually dunked in red wine before eating. They are made in Prato by the same firm that make *cantuccini (see p34)*. Various **herbal liqueurs** are produced by the monks of Monte Senario and Camaldoli, who also sell **honey**, **sweets** and **chocolate**. The Sieve and other rivers yield very fine **trout**. In the Casentino in particular, many shepherds make cheese and some of their **pecorino** and **ricotta** is as good as that produced in the Crete region, a popular cheese-making region to the south of Siena. **Schiaccioni** are a local large white bean worth trying. The Mugello, the pretty area to the north and east of Florence, has black truffles and the Valdarno region has white as well. The Empoli area produces fine vegetables, including **white asparagus**.

Wild Produce

PINAROLO
(Boletus luteus)

Winter *porcini* has a distinctive cap covered with a skin that comes away easily (the skin has to be removed before eating). Its skin is very slimy and brownish in colour, while the stalk has a broad ring. Found only in pine woods, it is one of the best *porcini* for preserving in oil as well as being excellent devilled fresh.

PORTENTOSO
(Tricholoma portentosum)

This silky grey mushroom is very common in late autumn and can be found in the stands of fir or pine trees mostly in Vallombrosa and Lunigiana. It is excellent preserved in oil or devilled, and is ideal in stews.

CROSTINI CON I CIMBALLI

600 g (1 lb 5 oz) caps of cimballi (funnel-cap mushrooms), chopped • 3 cloves garlic, chopped • pinch of chilli pepper • extra virgin olive oil • 1 dessertspoons chopped tomatoes • 1 sprig of parsley, chopped • salt • Tuscan bread

Place the mushrooms in a saucepan with the garlic and chilli, plenty of oil and salt. Cook over a high heat until the mushrooms shed their moisture, then lower the heat and cook until the moisture evaporates completely. Add the tomato pulp and parsley, and continue cooking for another 10 minutes. Toast slices of Tuscan bread, spread with olive oil and top with the mushrooms.

CIMBALLO
(Clitocybe geotropa)

In its early stages this mushroom – sometimes known as the Ridestone funnel-cap mushroom – looks like a large nail, then it grows into a tall, scented, coffee-coloured funnel. It grows in the mountains and meadows, in coastal areas under hedges, on heaths and in scrub where it forms zig-zag lines. The cap is exquisite; the dried stem is ground into a powder.

DORMIENTE
(Hygrophorus marzuolus)

This spring mushroom – sometimes known as silvery snowbank mushroom – is found in the mountains of Vallombrosa when the snow thaws, and around Siena and Arezzo in February and March. It is protected – only mushrooms larger than 2 cm (¾ inch) can be picked. It has a mild flavour and is excellent fresh, cooked in cream sauces or in flans, or preserved in oil.

CHIOCCIOLE ALLA NEPITELLA (SNAILS WITH CALAMINT LEAVES)

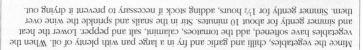

- *1 large onion* • *1 stalk celery* • *1 carrot* • *1 chilli* • *2 cloves garlic* • *extra virgin olive oil*
- *500 g (1 lb 2 oz) peeled tomatoes* • *calamint leaves* • *2 kg (4 lb 8 oz) small white*
snails, ready cleaned • *200 ml (7 fl oz) red wine* • *meat stock* • *salt* • *pepper*

Mince the vegetables, chilli and garlic and fry in a large pan with plenty of oil. When the vegetables have softened, add the tomatoes, calamint, salt and pepper. Lower the heat and simmer gently for about 10 minutes. Stir in the snails and sprinkle the wine over them. Simmer gently for 1½ hours, adding stock if necessary to prevent it drying out.

NEPITELLA
(Calamintha nepeta)

Gathered from early spring until the first frosts, calamint is found from the coast to the hills in Tuscany. It flowers in June and July. In Tuscan cooking it is used with mushrooms, snails, artichokes, or lamb. It must be used in very small quantities otherwise the dish will taste of caramel. It is often confused with mint, but the perfume is sweeter and heavier. Use calamint sparingly because it can cause sleeplessness and palpitations.

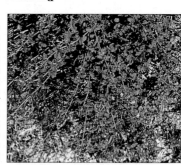

PIMPINELLA
(Sanguisorba minor)

A curious and unmistakable salad herb, *pimpinella* smells rather like melon peel. It is common at all altitudes, especially on the edges of pathways and vegetable patches. Use it raw in salads or add it to white wine for an intriguing aperitif.

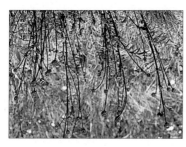

PEPOLINO
(Thymus serpyllum and other varieties)

Wild thyme is the commonest wild herb at all altitudes and latitudes. It is a tender plant that covers walls, stumps of trees and banks between woodland and pasture. The flowered tips are picked between May and October. It is excellent fresh or dried, for roasts, stews and meat sauces. Fresh thyme can be added to salads.

MORA DI ROVA
(Rubus species)

In Tuscany an abundance of blackberries can be found on the edge of thickets. They have large, flavoursome fruits, especially those growing on the Apennine range. They are ideal for jams and syrups and children enjoy picking and eating fresh blackberries.

Places of Interest

FLORENCE, AREZZO AND CASENTINO form a zone that runs the whole length of Tuscany and embraces a large city, cool, shady mountains along the crest of the Apennines, the forests of Casentino and the Mediterranean coast of the Basso Aretino. Its cuisine is a showcase for the region's food and drink, with outlets of notable quality in the Arezzo area – especially the butchers' shops. In the summer many shops close on Saturday afternoons.

AREZZO

🐂 Macelleria Corrado Falcinelli

Palazzo del Pero, 62/a
☎ 0575 369037.
◐ Wed pm.

Corrado Falcinelli, the heir to three generations of butchers and producers of salumi, *guarantees fine Chianina beef and also offers genuine Tuscan all-pork* salumi *completely free from preservatives. The pigs are raised in the traditional fashion locally. The excellent lamb sold here comes from local farms.*

🐂 Pollo San Marco

frazione San Marco,
via dei Frati, 12
☎ 0575 901601.
◐ Sat pm.

Here you will find beef, pork, lamb, an assortment of game birds and animals, plus a variety of other local produce including Chianina beef, the firm's own salumi, *free-range yellow-legged chickens from Valdarno (see p35), and ready-to-cook dishes, such as* collo ripieno *(stuffed neck of beef).*

🐂 Macelleria Sestini

via Romana, 130
☎ 0575 900067.
◐ Wed pm.

Local meat (including Chianina beef) is sold here, along with pork

from the firm's own farm and all kinds of classic salumi. *Specialities of the firm include* pancettone *made from Tuscan bacon and pork, plus suckling pig, stuffed local rabbits and other prepared meats.*

🌾 Panificio Tavanti

borgo Santa Croce, 15
☎ 0575 352354.
◐ Wed pm.

Bread sold here is made in the traditional way and then baked in a wood-fired oven.

🍇 Enoteca Torre di Nicche

piaggia San Martino, 8
☎ 0575 352035.
◘ after 6 pm.

This wine shop, bar and restaurant has a very good selection of Italian wines from all regions and a fine choice of

Tuscan produce. Try the salumi *and cheese or sample hot or cold dishes cooked traditionally. The cakes are home-made.*

BADIA TEDALDA (AR)

🐂 Macelleria Piegai

piazza Bonafede, 23
☎ 0575 714246.
◐ Wed pm.

You can buy Chianina beef from cattle that grazed on the company's farm at Caprile, an "agriturismo" (a place for farm or wine estate holidays). Likewise, the pork is from pigs from a nearby farm. Other specialities include pork and wild boar sausages.

BIVIGLIANO (FI)

🍁 Convento di Monte Senario

☎ 055 406441.
◐ Fri.

As well as their famous Gemma d'Abeto liqueur, the monks produce Elixir di China, Amaro Borghini and Alkermes from an ancient recipe.

PANZANELLA

12 slices stale bread • 2 teaspoons white wine vinegar • 12 anchovy fillets, chopped • 6 tomatoes, cut into wedges • 3 onions, sliced • fresh basil leaves, roughly torn • extra virgin olive oil • salt • pepper

Soften the bread by soaking it in cold water with the vinegar added. Squeeze it dry and divide it between six plates or bowls. Cover each slice of bread with some of the chopped anchovy, tomato wedges, onion slices and torn basil leaves. Drizzle olive oil over the top, season with salt and pepper, then repeat to make a second layer.

Fattoria Ambra

via Lombarda, 85
📞 055 8719049.

This estate's wine-making technique is based on a policy of separating the different varieties of grape so the wine-makers have more control over the combinations of grapes and are better able to harmonise the final blend. Much of the production is devoted to producing the estate's top wines, Carmignano Vigna Santa Cristina in Pilli and two Reserves: Le Vigne Alte and Elzana, all with good structure and a velvety texture. The Barco Reale makes excellent drinking.

STRACOTTO ALLA FIORENTINA

1 kg (2 lb 4 oz) braising steak or brisket in a single piece tied with string • 500 ml (17 fl oz) Chianti wine • sprigs of rosemary and sage • 1–2 bay leaves • 4 cloves garlic, chopped • 2 onions, chopped • 3 sticks celery, chopped • 3 carrots, chopped • extra virgin olive oil • 500 g (1 lb 2 oz) plum tomatoes, chopped • salt • pepper

Put the beef in a bowl with the wine, herbs and all the vegetables except the tomatoes. Leave to marinate in a cool place for 12 hours. Drain the meat and pat dry. Heat the oil in a flameproof casserole, add the meat and brown all over to seal it. Remove the vegetables from the marinade with a slotted spoon and brown them in a little oil in a second pan, then add to the beef. Pour in the wine from the marinade, add the tomatoes and simmer for 30 minutes. Remove the vegetables, purée them and pour the purée back into the pan. Simmer for a further 4 hours, adding water if necessary (but keep the gravy thick). Season with salt and pepper. Untie the meat and serve cut into thick slices, accompanied by the gravy.

La Pasta di Anna Paola

via Puccini, 237
📞 055 8879505. ● Mon.

Here you will find a wide range of flat and stuffed pasta specialities made from good quality fresh ingredients. The extensive selection varies according to the season and the produce available.

Antica Farmacia dei Monaci Camaldolesi

via Camaldoli
📞 0575 556143.
● Wed.

The Carthusian monks at the monastery produce various liqueurs flavoured with different herbs, an aperitif, a dessert liqueur made from fir cones, sweets (such as pine, barley, honey and fruit drops), and a wide variety of honey (with forest honey their local speciality). The monks also make chocolate from their own special recipe.

Tenuta Cantagallo

località Capraia Fiorentina, via Vallacarda, 35
📞 0571 910078.

The sea breezes that play over the hillside enable aromatic grapes to be grown successfully here. Alongside the production of the classic Chianti di Montalbano and a Reserve, Carleto is also produced from Rhine Riesling. For a more international style, there is Raffaello made from Sangiovese, Syrah and Merlot grapes. The olives yield a fine-scented and flavoursome oil – some is bottled as Laudemio and some is used to preserve fresh vegetables. The honey and the grape jam are very good.

Fattoria di Artimino

viale Papa Giovanni XXIII, 3
📞 055 8751424.

With about 70 hectares (173 acres) of vineyards and twice this area under olive groves, this is one of the most beautiful and interesting Tuscan estates. The Medici villa complex houses a four-star hotel (Hotel Paggeria Medicea) and two restaurants (Biagio Pignatta and Le Cantine del Redi). The vineyard's leading wines are Carmignano and Carmignano Riserva Villa Medicea, as well as Barco Reale and also Vin Santo, the rich sweet dessert wine which is made from Malvasia and Trebbiano grapes.

Fattoria Ambra at Carmignano

FAGIOLI AL FIASCO (BEANS IN A FLASK)

450 g (1 lb) dried cannellini beans • 1 sprig of sage • 2 cloves garlic, crushed • extra virgin olive oil • pepper • salt

Soak the beans in cold water overnight. The next day, drain them and put in a pan with all the other ingredients, adding plenty of oil. Add enough water to cover, bring to the boil and simmer for 1–2 hours. In Tuscany, the beans are cooked in a Chianti flask placed in the embers of a fire. Use fresh Sorana beans instead, if available (see p61).

CORTONA (AR)

🍷 Tenimenti D'Alessandro Luigi

viale Manzano, 15
C 0575 618667.

This is the former Fattoria di Manzano under a new name. The estate's policy is to produce wines from carefully selected grapes. Notable whites are Podere Fontarca (Chardonnay and Viognier) and Terrazze (Sauvignon Blanc, Grechetto and Chenin Blanc). The estate's gem is Podere il Bosco made from Syrah grapes, followed by Podere Migliare, from Sangiovese grapes.

FLORENCE

🍷 Enoteca Alessi

via delle Oche, 27/29
C 055 214966.
O Sat in July.

This large wine shop has two levels. The lower floor contains over 2,000 of the very finest Italian wines, sub-divided by region and commune. The serving counter is on the upper floor where you can find Tuscan and house specialities, particularly confectionery, as well as a choice selection of liqueurs and spirits.

CASTIGLION FIORENTINO (AR)

🫒 Frantoio Amatucci

località Noceta, 41/b
C 0575 657129.

This olive mill produces and sells the traditional extra virgin olive oil of the Colli Aretini. The oil is ideal for use in classic Tuscan soups and all dishes finished with a drizzle of good quality olive oil.

🍷 Tenuta Capezzana

via Capezzana, 100
C 055 8706005.

This is the largest farm property in Carmignano with about 90 hectares (222 acres) of vineyards and 150 hectares (370 acres) of olives surrounding a fine 18th-century Medici villa. The wines with the Carmignano label are Barco Reale, Rosso and Vin Santo Riserva. The rosé Vin Ruspo is delicious. The Ghiaie della Furba deserves special mention: made from Cabernet Franc, Cabernet Sauvignon and Merlot grapes in equal parts (a claret blend), it is one of the most prized wines (a "Super Tuscan") in Italy. The extra virgin olive oil is excellent.

🍷 Il Poggiolo

via Pistoiese, 76
C 055 8711242.

The vineyards here are scattered over the heart of the commune and the estate focuses on the whole range of Carmignano wines. This includes a traditional red (a reserve; a rosé called Vin Ruspo; and a younger Barco Reale and Vin Santo based on Trebbiano.

Il Poggiolo at Carmignano

✸ Boutique dei Dolci

via Fabroni, 18 r
📞 055 499503.
⬤ Mon.

*An original confectionery
shop founded and run
by an Italian-American.
The recipes are American,
English, French and
Dutch, all prepared with
organically grown
ingredients. The theme
cakes for kids, made
with original American
cake moulds of Disney
and Warner Brothers
cartoon characters, are
one of the shop's
specialities, as is the
classic cheesecake.*

⚖ Salumeria Del Panta

via San Antonino, 49 r
📞 055 216889.
⬤ Mon.

*This shop features a vast
assortment of traditional
Tuscan* salumi *and
cheeses, some of them
almost impossible to
find elsewhere. It also
offers excellent
international specialities.
Here you will find the
finest preserved fish –
anchovies, sardines,
herrings, dried or salted
cod. There are all sorts of
pickles, preserves in oil,
flour, pulses and cereals,
including some very
unusual ones, plus
different kinds of rice,
and spices sold loose.*

✸ Dolci e Dolcezze

piazza Beccaria 8 r,
📞 055 2345458.
⬤ Mon.

*This confectioner's and
café is renowned for its
very imaginative sweets
and cakes, as well as some
interesting savouries. All
ingredients are carefully
chosen from natural
produce and artificial
or chemical products are
rigorously excluded.*

Cantinetta Antinori

🥫 Fernando Primizie

via Don Minzoni, 38 r
📞 055 587540.
⬤ Wed pm.

*Here you will find a good
variety of vegetables and
fruit, organically grown
or from small local market
gardens. There are also
cheeses and preserves and
a fine selection of wines,
though Tuscans dominate.*

🍇 Enoteca Romano Gambi

via Senese, 21 r
📞 055 222525.
⬤ Sun.

*All the names that count
among local and Italian
wines, plus wines from
France and the US, can be
found here. There is also a
good selection of whisky
and grappa and a range
of sweets, cakes and
snacks. Salumi and cheese
are sold at Christmas.
Book for a tasting. A
second shop is in the town
centre at Via Borgo SS.
Apostoli, 21-23 r
(055 292646).*

❄ Gelateria Giorgio

via Duccio da Boninsegna, 36
📞 055 710849.
◻ Mon.

*This shop is celebrated
throughout Tuscany for its
quality ice-cream and the*
torta millefoglie *(vanilla
slice) and Florentine*
schiacciata *(bread).*

🍇 Marchesi Antinori

piazza degli Antinori, 3
📞 055 2359877.

*The grapes come from this
winery's various estates to
create a good range of
wines. The stars are the
famed Tignanello from
Sangiovese and Cabernet
grapes (a "Super
Tuscan"), and Solaia
(Cabernet Sauvignon and
Sangiovese grapes). There
are also very good
chiantis, including the
Chianti Classico Peppoli,
and the Reserves: Badia a
Passignano and Tenute
Marchesi Antinori. Note
the white Galestro, a wine
Antinori helped to create.
There is also a spumante:
Marchese Antinori Nature.
The extra virgin olive oil is
very good, especially from
the Fattoria Peppoli di
San Casciano Val di Pesa.
For purchases apply to:
La Cantinetta Antinori,
Piazza degli Antinori, 3
(055 292234).*

**LAMPREDOTTO
E TRIPPA IN ZIMINO**

*extra virgin olive oil •
3 cloves garlic , chopped
• 500 g (1 lb 2 oz)
tomatoes, peeled • 1 chilli,
deseeded and chopped •
1 kg (2 lb 4 oz) beet
leaves, cut into strips •
1 kg (2 lb 4 oz) plain
tripe (see below), cut into
strips • salt • pepper*

Heat some oil in a pan,
cook the garlic briefly,
then add the tomatoes
and cook for about 10
minutes. Add the greens
and cook for 3 minutes.
Add the tripe, season
and cook for 40–45
minutes. In Italy this dish
is made with half plain
tripe and half *millefoglie*
tripe (which looks like
the leaves of a book).

🍇 Marchesi de' Frescobaldi

via Santo Spirito, 11
☎ 055 27141.

Generations of the Frescobaldi family have been making wine in Tuscany for centuries. The Chianti Rùfina Montesodi and Riserva Castello di Nipozzano are well known. Also note the various versions of Pomino: Bianco, Rosso and Il Benefizio, of which the company is virtually the only producer. For purchases apply to the Enoteca Romano Gambi (see p41).

🌿 Pastificio Moretti

via Datini, 22 r
☎ 055 685607.

On offer here is a wide range of pasta, and also ready cooked food.

🏛 Gastronomia Palmieri

via Manni, 48 r
☎ 055 602081.

The variety and quality of its products make this one of Italy's most interesting cheese shops. This fine delicatessen offers an excellent choice of delicacies – caviar, pâté de foie gras, bread baked in a wood-fired oven, preserves, extra virgin olive oil, salumi and much else. There is a well-stocked enoteca (wine cellar) with some foreign wines and there is an excellent selection of ready cooked dishes on sale.

🏛 Gastronomia Pegna

via dello Studio, 26 r
☎ 055 282701.
⬤ Wed pm.

Pegna has been a household name in

BACCALÀ ALLA FIORENTINA

extra virgin olive oil • 3 cloves garlic, chopped • 1 onion, chopped • 450 g (1 lb) tomatoes, peeled • 1 kg (2 lb 4 oz) salt cod, presoaked • 1–2 tablespoons chopped fresh parsley • flour • salt • pepper • parsley, to garnish

Heat some oil in a pan, add the garlic and onion and cook until lightly browned. Add the tomatoes and season with salt and pepper. Meanwhile, bone the cod, leaving the skin on, and cut it into largish squares. Heat plenty of oil in a pan, Flour the pieces of cod, add them to the hot oil and fry until golden. Remove the fish from the pan, drain on kitchen paper and add it to the tomato sauce. Stir in the chopped parsley and serve garnished with extra parsley.

Florence for 140 years. The products are skilfully selected from Italy and abroad and include a choice of salumi, cheese, preserves, spices, terrines and confectionery.

🍇 Pitti Gola e Cantina

piazza Pitti, 16
☎ 055 212704.
⬤ Mon.

Close to Palazzo Pitti, this wine shop boasts a clientèle of Florentine connoisseurs who enjoy the wide range of wines, spirits, preserves and pickles, all strictly Tuscan produce. Visitors can browse through cookery books and there is an area for wine-tasting.

🌿 Forno di Marcello Pugi

viale De Amicis, 49 r
☎ 055 669666.
⬤ Fri pm.

This bakery is famous in Florence and the surrounding area for its delicious schiacciata all'olio (olive oil bread) and pizza slices. The excellent bread is made using fresh yeast.

✳ Bar Pasticceria Robiglio

via dei Servi, 112 r
☎ 055 212784.
⬤ Sun.

For almost 75 years Robiglio has delighted gourmets with its traditional confectionery and excellent coffee. There are two other branches, one in via Tosinghi 11 r (055 215013) and the other in viale Lavagnini 18 r (055 490886). A wide choice of delectable pralines and snacks is available at the bar.

🏛 Salumificio Senese

via Ugnano, 10
☎ 055 751611.
⬤ Wed pm.

This firm produces excellent fresh meat from pigs raised on its own farm at Lastra a Signa and by other local breeders. They make their own salumi, including the Tuscan classics, and serve aromatic sausages from other regions. They do roast suckling pig and cooked meats to order.

Macelleria Soderi Paolo

interno Mercato Centrale
San Lorenzo
055 2398496.
pm.

*Exceptionally good beef
(sometimes Chianina),
fine Fanano pork, lamb
from the mountains of
Pistoia and various ready
to cook cuts of meat plus
about 30 types of
hamburger are sold here.
Follow their instructions
for grilling the meat.*

Sugar Blues

via XXVII Aprile, 46/48 r
055 483666.
Wed pm.

*This shop specializes in
macrobiotic foods.
Gourmets looking for
wholesome, organically
grown produce, and both
fresh and preserved
specialities will find it
worth a visit. A selection
of natural essences are
also sold. Another shop
is in Cappalle, in the
"I Gigli" shopping centre
(055 898286).*

Pescheria Tirrena

via dei Cerchi, 20 r
055 216602.
Wed pm.

*The owner of this shop is
a real expert. Every day
he selects the pick of the
catch, especially shellfish
and top quality white fish.*

Fratelli Vettori

borgo San Jacopo,
63 r
055 212797.
Wed pm.

*Fruit and
vegetables
of outstanding
quality, including
spring vegetables, are
sold here. Prices are
high partly because of the*
*quality of the produce
and partly because of the
shop's well-deserved fame.*

Gelateria Vivoli

via Isola delle Stinche, 7 r
055 292334.
Mon. Sun.

*The same family still
oversees the high quality
of the ingredients used in
this ice-cream parlour,
which has been famous
in Florence for 70 years.
Today there are more
than 40 ice-cream
flavours to choose from.
The classics – cream,
chocolate, lemon and
torroncino (nougat) – are
based on recipes going
back to the 1920s. In the
café, the breads and
puddings are made from
natural ingredients.*

Macelleria Zagli

via Valori, 6 r
055 587571.
Mon pm, Wed pm.

*This butcher's shop stakes
its name on quality
Tuscan produce such as
Chianina beef (and not
just the rib steaks but
also the less prized cuts),
free-range Valdarno
chickens and pork from
Tuscan pigs. Various
ready-to-cook dishes are
also sold.*

FOIANO DELLA CHIANA (AR)

Caseificio Matteassi

via di Cortona, 66a
0575 649101.

*Here you will find an
excellent range of
pecorino and ricotta
cheeses made from milk
produced by local flocks
of sheep.*

MONTELUPO FIORENTINO (FI)

San Vito in Fior di Selva

località Malmantile
0571 51411.

*This estate is set in a
wonderful panoramic
position amid woods
just 20 km (12 miles)
from Florence. It is
farmed organically
and produces Chianti
Colli Fiorentini, plus Vin
Santo, spumante and
grappa. It also produces
good extra virgin olive
oil and honey. The
estate is one of many
agriturismo farms, with
holiday apartments for
visitors to rent, and it
serves a range of good
quality refreshments to
visiting tourists.*

CASTAGNACCIO (CHESTNUT CAKE)

**400 g (14 oz) chestnut flour • 4 walnuts, crushed •
75 g (2¾ oz) pine nuts • 50 g (1¾ oz) raisins
• 1 sprig of rosemary • extra virgin olive
oil • salt**

Preheat the oven to 200°C
(400°F/gas mark 6). Put the flour
and a pinch of salt into a mixing
bowl. Whisk in enough warm
water to make a paste. Pour into
a greased 20 cm (8 inch) cake tin
and bake in the oven for 5–6
minutes. Scatter the walnuts, pine
nuts, raisins and rosemary leaves
over the top and sprinkle with oil.
Bake for a further 20 minutes.

MONTEMURLO (PO)

Tenuta di Bagnolo
via Montalese, 156
C 0574 652439.

This 16th-century estate belongs to the Marquis Pancrazi, who inherited it from the Strozzi family of Montemurlo. The estate is well known for its Villa di Bagnolo extra virgin olive oil. It also produces good quality wine, which is bottled after two months of storage in oak barriques to soften it a little. The wine is made from Pinot Nero grapes. These vines were first planted here when they were mistakenly sold as Sangiovese in the 1970s. The Casaglia extra virgin olive oil from another family estate at Calamarcio is excellent.

PALAZZUOLO SUL SENIO (FI)

Dispensa della Locanda
via Borgo dell'Oro, 1
C 055 804019.
○ Wed.
○ Sun.

Among the firm's own specialities are prosciutto and salame from Cinta Senese pigs – these differ from the standard Cinta Senese breed because they have developed features that help them adapt to high altitudes. The firm also produces cocktail onions preserved in oil, quince jam, liqueurs from fruit and wild herbs, chestnut honey and various other local delicacies.

Azienda Agricola Lozzole
frazione Quadalto
Lozzole **C** 055 8043505.

A large number of goats, sheep and pigs that graze freely in chestnut woods are bred here. The estate sells a range of fresh and mature pecorino and caprino (goat's milk) cheeses, some scented with herbs, and chestnuts in season. The farm has not yet received a permit to butcher its own meat, however.

PIEVE AL BAGNORO (AR)

Villa Cilnia
località Montoncello, 27
C 0575 365017.

This medium-sized wine estate in the Aretine Hills offers a good Chianti Colli Aretini and Chianti Riserva. It also produces Mecenate, made from Chardonnay and Sauvignon Blanc grapes, and Vocato made from Sangiovese and Cabernet Sauvignon grapes.

PONTASSIEVE (FI)

Tenuta di Bossi
via dello Stracchino, 32
C 055 8317830.

The estate's star wine is its Mazzaferrata red made from Sangiovese and Cabernet Sauvignon in equal parts. Also interesting is its Chianti Rufina Riserva Villa Bossi matured in both small and large barrels, and the Colli dell'Etruria Centrale Vin Santo. The extra virgin olive oil – some of which is bottled as Laudemio – is noteworthy.

Tenimenti Ruffino
via Aretina, 42/44
C 055 83605.

This firm is owned by the Folonari family who are involved with a number of estates in Tuscany. The range of wines is good, with some notable highlights, such as Cabreo

---

CROSTINI ALLA TOSCANA

350 g extra virgin olive oil • ½ an onion, finely chopped • **300 g (12 oz)** chicken livers • **30 g (1 oz)** butter • **2** anchovy fillets • **20 g (⅔ oz)** capers • **1** glass white wine • meat stock • **4** slices Tuscan bread • chopped tomatoes and herbs (optional) • salt • pepper

Heat some oil in a pan, add the onion and cook until softened. Add the livers, pour in the wine and cook for 5 minutes. Drain the livers and purée with the anchovies and capers. Return to the pan, stir and add enough stock to make a creamy mixture. Season with salt and pepper. Remove the pan from the heat and stir in the butter. Toast the bread, spread with paté and cut each slice into several pieces. Top with chopped tomatoes and herbs, if liked.

di Borgo, made from Sangiovese and Cabernet Sauvignon grapes, and Cabreo La Pietra, from Chardonnay. There are also reds such as Nero di Tondo, a good Pinot Nero, and Romitorio di Santedame from Colorino and Prugnolo. Ruffino also produce Chianti and Vino Nobile di Montepulciano.

🍷 Fattoria di Galiga e Vetrice

località Montebonello
via Vetrice, 5
📞 055 8397008.

Fattoria di Galiga e Vetrice at Pontassieve

This estate is among the leading producers of Chianti Rùfina, and makes good quality wines. The estate also produces Vin Santo and an excellent extra virgin olive oil called "Il Lastro".

❄ Gelateria Sottani

località San Francesco,
via Forlivese, 93
📞 055 8368092.
⬤ Wed pm.

The owner of this ice-cream parlour boasts that only natural products – in particular, good quality fresh milk from the Mugello – go into the ice-creams. There is an extraordinary range of flavours – all the classics plus inzuppato al Vin Santo. Whatever fruit is

in the market – including exotic varieties and wild fruit – is included in their delicious sorbets.

🍷 Fattoria Torre a Decima

località Molino del Piano
📞 055 8317804.

This estate's strategy is to promote Malvasia Nera grapes, which are present in the Chianti Colli Fiorentini and the Rosso della Torre, combined with Sangiovese and Cabernet Sauvignon.

PRATO

🏛 Gastronomia Barni

via Ferrucci, 24
📞 0574 607845.
⬤ Wed pm.

Carefully selected Italian and French cheeses and fine Tuscan salumi are sold here. The wine shop sells wines from around the world and a selection of dessert wines. The ready cooked dishes are very good.

✴ Pasticceria Luca

via Lazzerini, 2
📞 0574 21628.
⬤ Tues. ◯ Sun.

This shop is owned by Gianluca Mannori, one of Italy's top pastry chefs. He offers numerous eye-catching, delectable specialities, including an Italian celebration cake. The pralines are exceptional, as is the whole chocolate range, especially the highly artistic, hand-painted eggs for Easter.

Oak barrels at the Fattoria Torre a Decima

RUFINA (FI)

Fattoria di Basciano
viale Duca della Vittoria, 159
📞 055 8397034.

The estate has about 20 hectares (49 acres) of vines and another 20 hectares of olive groves. Its produce is carefully made and the wine in particular is excellent value for money. The focus is on red wines with Chianti Rùfina in a standard version and Reserve, and two finer blends kept in new oak barriques for 12 months: I Pini made with equal quantities of Cabernet Sauvignon and Sangiovese, and Il Corso with a bigger proportion of Sangiovese.

CIBREO

1 kg (2 lb 4 oz) chicken livers, hearts, testicles and cock's combs or crests
• extra virgin olive oil
• 1 onion, chopped • 2 cloves garlic • 50 g (1¾ oz) salted anchovies
• 150 g (5½ oz) tomatoes, peeled
• 4 egg yolks • juice of 1 lemon • 1–2 tablespoons chopped fresh parsley
• salt • pepper

Clean and cut up the giblets. Heat plenty of oil in a pan and fry the onion, garlic and anchovies for a few minutes. Add all the giblets and cook until lightly browned. Add the tomatoes and salt and pepper and simmer for 2–3 minutes. Meanwhile, whisk the egg yolks, lemon juice and parsley with a little warm water in a bowl. Remove the pan from the heat. Still whisking, pour the egg mixture into the pan. Serve the mixture hot with rice or polenta.

REGGELLO (FI)

Vannucchi Ortofrutta
via Vincenzo da Filicaia, 2
📞 0574 36382
⏰ Wed pm.

Local produce is sold here in season, and at other times a variety of spring vegetables and exotic fruit from leading producers further afield. Local varieties of beans include cappoini or schiaccioni.

Frantoio di Santa Tea
località Santa Tea, frazione Cascia,
📞 055 868117.

The firm's olive oil has an intensely fresh, fruity bouquet and an aroma of newly mown grass. The flavour is strong and bitter with an aftertaste of the salad leaf rocket.

Primizie di Renato Palermo
via Gobetti, 18
📞 0574 30713
⏰ Wed pm.

This shop offers fruit and vegetables selected for their quality, with the emphasis on organically grown produce, and with trusted market gardeners favoured more than official certificates. As far as possible the produce is as Tuscan, but Renato Palermo also looks further afield to other regions where the produce is fresh, in season and of the finest quality. The same policy guides the selection of various other delicacies: dried pasta, preserves in extra virgin olive oil, traditional sweets and cakes. Note the local big white beans called schiaccioni, and the exotic and dried fruit.

Pasticceria Nuovo Mondo
via Garibaldi, 23
📞 0574 27765.
⏰ Mon. Sun.

Paolo Sacchetti is a top confectioner. He makes international specialities and at Christmas, although be it not Milanese or even from Lombardy, be makes one of the very finest panettoni (a Milanese cake) you can find anywhere.

Biscottificio Mattei
via Ricasoli, 20/22
📞 0574 25756.
⏰ Mon. Sun.

Since 1858, the place to buy biscuits in Prato has been "Mattonella", a store named after the firm's founder, Antonio Mattei. Sample the delicious cantuccini and cantucci all'anice biscuits.

Oil store at the Frantoio di Santa Tea

Azienda Agricola Colognole

via del Palagio, 15
☎ 055 8319870.

This is a family-run firm. The Spalletti name has always been linked with carefully balanced wines that age well, and so the wines marketed are generally a vintage older than average. The grapes from individual vineyards are vinified separately and then blended to make Chianti Rufina and Chianti Rufina Riserva del Don. A single white, Quattro Chiacchere, is made from Chardonnay alone. The estate also produces olive oil of excellent quality and offers agriturismo holiday facilities.

Fattoria Selvapiana

località Selvapiana, 43
☎ 055 8369848.

From a solid family tradition anchored in the land come some of the area's finest Chianti Rufina. The two single-vineyard wines, Bucerchiale and Fornace, both Chianti Rufina riserva, are excellent. Fornace contains a small proportion of Cabernet Sauvignon. The extra virgin olive oil is fabulous and there is also a delicious range of honey.

SANSEPOLCRO (AR)

Erboristeria di Aboca

località Aboca
☎ 0575 7461.
○ Mon.

This is the sales outlet for one of Europe's most important herbalists. Despite the firm's size, Valentino Mercatino has retained his passion for exclusively natural products. Sadly, the firm's current policy favours herbal cures over foodstuffs. All the same, in this wonderful old shop you will find essences (sweet and bitter orange) useful in cooking, plus naturally farmed dried herbs and herbal teas which are ideal for the end of a meal.

SCANDICCI (FI)

Fattoria Baggiolino

località La Romola,
via della Poggiona, 4
☎ 055 7689916.

This firm produces an excellent extra virgin olive oil. It is bottled as Laudemio and is one of the best sold under this name.

TERONTOLA (AR)

Mario Baldetti

località Case Sparse,
via Pietraia di Cortona, 21
☎ 0575 67143.

This winery produces a full-bodied Bianco Vergine della Valdichiana and a white Pietraia from Chardonnay vines. In addition, it makes an interesting red wine – the Rosso Baldetti, made from Sangiovese and Canaiolo grapes.

TRIPPA ALLA FIORENTINA

extra virgin olive oil • 2 stalks celery, finely chopped
• 2 carrots, finely chopped • 1 onion, finely chopped
• 1 kg (2 lb 4 oz) tripe, cut into strips • 300 g (10½ oz)
tomatoes, peeled and chopped • 100 g
(3½ oz) Parmesan cheese, grated
• salt • pepper

Heat some oil in a pan, add the celery, carrots and onion and fry until they have softened a little. Add the tripe and cook it for a few minutes. Add the chopped tomatoes, season to taste with salt and pepper and simmer for 25–30 minutes. Stir in the grated Parmesan cheese and serve at once.

Macelleria Betti

via XX Settembre, 98
☎ 0575 741077.
○ Wed pm.

Here you will find Chianina beef selected from herds in the Val Tiberina, traditional salumi, the firm's own produce (from pigs raised at Porto San Stefano), including excellent loin and sausages in oil. The lamb is from Badia Tedalda.

Gelateria Creperia Ghignoni

via Tiberina Sud, 850
☎ 0575 741900.
○ Tues.
○ Sun.

Not to be missed: the owner, Palmiro Bruschi, won the Italian ice-cream championship. As well as assorted ice-creams, there are delicious crêpes and mousses to try.

LUNIGIANA, GARFAGNANA AND VERSILIA

Lunigiana, Garfagnana and Versilia

R UNNING FROM THE COAST to the highest peaks of the Apennine
ridge, this area has something for everyone. Versilia has a
long tradition of excellent dishes made with fresh local fish. The
Garfagnana offers a very rustic way of life. The Lunigiana has a
cuisine that takes elements from the three bordering regions:
Tuscany, Liguria and Emilia-Romagna. In this area farming and the food industry
provide the greatest variety of gourmet pleasures. The area also shows great
inventiveness in the choice of vines for wine, and it is unrivalled in Italy (or the
world) for *porcini* (cep mushrooms). Mushrooms
are not the only woodland food to play a
part in the area's cuisine – chestnuts,
bilberries and raspberries are all widely
used. Finally, there is Pescia, not only
the centre of Italian flower culture but
also right in the middle of an area
producing wonderful
fruit and vegetables.

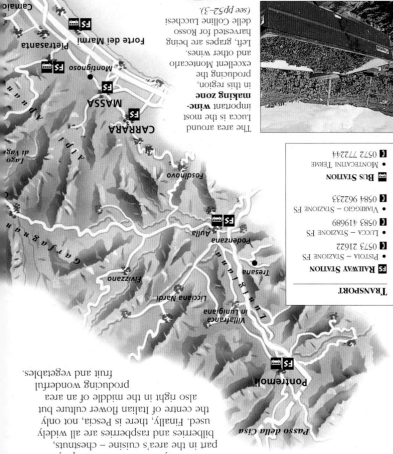

The area around
Lucca is the most
important **wine-
making zone**
in this region,
producing the
excellent Montecarlo
and other wines.
Left, grapes are being
harvested for Rosso
delle Colline Lucchesi
(see pp52–3).

PORCINI

The *porcini* at Garfagnana
are among the world's finest,
especially those from wooded
mountain slopes. They are
usually sold from September
to November.

▷ Drying grapes for the "governo" (fortifying) of wine

TRANSPORT

🚊 RAILWAY STATION

• PISTOIA – STAZIONE FS
  📞 0573 21622
• LUCCA – STAZIONE FS
  📞 0583 419689
• VIAREGGIO – STAZIONE FS
  📞 0584 962233

🚌 BUS STATION

• MONTECATINI TERME
  📞 0572 772244

VIAREGGIO 🚊

Lido di
Camaiore

Camaiore

Pietrasanta

Forte dei Marmi

Montignoso

MASSA

CARRARA

Fosdinovo

Lago di Vag

Alpi Apuane

Aulla

Podenzana

Fivizzano

Tresana

Licciana Nardi

Villafranca
in Lunigiana

Lunigiana

Garfagnana

Pontremoli

Passo della Cisa

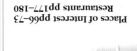

Places of Interest pp66–73
Restaurants pp177–180

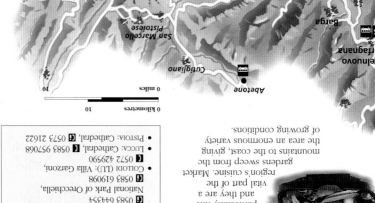

STAR ATTRACTIONS

- CAPANNORI (LU): Villa Torrigiani,
  ☎ 0583 928008
- CASTELNUOVO DI GARFAGNANA (LU):
  National Park of the Apuan Alps,
  ☎ 0583 644354
  National Park of Orecchiella,
  ☎ 0583 619098
  COLLODI (LU): Villa Garzoni,
  ☎ 0572 429590
- Lucca: Cathedral, **☎** 0583 957068
- Pistoia: Cathedral, **☎** 0573 21622

Tuscany's fresh **vegetables** are particularly fine and they are a vital part of the region's cuisine. Market gardens sweep from the mountains to the coast, giving the area an enormous variety of growing conditions.

Viareggio is not simply a fashionable seaside resort, it is also a very active fishing harbour where a splendid variety of **fresh fish and shellfish** (see pp54–7) is landed.

Agriturismo
(Farmhouse holidays) in the Garfagnana are very popular with visitors. The area is dotted with lovely old farmhouses, each with a fascinating history.

Wines

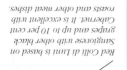

THE ALPI APUANE (APUAN ALPS), which run parallel with a stretch of the Tyrrhenian coast between Massa, Carrara and Viareggio, corral the warm sea breezes and create an ideal climate for vineyards. The same breezes flow up the lower part of the Arno Valley, creating equally good conditions for vines at Lucca. Further inland, toward Pistoia, the influence of the sea wanes, but the Apennine ridge gives shelter from the colder influences of the north and helps to provide a favourable climate for growing flowers. This area produces very respectable white wines from vines like Vermentino and Albarola, a link with nearby Liguria, as well as Trebbiano Toscano, Greco, Grechetto and Malvasia del Chianti vines. Certain French varieties have long been grown locally and are used in some of the DOC wines, such as Pinot, Semillon, Sauvignon and Roussanne. The same is true of reds: alongside Sangiovese, Canaiolo and rare vines like Ciliegiolo, Colorino, Malvasia Nera and Pollera Nera are Syrah, Cabernet and Merlot.

CANDIA DEI COLLI APUANI

This white wine is made in a tiny area at the foot of the Apuan Alps above Massa and Carrara, so production is limited. Made from two Ligurian vines, Vermentino and Albarola, the wine is straw-coloured with a fine scent and low alcohol content. It is perfect with *frittelline di cieche* (made with the fry of eels) and delicate fish dishes. There is also a Vin Santo version.

White Colli di Luni is based on Vermentino with some Trebbiano Toscano and other white grapes. It is perfect with fish antipasti and vegetable soups.

COLLI DI LUNI

This is a recent denomination. Its production straddles the two regions of Liguria and Tuscany.

Red Colli di Luni is based on Sangiovese with other black grapes and up to 10 per cent Cabernet. It is excellent with roasts and other meat dishes.

SCALOPPINE AI PORCINI

600 g (1 lb 6 oz) *porcini (cep mushrooms), sliced* • **2** *cloves garlic* • *extra virgin olive oil* • **50 g (1¾ oz)** *butter* • **1** *small onion, chopped* • **6** *veal escalopes* • *white wine* • *meat stock* • *salt* • *pepper* • **1** *sprig calamint or mint*

Fry the mushrooms in a shallow pan with one of the cloves of garlic, some oil and salt over a high heat until their moisture evaporates. In a separate pan, heat the butter with a little oil. Chop the second garlic clove and lightly fry with the onion in the butter. Add the escalopes and cook until browned on both sides. Season with salt and pepper and moisten with a little white wine . Cook until the meat is almost tender, then cover it with the mushrooms. Add a little stock and the calamint leaves and cook together for 1 minute before serving.

OTHER WINES WORTH TRYING

In the province of Pistoia you will find DOC Colli dell'Etruria Centrale and also DOC Chianti, some of which is made using the "governo" technique of adding dried grapes or must to the fermented wine to soften it.

Red Montecarlo (made from Sangiovese and Canaiolo, Syrah, Cabernet and Merlot) goes with spelt or mushroom dishes.

WINE TYPE	GOOD VINTAGES	GOOD PRODUCERS
Red Wine		
Super Tuscans (see p130)	98, 97, 95, 90	Moretti, Le Murelle di Lucca
Colline Lucchesi	99, 97	Valgiano di Capannori, La Badiola di Capannori
White Wine		
Montecarlo	00, 99	Fattoria del Buonamico, Fattoria del Teso

MONTECARLO

This wine is made from traditional Tuscan grapes together with some French ones, which give it a finer perfume and a well-balanced flavour.

The white (Trebbiano Semillon, Pinot Grigio and Bianco, Vermentino, Sauvignon and Roussanne) goes with delicate pastasciutte (pasta) and fried fish.

The white is made from seven varieties of white grapes, creating a wine with a subtle delicate perfume that is well-suited to soups and vegetable and omelettes.

CIONCIA

- **1 kg (2 lb 4 oz) veal** (traditionally flesh from the head, cheeks, tail, but use ready diced pie veal, if necessary) • **extra-virgin olive oil** • **3 stalks celery, chopped** • **3 carrots, chopped** • **1 onion, chopped** • **200 g (7 oz) tomatoes, peeled** • **chopped fresh parsley** • **chopped fresh basil** • **black olives** • **1 glass white wine** • **chilli pepper** • **salt**

Trim and wash the veal and cut into small pieces. Place in a pan, cover with water and simmer for about 30 minutes, then drain well. Heat some oil and fry the meat lightly, then add the chopped vegetables and tomatoes, herbs, olives and wine. Season with chilli pepper and salt and simmer for 3 hours.

COLLINE LUCCHESI

This denomination applies to wines produced on the hills around Lucca. In addition to the generic whites, rosés and reds, it includes varietals (wines made from single grape varieties): Vermentino and Sauvignon grapes for whites, Sangiovese and Merlot for the reds which have the Riserva label. The grapes for table wines are also used to make white and red Vin Santo.

The rosé and red are both made from Sangiovese and Canaiolo Nero. The red resembles a young, very drinkable Chianti and is perfect with suckling pig, fried chicken or roast rabbit.

Fish and Seafood

IT IS A PLEASURE to visit the outdoor market at the popular coastal resort of Viareggio when the sea is calm and the fishing boats have been out. With both rocky and sandy sea beds close at hand, and the seas around the island of Gorgona rich with fish, the catch is varied. There are excellent cheap fish on sale, as well as the seasonal ones that pass through these waters – fish that are hard to find even in the big city markets. The shellfish are nearly always sold still alive at the market. Viareggio has the same varieties of fish found in other Tuscan sea ports: those typical of Livorno's cuisine are described on *pp78–9*, others on *pp14–5* and *p161*. The local cuisine is noteworthy for its use of fewer spices than other regions – the fish is so fresh it does not need to be disguised with sauces or other artifice.

ORATA (GILTHEAD BREAM)

Gilthead are much sought after for their white firm flesh and fine flavour which comes from feeding mainly on shellfish. Those caught at sea, especially if well-grown (quite common in this area), are delectable. They are excellent grilled, baked and cooked *en papillotte* (in paper).

Generally small gilthead or portions of larger fish come from fish farms.

GALINELLA

There are various species of gallinella (also called "capone"), types of gurnard, and they are found on sandy sea beds. Their flesh is white, juicy and very tasty. They are ideal for soups, and are excellent baked or cooked with vegetables.

MORMORA (STRIPED BREAM)

Abundant, especially in summer, this is the commonest white fish on the sandy sea bed. It is less popular than other white fish because the flesh is not so firm. It can be baked or grilled.

Striped bream have dark vertical streaks on the scales.

POLPO DI SCOGLIO OR PIOVRA (ROCK OCTOPUS)

These are very common at the markets and are frequently sold alive. Large ones need to be pounded to tenderize the flesh. They are cooked, without water or seasoning, in a saucepan with the lid firmly closed, then seasoned to taste.

OMBRINA

Also known as *corvo* in Tuscany, this is a staple of the
seafood cuisine along the entire coastline. Its firm white flesh
is excellent grilled, baked, boiled or cooked in mixed dishes.
Even more highly prized is the *corvina* or
ombrina bastarda, which is similar
and equally good to eat. It is
caught almost only off Elba,
mainly in winter.

TOTANO
This variety of
squid is not as
highly prized or
costly as *calamari*.
It is excellent fried
or grilled.

*Flaps distinguish
this squid from
calamari.*

SGOMBRO (MACKEREL)
This tasty oily fish is very good grilled.
Those sold at the harbour in Viareggio are
particularly popular.

SUGARELLO OR SURO (SCAD)
Good value for money, the scad or horse mackerel is
ideal for grilling or cooking *en papillotte*.

OTHER MOLLUSCS WORTH TRYING
Moscardini (small squid) are valued for sauces, especially the autumn fry called
fragolini. There are numerous kinds of shellfish. The finest **cozze** (mussels) are
farmed at nearby La Spezia. **Coltellacci** or **cannolicchio** or **cannelli** (razor clams),
much appreciated in Versilia, have a long shell which contains a sweet, fleshy mollusc.
Telline and **arselle** are important in Viareggio's cuisine, but these smooth wedge-
shaped clams are very rare. The clams called **vongola grigia** or **cappa gallina** are
used in pasta sauces. The **tartufo di mare** (Venus clam), which is very expensive, is
sometimes eaten raw. The little cockles called **cuori**, picked up by children on the
beaches, have grooved shells and contain a hard red mollusc which is tasty when
cooked in seafood sauces. **Capesante** or **pellegrine** (scallops) are good but most are
imported. Also popular are the sea-snails (**chioccioline di mare**) called **maruzzelle**.

OTHER CRUSTACEANS WORTH TRYING

Gamberetti grigi (brown shrimps) are common at the markets: they are fried and eaten, shell and all. **Astici** (lobsters) are widely eaten but are not locally caught. **Aragoste** (crayfish) are caught off the islands and Argentario, but at the markets you will find mostly fine Sardinian ones. The big red crabs and granseola crabs are more typical of Italy's east coast, while here you find dark **granchi** (crabs) used in soups.

TRACINO OR PESCE RAGNO (WEEVER)

This fish is found on the sandy sea bed. The flesh is white, tasty and ideal for soups. It is very common and good value. The fish must be handled carefully because it has poisonous spines.

CICALO OR CANOCCHIA (MANTIS SHRIMP)

This common crustacean is cheap, with sweet flesh. It is excellent boiled and served in salads and is essential for soups, including *cacciucco*.

The mantis shrimp is best when bought alive.

SCAMPO (SCAMPI)

Scampi from Gorgonia reach the Tuscan ports alive. They are delicious, with sweet firm flesh. Excellent raw and in myriad classic recipes, or for creative cooking.

Buy scampi alive if you can.

ALICE OR ACCIUGA (ANCHOVY)

These small blue fish are very tasty when freshly caught. In Tuscany, they are eaten fried, marinated raw or baked in fishcakes, much as elsewhere in Italy. Salted, preserved anchovies are delicious with unsalted Tuscan bread.

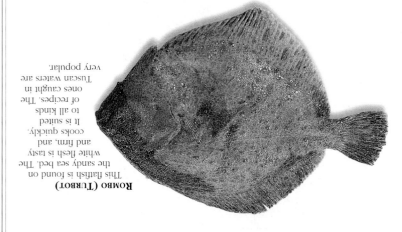

Anchovies are more slender than sardines.

ROMBO (TURBOT)

This flatfish is found on the sandy sea bed. The white flesh is tasty and firm, and cooks quickly. It is suited to all kinds of recipes. The ones caught in Tuscan waters are very popular.

BRANZINO OR SPIGOLA (SEA BASS)

Sea bass is the most sought-after fish on the market. Actively farmed, it is always excellent, but those caught with a hook and line, especially large ones, are definitely the finest. It is cooked *en papillote*, baked or grilled. Tuscans like to cook it with wild fennel.

OTHER FISH WORTH TRYING

Dentice (dentex) are often caught with depth lines. **Occhiata** (saddled bream), which live in schools along the coast, are good grilled. **Tonnetti** (small tunny fish) are sliced and grilled or stewed. **John Dory** (**sanpietro**, in Tuscany, but also **pesce gallo**) has delectable flesh. **Soglioline** (sole) caught along the coast are better than imported ones. **Cernie** (grouper) and **cernìole** (wreckfish) are caught off the islands, as are large fish such as **leccia** (amberjack) and **pesce castagna** (Ray's bream).

Game Birds

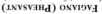

G AME BIRDS ARE an important part of Tuscany's gourmet tradition, and the marshlands near Torre del Lago ensure that this is an area rich in birds. The area offers unique recipes using ingredients that are not easy to find elsewhere, such as coot, mallard and small marsh ducks. In the market at Viareggio, and the ones in other cities in the area, you can buy all kinds of game birds which in other parts of Tuscany can only be found in specialist shops supplying the catering industry.

TORDO (THRUSH)

Songbirds such as song thrush, rock thrush, mistle thrush and fieldfare are appreciated for their tender, aromatic flesh, especially when the birds have been feeding on the sweet-smelling berries that grow wild. The birds are cooked on a spit, or in casseroles with olives, grapes and juniper berries, or they are made into pâtés.

This thrush and blackbird terrine includes both the liver and the giblets. Black truffles add extra flavour to the dish.

GERMANO (MALLARD)

Mallard is the commonest wild duck in Tuscany. Its flesh is much firmer than that of farm-bred duck, and it has a better flavour, but the birds are interchangeable in recipes.

Little bustard is cooked in a casserole with a sweet and sour pickle of sorb apples.

Wild duck goes well with fruit, as in this dish of duck breasts with raspberries and vinegar.

MERLO (BLACKBIRD)

Although blackbirds are widely hunted, they are not as popular as thrushes. They have a good flavour from feeding on berries, but the flesh is tough. The flavour comes out best in *pâtés* and dishes that require lengthy cooking.

FAGIANO (PHEASANT)

The pheasant is the hunters' favourite prey. It is unlikely to be a wild bird, since pheasants are bred for the game reserves. When newly released their flesh is pretty tasteless, but after living in the wild and feeding freely for some time they acquire a gamey flavour. Pheasants are roasted, cooked in casseroles with cream, truffles and fruit, or in traditional *salmi*, and are made into countless pâtés and terrines.

FOLAGA ALLA PUCCINI

- *1 coot • Juice of 1 lemon • extra virgin olive oil • 1 carrot, finely chopped • 2 onions, finely chopped • 1 stalk celery, finely chopped • 4 bay leaves • 1 sprig of thyme • 1 fresh chilli, finely chopped • a few leaves of calamint (or mint) • 1 salted anchovy, boned • red wine • meat stock • 1 dessertspoon flour • 1 sprig of basil • salt • pepper*

Pluck and skin the coot, then soak it for about 2 hours in cold water mixed with the lemon juice. Cut the bird into pieces, discarding the head, wing tips, and the cone of the rump with the tail feathers attached. Heat some oil and fry the carrot, onion, celery and bay leaves until the vegetables have softened. Add the coot flesh, thyme, chilli, calamint and anchovy. Brown the meat, then season with salt and pepper. Cover and cook slowly, moistening if necessary first with the wine and then the stock. When the coot is almost cooked, uncover the pan, add a ladleful of stock mixed with the flour, and allow to thicken. Stir in the basil and serve.

FOLAGA (Coot)

This water bird is very popular at Torre del Lago. It must be plucked and skinned as soon as it is killed. The coot has a distinctive, slightly fishy flavour and is used to make the classic recipe *folaga alla Puccini*, which dates back to the days of the Italian composer.

COLOMBACCIO (Wood Pigeon)

The wood pigeon has firm, aromatic and well-flavoured flesh. The bird is widely hunted in Tuscany, where one of the favourite ways of cooking it is in a casserole with olives.

Wood pigeon is cooked slowly in a rich gravy with wild cherries, which enhance the flavour of the meat.

BECCACCIA (Woodcock)

The woodcock is the most prized of the game birds. It is becoming increasingly rare and is hardly ever seen in any market. It is cooked undrawn and the entrails (apart from the crop) are eaten. There are many regional and international recipes for this bird, but the most popular dish is roasted woodcock with the entrails spread on toast.

OTHER GAME BIRDS WORTH TRYING

Other wild ducks shot in the marshy areas include **alzavola** (teal), **moriglione** (pochard), **fischione** (wigeon) and **codone** (pintail). The **tortora** (turtle dove) is appreciated for its delicate, tender flesh. Partridges are also hunted in Tuscany, both the common grey partridge (**pernice**) and the rock partridge (**coturnice**), but they are becoming increasingly rare. Wild **quaglia** (quail) are are much tastier than the farm-bred ones usually found in shops. **Beccaccino** (snipe) are smaller than woodcock, but just as tasty, and they can be used in the same recipes.

Traditional Produce

THIS AREA OF northern Tuscany has wonderfully varied landscapes: there are mountains with lakes and woods, and then hills that slope gently to the plains and the sea. The numerous delicacies are closely bound up with these natural settings and the climate, and the produce ranges from Mediterranean olives to spelt (a traditional type of grain) from the mountains. The popularity of the local produce has spread through a mixture of factors: a general concern for traditional qualities, the growth of *agriturismo* and specialist shops supported by a clientele capable of recognizing quality. It is worth finding trusted stores that specialize in good quality foods.

FILETTO DELLA LUNIGIANA
This dried pork fillet is seasoned with salt and pepper. It combines both Tuscan and Emilian traditions, being less dry and having less salt and pepper than other speciality meats of the region.

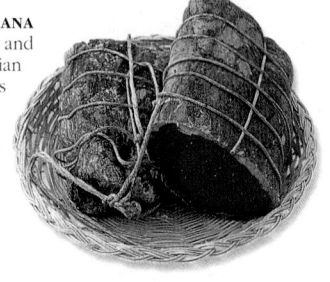

LASAGNE BASTARDE
These are *tagliatelle* and *pappardelle all'uovo* made with a mixture of white flour and chestnut flour for extra flavour. They are found in restaurants and on sale in small pasta shops, mainly in Lunigiana and around Monte Amiata.

TORTA DI PEPE
A speciality of Camaiore, this savoury tart is made with a *brisée* pastry and filled with beet leaves, rice, eggs, *ricotta*, *pecorino*, Parmesan and breadcrumbs, all seasoned with plenty of freshly ground pepper *(pepe)*.

BUCCELLATO
Lucca's traditional cake is sold by all *pasticcerie* and bakers in the city. It is a very simple cake, made with flour, sugar, muscatel raisins and aniseed. Traditionally it was a round loaf, but long shapes are now more common.

PANE DI ALTOPASCIO
This is one of the most prized Tuscan breads and is sold outside the area, reaching supermarkets in northern Italy. Loaves sold locally are normally round; when exported it is usually sold in long broad loaves.

CHESTNUT FLOUR

Chestnut flour (farina di castagne) is produced in various areas, including Lunigiana, the Mugello, the Casentino and Amiata, and is an ingredient of many traditional recipes.

TESTAROLI

A wholewheat flour and water dough is cooked in earthenware pans with lids called testi. The dough forms thick sheets which are boiled and served with pesto or tomato and mushroom sauce.

DRIED CHESTNUTS

Once a staple ingredient of traditional cooking in many mountain areas, dried chestnuts (castagne secche) are now a delicacy used in sweet and savoury dishes.

CANNELLINI DI SORANA

These white beans are common in Tuscan cooking. Sorana, north of Pescia, produces beans of slightly smaller than average size and these are much sought-after.

LUCCA OLIVE OIL

The area producing Lucca oil includes the coastal area of Versilia, above all around Carrara, the area north of Lucca along the Serchio, and other smaller zones near Camaiore and Ponte a Moriano. These oils are very fine and fruity. The flavour is of average intensity, full and balanced, sweetish though slightly peppery, with a lingering taste.

NECCI CON LA RICOTTA

500 g (1 lb 2 oz) chestnut flour • sugar • chestnut leaves • 500 g (1 lb 2 oz) fresh ricotta cheese • salt

Mix the flour with a pinch of salt and sugar to taste. Knead in enough water to form a thick but not solid dough. Heat several earthenware testi until sizzling hot, then place a chestnut leaf on each one. Spread with a ladleful of paste, then alternate leaves and paste to form layers. Leave to cool. Remove and serve the cheese with sugar.

FARRO (SPELT) FROM GARFAGNANA

Spelt is a very ancient cereal, which has been cultivated in the Garfagnana for over 7,000 years. Equally ancient is the gastronomic tradition of spelt soup (*minestrone di farro* or *zuppa di farro*), a trademark of this area.

TROUT

The Serchio river is celebrated for its fish, which is less commonly eaten now that the number of fishermen has declined. However, the tradition of using the excellent trout from the mountain streams remains strong.

MINESTRONE DI FARRO

200 g (7 oz) dried borlotti beans • 300 g (10½ oz) spelt • 50 g (1¾ oz) pancetta, chopped • 1 onion, chopped • 1 stalk celery, chopped • 1 carrot, chopped • ¼ of a Savoy cabbage, cut into strips • tomato purée • extra virgin olive oil • salt • pepper

Soak the beans in cold water overnight. The next day, drain them, put in a pan and cover with fresh water. Bring to the boil and simmer for 1½ hours. Drain the beans and set aside a quarter of them. Mince the rest with the cooking water, return to the pan, add the spelt and cook for about 1 hour. Sauté the pancetta, onion, celery and carrot in some oil. Add the cabbage, the tomato purée diluted in a little water, then the spelt and the whole beans and simmer for 15 minutes. Season and drizzle a little oil over the soup before serving.

PECORINO FROM GARFAGNANA AND LUNIGIANA

This *pecorino* is generally drier than the similar cheese from the Crete to the south. It has a strong milky scent and a distinctive flavour from the mountain grasses the sheep feed on, quite different from that of cheese from the more arid coastal areas.

RICOTTINE DELLA LUNIGIANA

This cheese is eaten very fresh. It is also a traditional cheese for making cakes, especially with chestnuts.

Agnello al Testo

1 leg of lamb • 100 g (3½ oz) lardo
*(lard) • sage • rosemary • garlic
• 1 kg (2 lb 2 oz) potatoes • extra
virgin olive oil • salt • pepper*

Make incisions in the
leg of lamb with the
tip of a knife. Make
a paste with the
lard, herbs and
garlic and push it
into the incisions.
Season with salt and
pepper. Put the lamb
in a *testo* (earthenware
pan with a lid) and pour over
plenty of oil. Sink the pan into hot
wood embers; heap them over the
lid. Cook for 30 minutes, renewing
the hot embers frequently.

*Rosemary and garlic are
often used in curing* lardo.

Lardo from Colonnata
Among the pinnacles of Tuscan
gastronomy, this *lardo* (lard) is
highly rated. The lard is matured
in tubs of marble from nearby
Carrara. Once removed, it quickly
loses its flavour, so it is cut only
when needed. It may be used in
cooking or thinly sliced and eaten
sprinkled with pepper.

Rolled Pancetta from Lunigiana
A combination of the
Tuscan style mixed with
the traditional styles of the
nearby valleys of Parma
and Piacenza produces
this *pancetta* (bacon
cured from belly of pork).
Tuscan custom is reflected
in the use of herbs,
especially rosemary, while
the Emilian influence is the
technique of rolling the bacon and
salting it only lightly, to keep it moist.

What to Sample
Black-headed lambs, a breed called **Massese** from the Garfagnana and the Lunigiana,
are much appreciated and sought-after outside the region. In the Pescia district there is
excellent **asparagus** and **fruit** such as **cherries**. Some producers have begun to
specialize in herbs. There are a number of **soft fruit** farms. Pistoia has its traditional
cakes and **sweets**, such as **sugared almonds**, **brigidini** (aniseed-flavoured wafers)
and **berlingozzi** (carnival cakes). The Garfagnana has **truffles**, black and white.
Around Abetone there are locally produced **aromatic grappas** scented with berries
and herbs. The **table olives** are excellent; many types are small and a brownish-black
colour, rather like Ligurian *taggiasca* olives. **Biroldo** is a blood sausage, its more
authentic versions containing raisins and pine nuts, which is eaten raw if very fresh.

Wild Produce

PRUGNOLO
(Lyophyllum georgii)
Even in antiquity this spring mushroom was prized. Now it is protected and it is forbidden to pick any under 2 cm (¾ inch) high. Whitish with tender flesh and an intense scent of fresh flour, it is sliced and eaten raw on risotto or pasta or quickly cooked in white sauces. It forms circles in mountain meadows or under thorn bushes in the hills.

GRIFOLA
(Polyporus frondosus)
This is a giant fungus that can weigh up to 50 kg (110 lb). From a single stalk growing at the foot of broadleaf trees, it fans out into numerous branches forming a kind of dense bush. When young, it is good preserved in oil.

COLOMBINA
(Russula cyanoxantha)
Easily found, even at markets, this mushroom has distinctive white gills, and is firm and springy to the touch. Commonly known as "the charcoal burner", it grows in woods, especially beech, and is excellent grilled, baked with potatoes or in devilled dishes.

COCCORA
(Amanita caesarea)
The most expensive mushroom on the market, also known as *orolo*, grows in broadleaf woods and is protected by a ban on picking specimens under 4 cm (1½ inches). When closed it forms a white ball. If this is cut open, it reveals embryo mushrooms already coloured with orange cap, yellow stalk and gills. It is not true that they are tastier when closed: open ones have more flavour whether raw or cooked.

COCCORA IN INSALATA (MUSHROOM SALAD)

1 clove garlic • 500 g (1 lb 2 oz) coccore or orolo, thinly sliced • juice of 1 lemon • extra virgin olive oil • salt • pepper

Cut the garlic clove in half and rub the individual serving plates with the cut surfaces. Arrange the mushrooms on the plates. Mix together the lemon juice, oil and salt. Season with pepper, pour the dressing over the mushrooms and serve at once.

MINESTRA DI CECI

*400 g (14 oz) chickpeas • 1 small onion,
chopped • 1 small carrot, chopped
• 1 small celery stalk, chopped • 2 cloves
garlic, chopped • 1 sprig of rosemary
• 1 sprig of winter savory • extra virgin
olive oil • grated parmesan cheese
(if preferred, mix it with some mature
pecorino) • 1 piece of the cotenna (skin)
from a prosciutto • salt • black pepper*

Rinse the chickpeas, then soak in water
for 24 hours. The next day, heat some oil
and lightly fry the onion, carrot, celery,
garlic and rosemary leaves. Drain the
chickpeas, reserving the liquid, and stir
them into the vegetables with the
cotenna. Strain the soaking water and
add enough to the pan to cover the
beans. Cover the pan and simmer until
the chickpeas are tender. Remove the
cotenna and purée the soup in a blender.
Return it to the pan, add the savory,
season and simmer for 10 minutes. Serve
with the cheese and extra oil to drizzle.

MIRTILLO NERO (BILBERRY)
(Vaccinium myrtillus)
This summer berry is abundant on the
Apennine ridges in high-altitude woods
of beech or chestnut. It can be eaten
fresh – it has a high vitamin C content –
or used in jams and liqueurs.

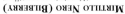

TIMO (THYME)
(Thymus communis)
Thyme is found all over Tuscany and is
used a great deal in cooking – in fact, it is a
staple of numerous traditional recipes. The
flowering sprigs are better than the leaves
alone. It is excellent fresh or dried.

SANTOREGGIA (WINTER SAVORY)
(Satureja montana)
Commonly found on dry, stony slopes,
this herb is similar to thyme but has
different spear-shaped leaves. It has
long been noted for its supposed
aphrodisiac qualities. It is excellent
fresh or dried with sauces, and braised,
roasted or grilled meat.

OLIVELLO SPINOSO (SEA-BUCKTHORN)
(Hippophae rhamnoides)
Wear gloves if you want to pick these
orange berries as there are plenty of thorns
concealed among the blue-green leaves.
However, they are well worth the trouble,
being rich in vitamin C, and they make
exquisite jam. The plants are found in the
Apennines on open ground and along
escarpments and waterways.

Places of Interest

THIS IS A GOOD area for shopping, though prices at Versilia are often inflated because it is such a fashionable tourist spot. The shopkeepers are accustomed to catering for a clientele in search of traditional speciality foods, and many are very knowledgeable. In addition to the addresses given below, the outdoor market at Viareggio is well worth a visit.

AGLIANA (PT)

Ⓒ Arte del Cioccolato di Catinari

via Provinciale, 378
☎ 0574 718506.
● Mon am.

Roberto Catinari is one of the great Italian and European pastry chefs. Here you will find 120 types of chocolates, such as ones with liqueur centres (grappa, Vin Santo, whisky, Gemma d'abeto, amaretto liqueur and coffee), or wrapped chocolates weighing 30 g (1 oz) each. The gianduia tortine (chocolate cream cakes) are excellent. Numerous trainees come here from as far away as America, and Catinari has produced creations to order for famous designers like Armani.

BERLINGOZZO

*100 g (3½ oz) butter •
400 g (14 oz) plain flour
• 2 eggs • 2 egg yolks •
200 g (7 oz) sugar •
grated zest of 1 lemon •
100 ml (3½ fl oz) full-fat
milk • 1 teaspoon baking
powder • salt*

Preheat the oven to 180°C (350°F/gas mark 4). Grease and flour a 20 cm (8 inch) cake tin with 20 g (¾ oz) each of the butter and flour. In a bowl, vigorously mix the rest of the flour and butter, eggs and yolks, sugar, zest, milk, baking powder and a pinch of salt. Pour into the tin and bake for 40 minutes.

🍇 Enoteca Lavuri

via Provinciale, 154/g
☎ 0574 751125.
● Tue am.

This wine store has a wide selection of the most significant Tuscan wines. Its guiding policy is to comb the region for new products, provided they have a good pedigree. There are also interesting Italian and foreign wines. Lavuri also offers a fine selection of cheeses, coffees and spirits, including some collector's items.

🐖 Marini

località Ferruccia
via Selva, 313
☎ 0574 718119.
● Wed pm.
○ in summer: only am.

Marini is a delicatessen and butcher's shop, family-run since 1904, selling Chianina beef and local salumi, which includes traditional specialities no longer found elsewhere.

BORGO A MOZZANO (LU)

🐟 Lago la Macchia

frazione Valdottavo
☎ 0583 835444.

This fish farm with agriturismo facilities sells the fry of mountain and rainbow trout, sturgeon, eels (including the much prized large female eels called capitoni), freshwater crayfish and small trout for frying.

CAMAIORE (LU)

🐖 Bonuccelli Salumi

via Vittorio Emanuele, 9
☎ 0584 989680.
● Wed pm.

Here you can find traditional salumi, both local and Tuscan (and some made with wild boar's meat). Particularly interesting products include salt ham, lardo and biroldo (a Tuscan blood sausage). There is a range of Italian and imported cheeses and a selection of fine wines. The butcher specializes in pork and ham.

♠ Gastronomia Claudio

via Provinciale, 45
☎ 0584 989069.
● Wed pm.

Angelo Torciglioni is a great enthusiast for cheeses, scouring Italy for them from Val d'Aosta to Sicily. He makes a point of stocking many fine cheeses produced by small traditional dairies in different regions. The delicatessen also stocks ready-made delicacies (try the torta di pepe and the ravioli), plus various specialities of Torciglioni's own, such as the quite remarkable cantucci, as well as much local produce (olives, oil, flour) and delicacies from other regions. Everything is chosen with knowledge and passion. The selection of wines is also excellent.

🍇 Enoteca Nebraska

strada provinciale per Lucca, bivio per Nocchi
☎ 0584 983805.
● Tue. ○ Sun pm.

The owners of this wine shop are friendly and affable, and they never compromise on the quality

PATTONA AL TESTO

dry chestnut leaves •
500 g (1 lb 2 oz)
sweetened chestnut flour
• salt

Soak the leaves in warm water for 10 minutes. In a mixing bowl, mix the flour with a little salt and enough water to make a paste. Drain the leaves and pat dry. Pour 2 dessertspoons of the mix onto the smooth surface of two overlapping leaves. Fold the leaves over the mixture and place in an earthenware *testo*. Repeat until the mix is all used up. Cover the *testo* and bake the discs for 30 minutes under smoking embers.

of their products. The big names in Tuscan, Italian and foreign wines can be sampled with excellent cheese and salumi, *local products above all.*

CAMPORGIANO (LU)

🐦 Mulin del Rancone

località Rancone
📞 0583 618670.

This splendid farm, which offers agriturismo *facilities in an old converted watermill on the banks of the Serchio, rescued the local Pontremolese breed of cattle when they were on the verge of extinction. As part of the same philosophy, it produces and sells many traditional local products, such as conserves, lentils, spelt, fruit and vegetables preserved in oil. Then there are the biscuits:* neccini *(made from chestnut flour),* farrini *(spelt flour),* formentini *(maize flour). They also sell* salumi, *cheese and honey which comes from the Garfagnana.*

CAPANNORI (LU)

🍇 Azienda Agricola La Badiola

località San Pancrazio
📞 0583 309633.

This estate produces an interesting red wine, Vigna Flora, which is made from Cabernet Sauvignon and Merlot grapes, and a promising Stoppielle, from Chardonnay and Pinot Bianco. The extra virgin olive oil is not bad, if perhaps rather sweet.

🍇 Fattoria Colle Verde

località Castello
frazione Matraia
📞 0583 402310.

The estate aims to produce white wines with low acidity, which are well-structured and richly perfumed. A good example is the Brania del Cancello Bianco, made from equal quantities of Trebbiano and Chardonnay grapes. Another notable wine is the Colline Lucchesi Rosso Brania delle Ghiandaie, which is made from a careful selection of red grapes. The estate also produces a very fine extra virgin olive oil.

♠ Cooperativa del Pastore

via Sarzanese, B45
Castelvecchio di Compito
📞 0583 979804.

The dairy on this estate produces various ewe's milk cheeses best eaten fresh. It also sells, to order, the excellent Massese breed of black-headed lambs.

🍇 Fattoria di Fubbiano

località San Gennaro
📞 0583 978011.

This corner of Tuscany enjoys an unusual microclimate and has been chosen for the grafting of experimental varieties of vines by the Regional Authority. These include a Vermentino used to produce Colline Lucchesi Vermentino. The Teroldego grape has been imported to boost the Sangiovese in making the red Pàmpini, which is aged in barriques. The estate also makes two finer blends of the Rosso delle Colline Lucchesi, from vines with a western exposure for the Villa and a southern for the San Gennaro. The extra virgin olive oil is excellent. There are splendid agriturismo *facilities on the estate with farmhouses available to rent.*

The Fattoria di Fubbiano at Capannori

Fattoria Maionchi

località Tofori,
via di Tofori, 81
☎ 0583 978194.

This is a late-17th-century farm with agriturismo accommodation in farmhouses which have been renovated to preserve their original features. Various DOC wines and table wines, traditional extra virgin olive oil from Lucca, olives in brine, conserves from the farm's own fruit (try the pear and grappa jam), and grappas are sold here.

GRAN FARRO (SPELT AND BEAN STEW)

400 g (14 oz) dried borlotti beans • 300 g (10½ oz) spelt • extra virgin olive oil • 2 cloves garlic • 1 onion • 1 stalk celery • 3 leaves sage • 1 sprig of marjoram • 1 sprig of rosemary • 150 g (5½ oz) diced cotenna (skin) of prosciutto • 300 g (10½ oz) ripe tomatoes • salt • pepper

Soak the beans in water for 12 hours. Drain the beans, put in a pan and cover with fresh water, then simmer until tender. Drain, reserving the cooking water. Press the beans through a sieve to purée them. Heat some oil in a pan, add the vegetables, herbs, tomatoes and cotenna. Season to taste and fry for a few minutes. Add bean purée and the spelt. Simmer for 40 minutes, adding some of the bean cooking water, as necessary. Drizzle with olive oil to serve.

 Tenuta di Valgiano

frazione Valgiano
☎ 0583 402271.

This estate produces a range of straightforward, good wines: Bianco delle Colline Lucchesi Giallo dei Muri (from Trebbiano and Chardonnay) and Rosso delle Colline Lucchesi and Rosso dei Palistorti (Sangiovese and Syrah). In addition there are two regional classics: a single-grape Merlot and the Scasso dei Cesari. The estate also produces excellent extra virgin olive oil.

CARRARA

 Pescheria Elda

frazione Marina di Carrara
viale Colombo, 9/c
☎ 0585 785060.
● Mon pm.
○ Sun am.

Quality counts here and this depends not just on freshness but also the origin of the produce. For example, the farmed fish comes from very carefully selected hatcheries: sea bass and bream from Portovenere, mussels from

La Spezia, and shellfish from a select group of producers in the northern Adriatic. The fresh fish is all local, coming from Viareggio and La Spezia.

 Pasta e Gastronomia di Grandi Patrizia

via Santa Maria, 1
☎ 0585 72195.
● Tues.

Here you can buy take-away dishes, most of them typical of Carrara, such as marinated salt cod, stockfish, taglierini ai fagioli (pasta with beans), rice cakes, plus fresh pasta, especially tordelli, and seasonal specialities including fish. On Sunday an interesting, complete menu is on offer, from antipasto to dessert, at very reasonable prices.

Lardo di Colonnata di Giannarelli Marino

frazione Codena
piazza Fratelli Rosselli, 10
☎ 0585 777329.

This is a specialist producer of the typical local lardo (cured pork

fat), which is processed here but then matured at Colonnata, its place of origin. It is sold at the firm's butcher's shop at number 11 on the piazza.

FIVIZZANO (MS)

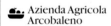 Azienda Agricola Arcobaleno

località Rosara di Sopra
☎ 0585 92508.

Organic raspberries, woodland berries and vegetables are produced here. They are sold fresh or made into liqueurs and conserves. Other organic products, including spelt and various cereals, soups with cereals, pulped tomatoes and chestnut flour, are also available.

Farmacia Clementi

via Roma, 109
☎ 0585 92056.
● Wed pm.

This pharmacy, with its fine old furnishings in Empire style from the late 19th century, is well worth visiting even if you are not in search of medicines. The Elixir

di China is made to a
recipe belonging to the
great-grandfather of the
present owner, and the
fruit syrups are made of
berries from the local
woods or fruit cultivated
on the firm's own soft
fruit farm.

Azienda Agricola Giardino

Colle di Cerignano, 1
0585 92441.

This estate produces
organically grown fruit
and vegetables, potatoes,
cherries, apples, apricots,
pears and San Giovanni
plums, a local variety.

Azienda Agricola il Pino

località Pastena
di Ceserano
0585 982355.

This farm grows and
sells organic courgettes
and strawberries.

FOSDINOVO (MS)

Barbero Nanni

località Fornello
via Fravizzola, 17
0187 68410.

This agriturismo offers
accommodation in five
bedrooms, in a hillside
setting. The owner selects
a clone of the Vermentino
grape for the Colli di Luni
Vermentino di Fravizzola
and puts Mammolo grapes
to use in the Colli di Luni
Rosso del Fornello.

LAMPORECCHIO (PT)

Pasticceria Carli - da Pioppino

piazza Berni, 20
0573 82177.
Wed. Sun.

For well over a century
now, this confectionery
shop has made authentic
brigidini and berlingozzi
to the same recipe.

LICCIANA NARDI (MS)

Apicoltura Dell'Amico e Amorfini

località Amola
0187 471502.

Local honey – aromatic
chestnut, dandelion,
acacia, honeydew and
meadow – is produced
and sold here, along with
jars of local dried fruit
preserved in honey.

Montagna Verde

località Apella
0187 421203.

This is an agriturismo
where refreshments are
available. Chestnuts,
chestnut flour, honey,
pecorino cheese and
mushrooms (from the
estate's woods) are sold.

LIDO DI CAMAIORE (LU)

Gastronomia Giannoni

viale Colombo, 444
0584 617332.
Wed pm.

Ready-to-eat dishes made
only from fresh produce,
including fish, can be
found here. There is a
fine selection of salumi,
including well-matured
prosciutto di Langhirano.

LUCCA

Antica Bottega di Prospero

via San Lucia, 13
Wed pm.

This 200-year-old shop
sells all kinds of different
beans, spelt and other
cereals, plus pulses and
chestnut flour.

La Cacioteca

via Fillungo, 242
0583 496346.
Wed pm.

On sale here is a wide
range of Tuscan
pecorino, especially from
the Garfagnana, some of
it matured by the owner
Aldo Pieracci by storing
in caves and barrels.
There is also a selection
of Tuscan salumi, oil
and wine from around
Lucca and cheeses from
all over Italy.

TORDELLI LUCCHESI

*1 kg (2 lb 4 oz) plain flour • 7 eggs • 300 g (10½ oz) loin
of pork • rosemary • 500 g (1 lb 2 oz) rump steak • 150 g
(5 oz) veal brain • 100 g (3½ oz) beet leaves • thyme •
1 slice Tuscan bread • meat stock • grated nutmeg • grated
Parmesan cheese • extra virgin olive oil • pepper • salt*

Preheat the oven to 180°C (350°F/gas mark 4). Make
incisions in the pork and insert rosemary leaves. Place the
pork and the steak in a roasting tin, brush with a little oil
and season. Roast for 30 minutes, basting with stock, if
necessary. Meanwhile, steam the beet leaves and brains
until cooked. Soak the bread in some meat stock. Mince
all the meat and the leaves. Mix with the bread, 1 egg, the
cheese, thyme and nutmeg. Season. Mix the flour,
6 eggs and salt, knead the dough and roll it out. Fill with
the meat to form large ravioli. Cook in boiling salted
water for 4 minutes. Serve with butter and cheese.

Piazza del Mercato in Lucca, once a Roman amphitheatre

mainly based on non-
native vines: Sauvignon
Blanc and Chardonnay
for whites and a blend of
Cabernet and Sangiovese
for the red. The estate has
recently started letting
renovated farmhouses
on its land.

⊛ Taddeucci

piazza San Michele, 34
📞 0583 494933.
● Thurs. ▢ Sun.

This pasticceria has been
in the same family for
120 years. Specialities are
buccellato (Lucca cake,
which looks more like
bread than cake) and
traditional vegetable pies
(spicy but sweet, made
with beet leaves).

⚖ Delicatezze di Isola

via San Giorgio, 5/7
📞 0583 492633.
● Wed pm.

A wide range of delicacies,
some typical of Lucca and
others from all over the
world, including cheese
and some unusual salumi
(made from game and
turkey), smoked fish and
wines are sold here.

🏺 Tenuta di Forci

via per Pieve San Stefano,
7165
📞 0583 349001.

This 14th-century farm
offers its fine extra virgin
olive oil under the label
Olio dell'Antico Frantoio
di Forci.

⚖ Lucca in Tavola

via San Paolino, 130/132
📞 0583 581022.
● Wed pm.

Here you will find all the
specialities of the Lucca
area, chosen by the owner,
a sommelier and oil-taster,
including wines, oils, spelt
and spelt products, honey,
preserves and olives.

🍇 Azienda Agricola Moretti Daniele- Le Murelle

località Cappella, via per
Camaiore, traversa V
📞 0583 394055.

This estate has 30 hectares
(74 acres) of vineyards,
olive groves and woodland.
Wine production is

🍇 Enoteca Vanni Giulietta

piazza San Salvatore, 7
📞 0583 491902.
● Mon am.

Within the stone walls
and vaulted ceilings of
this shop is stocked a wide
choice of local and other
Italian wines. One section
is devoted to whisky
(including collector's
items) and grappas. Book
for a tasting. Lucca olive
oil is also sold.

ZUPPA FRANTOIANA (BEAN SOUP)

**600 g (1 lb 5 oz) dried cannellini beans • 3 cloves garlic •
sprigs of sage • extra virgin olive oil • 1 onion, sliced •
100 g (3½ oz) rigatino (bacon), sliced • 400 g (14 oz)
black cabbage (cavolo nero), sliced • 2 potatoes, chopped •
2 carrots, chopped • 1 stalk celery, chopped • 200 g (7 oz)
pumpkin, chopped • 1 bead chicory, chopped • 1 bunch of
mixed herbs, chopped • 6 slices crusty bread • salt • pepper**

Soak the beans in water overnight. The next day, drain
and place in a pan with 2 garlic cloves and the sage.
Cover with water and simmer for 2 hours. Drain the
beans and reserve the water. Heat some oil in a pan, add
the onion and bacon and fry until browned. Add the
vegetables and the bean water and cook for 30 minutes.
Crush half the cooked beans and add the crushed and the
whole beans to the soup. Season with salt and pepper.
Rub the bread with the remaining garlic and sprinkle with
oil. Place the slices in a tureen and pour the soup on top.

➤ Polleria
Fratelli Volpi

via San Paolino, 42
☎ 0583 56689.
● Wed pm.

*Free-range chickens,
ducks and pigeons, rabbits
from the Garfagnana,
wild game, Pratomagno
hams, pork sausages, wild
boar, goose and game
from small local producers
can all be found here.
There are also various
poultry and game dishes
prepared, ready for
cooking in the oven.*

MASSA

❄ Gelateria Eugenio

località Ronchi,
Marina di Massa, via Pisa
☎ 0585 240369.
● Mon in winter.
○ Sun.

*This ice-cream parlour
is famed for the excellent
quality and the sheer
variety of its many ice-
creams, some of them
quite sublime.*

🍇 Podere
Scurtarola

via dell'Uva, 3
☎ 0585 831560.

*This is one of the few
producers who still bottles
the rare white wine
Candia dei Colli Apuani
in both the dry and the
semi-sweet versions.
The Scurtarola Rosso
is made from almost local
vines such as Massaretta
and Buonamico plus
Ciliegiolo and a fair
proportion of Sangiovese.
It is drunk young. A
small quantity of
Vermentino Rosso wine
is made from the local
grapes. The farm also
sells two different kinds
of honey (chestnut and
acacia flavours) as well
as olive oil.*

TORTA DI ERBE (HERB PIE)

*2 kg (4 lb 8 oz) mixed green leaves and herbs • 50 g
(1¾ oz) cured pork fat (lardo) • 50 g (1¾ oz) mortadella
(or local salami) • 50 g (1¾ oz) pecorino cheese • 100 ml
(3½ fl oz) extra virgin olive oil • 200 g (7 oz) flour •
extra virgin olive oil • pepper • salt*

Preheat the oven to 200°C (400°F/gas mark 6). Cook the
leaves and herbs in boiling water until tender. Squeeze
dry and chop with the pork fat and mortadella. Mix in the
cheese and oil and season. Mix the
flour, water, a little oil and salt
into a dough. Line a pie dish
with half the dough, add the
cooked leaves and herbs
and cover with the rest
of the dough. Bake for
10 minutes then lower
the temperature to
180°C (350°F/gas mark 4)
and cook for a further
20 minutes. Serve warm.

🍶 Drogheria
Caffè gli Svizzeri

via Cairoli, 53
☎ 0585 43092.
● Wed pm.

*This long-established
grocery store has two
main sections: a choice
selection of local produce
from the land – spelt,
testaroli (pasta discs like
pancakes), chestnut flour,
ricotta cheese – and, in
response to consumer
demand, a rich choice of
pulses and cereals. They
also sell teas and spices.*

MONSUMMANO TERME
(PT)

🍫 Slitti Caffè
e Cioccolato

via Francesca sud, 268
☎ 0572 640240.
● Sun.

*In Italy, chocolate
confectioners are rare,
but Monsummano has a
world champion. Andrea
Slitti has won countless
awards, cups and
championships, in well-
earned recognition of the
taste and attractive
appearance of his
creations, which are true
works of art. This shop
and café has wonderfully
luscious and imaginative
pralines, chocolate bars,
Arabian coffee beans
swathed in chocolate,
chocolate teaspoons for
stirring coffee, creamy
spreads and flavoured
chocolate sculptures.*

MONTECARLO
(LU)

🍇 Carmignani

località Cercatoia
via della Tinaia, 7
☎ 0583 22381.

*Lorenzo and Gino
Carmignani produce
Duke Vermiglio, made
with Syrah, Merlot and
Sangiovese grapes and
aged in wood. There is
also a Vin Santo version,
Le Notti Rosse di Capo
Diavolo, plus Montecarlo
Rosso Sassonero and
Bianco Pietrarchiara.
Output is limited to a few
thousand bottles of each.
There is agriturismo
accommodation to rent
in the summer.*

🍇 Fattoria del Buonamico

località Cercatoia
via Provinciale di
Montecarlo, 43
☎ 0583 22038.

This is a leading producer of Montecarlo Bianco and Rosso, backed up by a white, Vasario, from Pinot Bianco fermented in wood and aged in barriques. *There are also two reds: Cercatoia, with a good proportion of Sangiovese Grosso followed by Cabernet Sauvignon, Merlot and a little Syrah; and Il Fortino, from pure Syrah grapes from a 30-year-old vineyard.*

🍇 Fattoria del Teso

località Teso
via Poltroniera
☎ 0583 286288.

Montecarlo Bianco and Rosso are on offer at this estate, both excellent quality for the price.

MONTIGNOSO (MS)

La Bottega di Adò

via Vecchia Romana Est, 66
☎ 0585 348315.
● Wed pm.

The traditional Tuscan hams and sausages of this long-established salame *producer have a slightly sweet flavour, in the Emilian style. The*

company pursues a policy of good quality and is best known for its sausages, made to the highest standards. They should be eaten fresh and raw. Note also the firm's salamis – traditional soft Tuscan mortadella, *its* biroldo *(a blood sausage similar to* buristo*),* soppressata, *excellent* cotechini *plus, of course,* Colonnata lardo.

🍴 Gastronomia Osvaldo

località Cinquale
via Gramsci, 32
☎ 0585 309193.
● Wed pm.

Here you can find a well-chosen range of often quite exclusive delicacies from every corner of Tuscany. There are wonderful specialities, like the salumi *and* pecorino *cheeses, always of the very highest quality.*

PIEVE A NIEVOLE (PT)

🏺 Frantoio Del Ponte

via Poggio alla Guardia, 12
☎ 0572 67095.

The Del Ponte Gold extra virgin olive oil is this firm's premium product. The oil is made from olives from the Val di Nievole and Monte Albano. The estate has its own olive presses.

PISTOIA

🌾 Panetteria Capecchi

via Dalmazia, 445
☎ 0573 400208.
● Wed pm.

This firm claims that a brick oven using gas, not wood-fired, bakes the best cakes and bread, and sampling their wares it is impossible to disagree. The Tuscan bread and other types of traditional Italian bread are excellent, as is the schiacciata *baked on the floor of the oven. The* cantucci, *made with natural ingredients of high quality, are exceptional. The range of foods is completed with various Italian cheeses and* salumi.

🍲 Primizie e Funghi Sauro e Assunta

piazza della Sala, 11
☎ 0573 21663.
● Wed pm.

Excellent local fruit and vegetables are stocked by this greengrocer, plus best quality produce from further afield, including an unusual range of exotic fruit. In addition, all kinds of dry fruit, a large assortment of pulses, cereals, flour, mushrooms from Abetone and a selection of gastronomic specialities are sold.

PONTREMOLI (MS)

🐂 Macelleria Mori

via Pietro Bologna, 23
☎ 0187 830858.
● Wed pm.

The meat sold by this specialist butcher's shop includes very fine lamb, raised locally. Mutton is also sold but only in the winter months.

The Fattoria del Teso at Montecarlo

TRESANA (MS)

 ### Tomà Rita

località Groppo, via Bola, 41
 0187 477946.

*This is the place for fresh
chestnuts in season, plus
dried chestnuts and
chestnut flour.*

VIAREGGIO

Forno Benzio
e Pancaccini

via Mazzini, 75
0584 962439.
Wed pm.

*Many excellent kinds
of bread are sold here,
especially pane brutto (the
Tuscan name for oddly
shaped loaves), ciabatta
(loaves containing lard),
and ciabatta polesana
(loaves made with a flour
that can be left to rise for
a long time). Biscuits like
anicini and pratolini are
also available.*

Rolando Bonini

via Mazzini, 181
0584 44175.
Wed pm.

Il Puntodivino wine store

*Seemingly a small
butcher's shop opposite
the celebrated Ristorante
Romano, but in reality
this is a shop run by a
great game expert who
sells game caught by
various hunters in this
area and also the
Maremma, and who has
contracts (contratti) with
the forestry guards. As
well as fresh game birds
and animals (plus all cuts
of free-range Hungarian
geese), it has a selection of
dry meats and bottled
sauces based on game.*

 ### Gelateria Mario

via Petrolini, 1
0584 961349.
Mon.

*The specialities of this shop
are whipped ices and
fresh fruit sorbets. They
also sell fruit that is filled
with ice-cream flavoured
with the same fruit. A
second shop on via dei
Lecci 132 sells semi-freddi
(ice-cream and sponge
desserts) and cakes.*

 ### Il Puntodivino

via Mazzini, 229
0584 31046.
Mon.
Sun.

*This is a particularly
charming wine shop with
tasting counter and an
excellent restaurant run
by Roberto and Cristina
Franceschini. It stocks 700
wines and spirits from all
over the world. It also has
very fine extra virgin olive
oil. Snacks made with
Colonnata lardo are
served with the wines.*

 ### Pescheria Volpi

Mercato Centrale
0584 32221.
Mon.

*At the well-stocked fish
market of Viareggio this
is the most interesting
fishmonger, with scampi
from Gorgona, Sardinian
crayfish, local red prawns
sold live, and all the fish
you need to make a real
cacciucco (fish soup).*

VILLAFRANCA
IN LUNIGIANA (MS)

Pan Art

località Filetto,
via San Genesio, 21
0187 495124.
Wed pm.

*This the place to buy real
testaroli (pasta discs like
pancakes), torta d'erbe
(herb pie) and, above all,
Carsenta flat peasant
bread cooked on chestnut
leaves in a testo.*

CACCIUCCO ALLA VIAREGGINA

*extra virgin olive oil • 4 cloves garlic • 1 fresh chilli,
seeded and chopped • 500 g (1 lb 2 oz) octopus • 500 g
(1 lb 2 oz) cuttlefish • 1 glass red wine • 800 g
(1 lb 12 oz) ripe tomatoes, chopped • 800 g (1 lb 12 oz)
mixed fish (scorpion fish, gurnard, hake, weever, white
bream, small ombrine) • 600 g (1 lb 5 oz) shark steaks
and conger eel • 10 razor clams • slices of bread • 1–2
tablespoons chopped fresh parsley • salt*

Heat some oil in a pan. Chop two of the garlic cloves and
lightly fry with the chilli. Cut the octopus and cuttlefish
into largish pieces and stir into the pan. Add the wine and
cook over a low heat until the wine has evaporated. Add
the tomatoes; cook for 15 minutes. Add all the other fish,
cutting up the large ones so they cook uniformly. Cover
with hot water and simmer without stirring. When the fish
is nearly cooked, add the razor clams and cook until all
the fish is tender. Season with salt. Toast the bread, rub
with the remaining garlic and use to line a tureen. Pour in
the soup, garnish with parsley and serve.

PISA
AND
LIVORNO

Pisa and Livorno

THE PROVINCES OF Pisa and Livorno are strongly influenced by the sea, for better, for worse. On the plus side is the fact that Livorno (which is still known by its anglicized name of Leghorn in many tourist brochures) is one of the most important fishing harbours on the Tyrrhenian and that means plenty of fresh fish. It owes its prosperity to Cosimo I, who chose Livorno – a tiny fishing village in 1571 – as the site for Tuscany's new port when Pisa's harbour silted up. The other plus is that the sea air suits some types of vegetables and fruit. On the minus side, the salt air has an unfavourable effect on the quality of the extra virgin olive oil produced along the coast. However, the benefits of the sea are felt further inland where the warm air from the sea, the hilly ground and the quality of the soil make for good growing conditions. The flourishing undergrowth in the extensive woodlands along the coast and inland is rich in scents and wildlife, as well as mushrooms and berries. This is an area where agriculture, food production and gastronomic tradition reflect a marriage of land and sea and a balance between agriculture and nature.

There is a plentiful supply of excellent **fish** at Livorno thanks to the good quality of the water and the sheer abundance of fish in the seas of Vada, Formiche Grosseto, Gorgona and the other islands (*see pp 78–79*).

TRANSPORT

FS RAILWAY STATION
- PISA – STAZIONE FS
  (050 500707
- LIVORNO – STAZIONE CENTRALE
  (0586 898111

BUS STATION
- VOLTERRA
  (0588 86099

STAR ATTRACTIONS

- PISA: tower and Cathedral, (050 560921
  Baptistry and Camposanto, (050 560464
  Santa Maria della Spina, (050 910510
- SAN MINIATO (PI): Cathedral, (0571 42745
- SAN PIERO A GRADO (PI): church of San Piero
- TENUTA DI SAN ROSSORE (PI): nature park,
  (050 525500
- VOLTERRA (PI): Museo Etrusco Guarnacci,
  (0588 86347
  Roman amphitheatre, (0588 86150
  Gallery and civic museum, (0588 87580

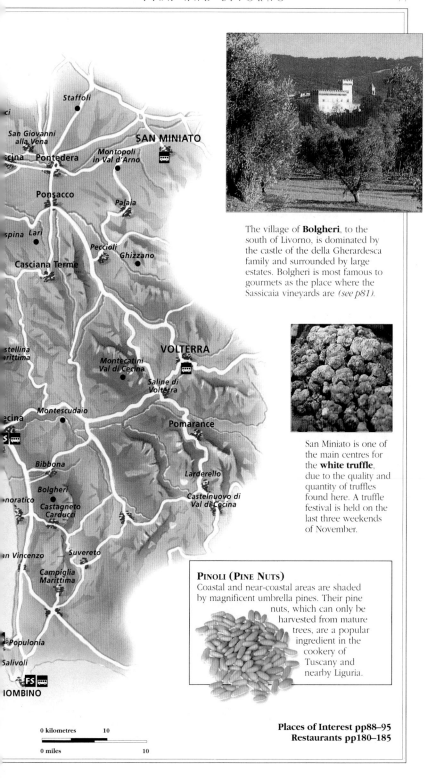

The village of **Bolgheri**, to the
south of Livorno, is dominated by
the castle of the della Gherardesca
family and surrounded by large
estates. Bolgheri is most famous to
gourmets as the place where the
Sassicaia vineyards are *(see p81)*.

San Miniato is one of
the main centres for
the **white truffle**,
due to the quality and
quantity of truffles
found here. A truffle
festival is held on the
last three weekends
of November.

PINOLI (PINE NUTS)

Coastal and near-coastal areas are shaded
by magnificent umbrella pines. Their pine
nuts, which can only be
harvested from mature
trees, are a popular
ingredient in the
cookery of
Tuscany and
nearby Liguria.

**Places of Interest pp88–95
Restaurants pp180–185**

0 kilometres   10

0 miles   10

Fish

FRESH FISH IS LANDED at Livorno harbour from all types of fishing grounds nearby – the sandy shallows, especially those at Vada, and the deep waters with sea beds of stone or gravel off the islands. But Livorno is not the only fishing harbour on this part of the coast: fishing is also an important industry in the islands. The waters around Elba, in particular, contain many rare fish in season, such as meagres and amberjack. Piombino also has a busy fishing harbour, and some small boats call in along the Riviera degli Etruschi.

PALOMBO OR NICCIOLO (SMOOTH-HOUND SHARK)
This shark has delicate flesh which is always tasty and firm and Italians consider it suitable for children. *Palombo* is a basic ingredient in the local *cacciucco* (fish soup). It is sold ready skinned. Often other sharks are passed off for *palombo*, which is acceptable in the case of *spinarolo* (spur dog) or *smeriglio* (porbeagle shark) because they are also tasty, but the *gattuccio* (lesser spotted dogfish) is far inferior.

RAZZA OR ARZILLA (SKATE)
Various kinds of skate are caught in these waters. Only the wings are eaten. Some regional recipes suggest boiling the fish and serving it with a sauce or stewing it.

GRONGO (CONGER EEL)
This typical coastal fish is similar to the ordinary eel but it is bonier and the flesh is less fatty. It grows to an enormous size and is used in soups and sauces.

CODA DI ROSPO OR RANA PESCATRICE (MONKFISH)
Fierce-looking *(see lower part of the photograph)* but delicious, this is one of the most versatile fish in the kitchen. Usually only the tail end is sold in slices, which is a pity as it makes a splendid soup when cooked whole. The liver is regarded as a delicacy.

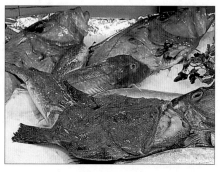

STRIGLIA DI SCOGLIO (RED MULLET)

This fish is a prime ingredient of Tuscan fish cuisine. Freshly caught and lightly cooked, smaller red mullet are always cooked whole. Larger red mullet are excellent grilled or baked in paper; or they may be fried or filleted as an *antipasto* (appetizer or starter). The related, very similar *triglia di fango* is a duller colour, but has a stronger flavour. Red mullet liver is highly regarded.

SARAGO (A TYPE OF BREAM)

This white fish is typical of the coast and is highly prized. Its flesh is very tasty. *Sarago* is usually grilled or baked.

Hake have numerous relatives. Small hake (merluzzetto) are delicious when fried.

NASELLO OR MERLUZZO (HAKE)

Some fine specimens of hake are sold at the markets of Viareggio and Livorno, and when the fish is that fresh, it is excellent in all kinds of recipes. Hake is a delicate fish, easy to digest.

SEPPIA (CUTTLEFISH)

The commonest of the squid family, *seppie* are usually inexpensive in markets. Cuttlefish is very versatile and is used in numerous regional recipes and special-occasion dishes. It is excellent boiled and dressed for a salad, or it can be grilled, or baked. Pick one with the dark outer skin intact and avoid those already cleaned. The ink sac is used for colouring and flavouring risottos and fresh pasta, although this is not a Tuscan tradition.

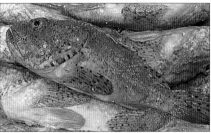

SCORFANO (SCORPION FISH OR RASCASSE)

This fierce-looking fish, considered the best fish for soup, is also delicious baked with rosemary. The flesh is white, tender and juicy.

Wines

THE WEATHER IN the provinces of Pisa and Livorno is affected by the warm air currents of the Tyrrhenian Sea and, consequently, the wines produced along the coast have always been fair but not excellent, light-bodied and rather short on bouquet. The lack of first-rate wines changed in 1968 with the creation of Sassicaia, the most influential of modern Italian red wines, and the one which paved the way for the creation of other wines based on Cabernet Sauvignon. As in most parts of Tuscany, local vines are cultivated alongside foreign vines imported in the late 19th century.

The traditional whites include Trebbiano Toscano, Vermentino, Malvasia del Chianti and Bianco Pisano di San Torpé; with Sauvignon as an import. Among the local reds are Sangiovese, Canaiolo Nero, Malvasia Nera, and the imports Cabernet Sauvignon and Merlot. Elba with its iron-rich soil and briny breezes produces wines rich in flavour but lacking in perfume. Also, the difficulty cultivating the vines means that the wine is more expensive. Typical white grape vines grown on the island include Trebbiano Toscano (Procanico), Ansonica, and Moscato; the red grape vines include Sangioveto or Sangiovese and Aleatico.

The red (Rosso) goes well with pork chops and spare ribs; the Rosso Superiore with grilled red meats.

The whites and the rosé (Rosato) are the perfect accompaniments for first courses with light sauces.

BOLGHERI
The Bolgheri area is limited to the region of Castagneto Carducci. It produces Bianco from Trebbiano Toscano, Vermentino and Sauvignon, with Sauvignon and Vermentino from the same vine contributing at least 80 per cent; Rosato, Rosso and Rosso Superiore from Cabernet Sauvignon, Merlot and Sangiovese grapes; and a Vin Santo Occhio di Pernice, ordinary and Riserva, from Sangiovese and Malvasia Nera.

MONTESCUDAIO
This wine is produced in the hills, where the soil gives it a special fragrance.

The red, based on Sangiovese, is very similar to Chianti. It differs by having an intensely fruity perfume and because it is aged for only a short time, no more than about 4 years. Serve it with meat stews, mushrooms and pasta with meat sauces.

The white, from Trebbiano Toscano, Malvasia and Vermentino grapes, goes well with full-flavoured fish dishes and eels.

BIANCO PISANO DI SAN TORPÉ

The Arno valley around Pisa and Livorno produces this delicately perfumed light white wine. Its name comes from a variety of Trebbiano named after the first holy martyr of Pisa. This wine is ideal as an aperitif and with vegetable dishes. The Vin Santo and Vin Santo Riserva versions are perfect with sweet biscuits.

CHIANTI COLLINE PISANE

This wine is subtly perfumed with a lighter body than other Chiantis, so it makes an excellent accompaniment to a wider range of dishes, including white meats with sauces. It is also produced in Superiore and Riserva versions.

BOLGHERI SASSICAIA

This is the great wine of the Super Tuscan category. It owes its success to the Cabernet Sauvignon vine which develops an unusual bouquet and body in the soil in this area. The wine has to age at least 2 years in wood, of which at least 18 months is spent in small casks holding no more than 225 litres (50 gallons). It is good with *bistecca alla fiorentina*, but its perfect match is game.

CACCIUCCO ALLA LIVORNESE

extra virgin olive oil • 2 onions, finely chopped • 1 carrot, finely chopped • 1 stalk celery, finely chopped • 4 cloves garlic • 1 handful of minced parsley • 1 kg (2 lb 4 oz) small reef-fish suitable for soups, including a few mullet • 1 larger fish (scorpion fish, weever, gurnard, slices of conger and palombo) • 400 g (14 oz) octopus, cut into pieces • 400 g (14 oz) cuttlefish, cut into pieces • a few scampi, cockles and slices of squid (optional) • 400 g (14 oz) mantis shrimps • 1 kg (2 lb 4 oz) ripe tomatoes, peeled and seeded • chilli pepper• 3 glasses red wine • 3 dessertspoons wine vinegar • slices of Tuscan bread • salt

Heat some oil in a large pan (preferably a terracotta one) and lightly fry the chopped vegetables, garlic and parsley. Clean the small fish and add them with the chilli. Fry lightly and season with salt. Add the vinegar and let it evaporate, then add the wine and the tomatoes. Simmer for 10 minutes then pass the mixture through a sieve. Heat some oil and fry the cuttlefish, octopus and squid, if using, then add the sieved mixture and gradually all the other fish, calculating the cooking time for each (adding mantis shrimps, scampi and cockles last). Add water, if necessary. Toast the bread and line a tureen with the slices. Pour the cooked soup over the bread and serve.

ELBA ANSONICA
Made with at least 85 per cent Ansonica grapes, this is a dry white wine with a good body. It is well suited to a fish *antipasto* and delicately flavoured first courses. There is also a sweet *Passito* (raisin wine) version.

ELBA BIANCO
This dry white wine, which is made chiefly from Trebbiano grapes, goes well with the island's traditional herb soups. There is also a spumante version.

ELBA ALEATICO
Considered the pearl of Elba's output – partly because of the difficulty of working the grapes – this is a pleasantly sweet red wine. Drink it with *torta ubriaca*, a fruit cake that is sprinkled with Elba Aleatico.

ELBA ROSSO AND ROSSO RISERVA
Sangiovese predominates, with small quantities of other red grapes in these wines. The young Rosso is good with white meats, especially rabbit in sauce, while the Riserva goes well with game – try it with hare.

WINE TYPE	GOOD VINTAGES	GOOD PRODUCERS	WINE TYPE	GOOD VINTAGES	GOOD PRODUCERS
Red Wine			**Red Wine**		
Bolgheri	97, 96, 90,	Podere Grattammacco di Castagneto Carducci, Ornellaia di Bolgheri, Le Macchiole di Bolgheri	Montescudaio	97, 96, 90	Sorbaiano di Montecatini Val di Cecina
Bolgheri Sassicaia	97, 96, 90	Tenuta San Guido di Bolgheri	Supertuscans *(see p. 130)*	98, 97, 95, 90	Tua Rita di Suvereto, Tenuta del Terriccio di Castellina Marittima, Michele Satta di Castagneto Carducci
Chianti delle Colline Pisane	97, 90	Tenuta di Ghizzano			

Traditional Produce

MOST OF TUSCANY grows excellent vegetables but the rural areas of Livorno and the Arno Valley between Pisa and Florence are particularly productive. One of the reasons market gardening here is so successful is the length of the growing season, which covers almost every month of the year except perhaps dry periods in high summer. The most distinctive Tuscan dishes are the soups (*minestre* and *zuppe*) and fresh vegetables are such an important ingredient in local cooking that nearly all the *trattorie* grow their own produce. The areas around San Miniato and Volterra are renowned for white truffles.

BLACK-EYED BEANS
These beans were widely used in Europe before the discovery of America. In Italy they have been replaced by *cannellini* and *borlotti* beans, but they are still grown in Tuscany, in the area around Pistoia.

ELVERS
Elvers, the fry of eels (*cée* in the local dialect), have long been caught in Tuscan river estuaries. In local recipes they are cooked quickly in a covered pan or used to make stuffed omelettes. Elvers are now protected in Italy but not in Spain, where they are called *angulas*.

CÉE ALLA PISANA

extra virgin olive oil • 4 cloves garlic, crushed • 4 sage leaves , chopped • 500 g (1 lb 2 oz) elvers • 1 piece of fresh chilli, chopped • salt

Heat plenty of oil in a pan and sauté the chopped garlic and the sage leaves. Add the elvers and cover the pan at once, holding the lid down firmly and shaking the pan to prevent them sticking. After a few seconds, uncover the pan and stir the elvers. Add the chilli and season with salt. Re-cover the pan and cook the elvers on a low heat for a few minutes.

Cée alla pisana *is a Viareggio-style dish of elvers , cooked with garlic and sage.*

OLIVE OIL FROM THE LIVORNO MAREMMA
The area of production for this oil lies inland from the Tyrrhenian coast and comprises Castagneto Carducci, Bibbona, Sassetta and Monteverdi Marittimo. The oil is light and fruity with floral notes and a hint of the aroma of hay. It has a balanced flavour without marked intensity.

GOBBI IN GRATELLA

*1 kg (2 lb 4 oz)
cardoons • extra
virgin olive oil • wine
vinegar • salt • pepper*

Cut the cardoons into
pieces about 12 cm
(4½ inches) long and
cook in boiling water
until tender. Drain and
rinse under cold
running water, then
remove the strings.
Season with plenty of
oil, salt and pepper and
a few drops of vinegar.
Leave for 2 hours and then
grill the cardoons over
very hot charcoal.

GOBBI (CARDOONS)
Cardoons with their silvery
white stalks look like prickly
celery. Those from the Arno
Valley – the area bordering the
province of Florence – are
particularly sought-after.

OIL FROM THE HILLS OF PISA
Oil from olive
groves south of Pisa
and east of Livorno
has a delicate, yet
somewhat peppery
and fruity flavour.
It has a flowery
scent and a
sweetish aftertaste
of almonds.

PASTA SECCA (DRIED PASTA)
Lari produces some of the finest
dried pasta in Italy. The pasta is
sent to specialist shops the world
over.

Tagliatelle.

Pappardelle.

PASTA SECCA ALL'UOVO (DRIED EGG PASTA)
Many small
producers make
different egg-
based long
pastas. Although
these pastas are
dried, they have all the
flavour of fresh pasta.

Tagliolini.

WHAT TO SAMPLE
The **wild game**, especially boar, hare, wood pigeons and woodcock, in this area – and
especially in the Maremma around Livorno – is as fine as that found in Grosseto. Inland,
and on Elba, there are areas that are good for vegetables and for **fine fruit,** including
yellow freestone peaches, white peaches (on Elba), figs, table grapes, and cherries (on
Monte Pisano and in the Lari area). In the hill areas there is excellent **prosciutto crudo**,
ham from shoulder of pork and **pecorino** cheese at Volterra. The **farinata di ceci**
(chickpea polenta) is a speciality of Livorno. Local confectioners make and sell marzipan
fruits. On Elba the production of **honey** and **extra virgin olive oil** is considerable.

At the start of the season, the early artichokes do not have any spines.

CARCIOFINI SOTT'OLIO

36 artichokes (late-season ones) • 1 litre (1¾ pints) wine vinegar • 2 bay leaves • 1 clove • 4 juniper berries • 1 dessertspoon black peppercorns • extra virgin olive oil • salt

Clean the artichokes, removing the tough outer leaves. Dilute the vinegar with 1½ litres (2¾ pints) of water and pour it into a tall saucepan. Add the spices and plenty of salt. Bring to the boil, add the artichokes and simmer for 6–7 minutes. Drain carefully and leave to cool. Dry the artichokes and transfer to one or more clean jars. Cover with oil, taking care not to trap air bubbles inside. Store in a cool dry place.

By the time the cold weather sets in, the artichokes have developed spines.

CARCIOFI (ARTICHOKES)
Artichokes are an essential ingredient in many traditional dishes, including fish ones, in the area; *Violetto* artichokes are a traditional Tuscan variety.

CAVOLFIORE (CAULIFLOWER) FROM CASCIANA
Casciana is a spa town renowned for cultivating cauliflowers, some of which grow to a very large size.

SPINACI (SPINACH)
Inland from Livorno, tasty spinach grows all the year round. In the springtime it is eaten raw in salads; the rest of the year it is cooked in traditional dishes.

OTHER PRODUCE WORTH TRYING
All summer the vegetables in this area are full of flavour, and the **aubergines** are exceptional. Look out for **fennel**, **peas**, **potatoes** from Santa Maria a Monte, **white asparagus** from the Valle d'Arno, **courgettes** and **celery**. Along the coast there are sweet, juicy **tomatoes**. The **basil**, both the large-leaved variety and small-leaved Ligurian basil, has a wonderful scent. Specialist producers grow **garlic**, **onions** and **shallots**.

Wild Produce

MILK-CAP MUSHROOM
(Lactarius sanguifluus)
This mushroom is called *pineggiole* locally, but *sanguinello* in the rest of Italy. Easily recognized because the gills shed a thick, red liquid, it is an orangey colour with green patches, and has chalky flesh. They are common in woods along the coast and the best ones are found under pine trees. Excellent preserved in oil, they can also be grilled or cooked in pasta sauces.

BLACK MOREL
(Morchella conica)
When the spring flowers bloom, these mushrooms *(spugnole)* sprout along the coast under pine and heathland trees, and inland in vineyards, orchards and wherever there have been fires in pine woods. They are exquisite, fresh or dried, in risottos, sauces, savoury pies and casseroles.

TRIPPA CON LE SPUGNOLE

extra virgin olive oil • 500 g (1 lb 2 oz) morels, sliced • 1 sprig of calamint (or mint) • 3 cloves garlic, finely chopped • 700 g (1 lb 9 oz) tripe, cut into strips • light meat stock • salt • pepper

The traditional recipe uses *porcini* (cep mushrooms) but morels are better. Heat plenty of oil, add the mushrooms, calamint and garlic, and season with salt and pepper. Cook until the mushrooms shed all their water. Lower the heat, add the tripe and cook until all the liquid has evaporated and the tripe is tender, moistening with a little meat stock, if necessary. Adjust the seasoning.

YELLOW MOREL
(Morchella esculenta)
The yellow morel *(spugnola gialla)* is highly prized in international cuisine. It is common in the coastal scrub of Tuscany in springtime, then in damp inland valleys under elm and ash trees and in vineyards. Usually sold dried at the markets, this morel is excellent in pies, risottos, soups and with eggs or meat.

SADDLE FUNGUS
(Helvella monachella)
In spring this mushroom forms clusters under poplars where the ground is sandy, especially at the coast. It is picked along with morels. While the perfume and taste are not exceptional, it adds a pleasant flavour to sauces.

SUMMER BOLETUS
(Boletus lepidus)
Distinguished from other ceps by its yellow stalk
and scaly surface, this mushroom has rubbery
yellow flesh when ripe, but turns a pinkish colour
when cut. It is nothing special but is picked
because of the thrill of finding a cep in summer,
when no other boletus mushrooms are to be
found. If young, they are quite good fried.

BORAGE
(Borago officinalis)
One of the best-known and prettiest of the
wild herbs, borage *(borraggine)* grows on
waste ground on the Tuscan plains. It has a
pleasant taste of cucumber and the leaves
are cooked in many of the classic soups of
the region and added to spinach dishes.
The pretty blue flowers add a lovely splash
of colour to leafy salads.

CAPERS
(Capparis spinosa)
Caper plants *(capperi)* scramble
over sea-facing rocks and walls.
Their flower buds, salted and
pickled, are one of the classic
Mediterranean condiments.

PINE NUTS
(Pinus pinea)
Pinoli are found in abundance all year
round in Tuscany, growing inside the
cones of the majestic umbrella pines. Sadly,
they are harvested by machine, which is
very damaging to the undergrowth and
threatens to kill off the coastal pine woods.
Left on the tree, the large cones fall as they
open, so the pine nuts can be picked up
from the ground.

BACCALÀ IN DOLCEFORTE (SALT COD IN SWEET AND SOUR SAUCE)

*1 glass white wine • 1 small glass wine vinegar • 2 dessertspoons pine nuts •
2 dessertspoons sugar • 1 dessertspoon sultanas • a few calamint (or mint) leaves • extra
virgin olive oil • 800 g (1 lb 12 oz) salt cod, pre-soaked and cut into pieces • plain flour*

Put the wine, vinegar, pine nuts, sugar, sultanas and calamint in a pan. Bring to the boil
and boil until the liquid is reduced by half. Heat the oil in a separate pan. Coat the cod
pieces in flour and fry in the oil for 6–7 minutes on each side. Drain the cod and put in
another pan with a little of the oil and the sauce. Sauté over brisk heat for 3–4 minutes.

Places of Interest

THE FOLLOWING PLACES sell an extensive range of foods produced in this region – fruit, vegetables, meat, fish, cheeses, pasta, honey and preserves. They also include excellent wine-makers. In addition, it is always worth stopping wherever you see a hand-written sign outside a farm, as many farmers will sell their produce directly to callers. You may even find some who will let you pick fruit from the trees and gather vegetables in their kitchen gardens.

ASCIANO (PI)

 Fattoria di Asciano

via Possenti, 87
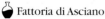 050 855924.

This large estate has its own olive press, once the property of Lorenzo il Magnifico. It produces Monti Pisani Colle di Bellavista extra virgin olive oil, which is one of the finest olive oils in Italy. More versatile than the classic Pisan oils, it is very good for making mayonnaise and dressing fish grilled over charcoal or poached.

BIBBONA (LI)

 Fattoria San Anna

località Sette Fattorie
via Aurelia Sud
0586 670230.

The fruit and vegetables grown on the farm here are used for making preserves, jams and fruit in syrup. Sauces and soups are sold ready to heat up and serve. All the products are carefully packaged in glass jars and they are guaranteed to keep well.

BOLGHERI (LI)

 Tenuta Belvedere

località Belvedere
0565 749735.

This property is owned by Piero Antinori, who uses it for growing local vines. His Bolgheri Bianco Belvedere and Bolgheri Rosato Vigneto Scalabrone are notable wines. The best known, however, is a red, Guado al Tasso. The wines can be bought at Enoteca Tognoni (see opposite page).

The gateway to Bolgheri

 Azienda Agricola Le Macchiole

via Bolgherese, 189/A
0565 766092.

By tending the vines and careful wine-making this estate has produced a range of fine wines. The prime one is Bolgheri Rosso superiore Paléo Rosso, well supported by Paléo Bianco (Sauvignon, Chardonnay and Vermentino) and two single-grape reds: Messorio (Merlot) and Scrio (Syrah).

Tenuta dell'Ornellaia

via Bolgherese, 191
0565 7181.

Owned by the Marquis Lodovico Antinori, this estate is known for a good wine, Ornellaia (from Cabernet Sauvignon, Merlot and Cabernet Franc), accompanied by other noteworthy wines – Masseto (from Merlot alone), Le Volte (Sangiovese, Cabernet Sauvignon and Merlot), and Poggio alle Gazze (Sauvignon Blanc). The extra virgin olive oil is also excellent. Purchases can be made at Enoteca Tognoni (see opposite).

 Tenuta San Guido

località Capanne, 27
0565 762003.

This estate gave birth to the first wine to be called a "Super Tuscan", Sassicaia. The owner, the Marquis Niccolò Incisa della Rocchetta, assisted by his skilled staff, chose Cabernet Sauvignon vines and achieved excellent results. At present this is the only wine made here, with the 180,000 bottles

The cellar of the Tenuta dell'Ornellaia at Bolgheri

always booked well in advance. The extra virgin olive oil is not always of the highest quality – it depends on the year. Purchases can be made at Enoteca Tognoni (see below).

Enoteca Tognoni

via Giulia, 6
C 0565 762001.
● Wed.
□ Sun.

This wine shop stocks a good selection of the great wines of Bolgheri and Tuscany as well as various other Italian wines. You can sample and buy cheeses, Maremma salumi, and other local delicacies. Hot and cold dishes are served: the former include soups made with spelt.

CALCI
(PI)

Il Colletto

località Par di Rota
via dei Pari, 14
C 050 939320.

Excellent extra virgin olive oil, produced from the firm's own organically grown olives, is sold here.

CAMPIGLIA MARITTIMA
(LI)

Azienda Agricola Jacopo Banti

località Citerna
C 0565 838802.

The small range of red and white wines sold here includes a noteworthy Val di Cornia Bianco Il Peccato, made from Vermentino grapes alone, and Ceragiolo, an unusual red from Ciliegiolo grapes alone. The olive oil comes from the olive groves dotted on the hillsides.

The Elixir China Calisaja shop at Castagneto Carducci

CAPOLIVERI – ELBA
(LI)

Azienda Agricola Mola

località Gelsarello, 2
C 0565 958151.

This is a mixed farm, producing a range of vegetables, fruit, oil and wine. The wines produced here are Elba Bianco Vigna degli Aiali, Elba Rosso Gelsarello, a pure Sangiovese, and two sweet wines: Elba Aleatico and Passito di Moscato.

CASTAGNETO CARDUCCI (LI)

Enoteca Il Borgo

via Vittorio Emanuele, 25/27
C 0565 766006.
● Mon.
□ Sun.

Only Italian wines – the premier wines of the Bolgheri area and the leading estates – are stocked by this wine shop. The range includes a selection of grappas and spirits and olive oil from local producers.

Elixir China Calisaja

via Garibaldi
C 0565 766017.
● Wed pm in winter.

This is the sales outlet for a long-established firm. They import quinine bark, which is then processed by hand in the traditional way, by pounding in a mortar and soaking in alcohol. The resulting elixir is then stored in wood. The firm also produces an infusion made from vanilla pods, sugar, lemon and milk, which is called "Gran liquore del Pastore". The shop sells a wide range of local produce, including honey, preserves and pasta, much of it organically produced.

SEPPIE IN ZIMINO

extra virgin olive oil
• *1 onion, chopped*
• *2 stalks celery, chopped*
• *1 kg (2 lb 4 oz) beet leaves, sliced into large pieces • 1 kg (2 lb 4 oz) cuttlefish, cut into strips*
• *300 g (10½ oz) tomatoes, peeled*
• *chopped fresh parsley*
• *salt • pepper*

Heat some oil in a pan, add the onion and celery and cook until softened slightly. Add the beet leaves, cover and cook for about 15 minutes. Add the cuttlefish, cook for a few minutes and then add the tomatoes. Season with salt and pepper and simmer until the cuttlefish is tender. Garnish with the parsley.

**Podere
Grattamacco**

località Grattamacco
 0565 763840.

*The peak of this estate's
wine production is the
Bolgheri Rosso Superiore
Grattamacco from
Cabernet Sauvignon,
Merlot and Sangiovese
grapes, followed by
Bolgheri Bianco
Grattamacco from
Vermentino, Trebbiano
and Sauvignon. The estate
produces a fine oil, one of
the best in the district.*

**Fattoria Poggio
Lamentano**

località Lamentano, 138/b
0565 766008.

*This estate is owned by a
Scot called Michael Zyw,
who devotes himself to
painting and the land.
He produces a fine,
intense, fruity extra
virgin olive oil, which is
well-known abroad and
appreciated by leading
restaurateurs in Italy.*

**Azienda Agricola
Michele Satta**

località Vigna al Cavaliere
0565 763894.

*Reconciling style with a
commitment to quality is
the aim of this estate. The
Bolgheri Rosso Piastraia
blends four types of grape:
Merlot, Cabernet, Syrah
and Sangiovese. The red
Il Cavaliere is from
Sangiovese alone. Among
the whites, Bolgheri
Vermentino La Costa di
Giulia is of note.*

CASTELLINA
MARITTIMA (PI)

**Tenuta del
Terriccio**

via Bagnoli
 050 699709.

*The Lupicaia '95 available
here is a well-structured
red made from Cabernet
and Merlot grapes. There
is also its younger brother,
Tassinaia, containing
some Sangiovese. The
Montescudaio Bianco
and the Saluccio, from
Chardonnay and
Sauvignon Blanc, and
fermented in wood, are
also noteworthy.*

CASTIGLIONCELLO (LI)

 **Gelateria Dai Dai**

via del Sorriso, 8
0586 753390.

*Delicious ice-creams
made from good quality
ingredients are on offer
here. Try the ice-cream
bricks, tartufini, cassatas,
vanilla ice-cream, sorbets
and bocconcini.*

CAVO – ELBA (LI)

Apicoltura Ballini

strada provinciale
della Parata
0565 949836.

*Here is a leading breeder
of queen bees, exported
world-wide, and a
producer of outstanding
honey from unusual
flowers, mostly aromatic
herbs: rosemary, lavender,
cardoons, heather,
arbutus (strawberry tree),
helichrysum, eucalyptus,
sweet chestnut, and wild
flowers. There is another
shop at via Michelangelo
11 in the village.*

CRESPINA (PI)

 Fattoria di Celaja

località Cenaja
via Lustignano, 4
050 643949.

*Production here is based
on two main lines,
Chianti and a Bianco
Pisano di San Torpé from
Trebbiano grapes alone.*

DONORATICO (LI)

Maestrini

via Aurelia, 1
0565 775209.
Mon. Sun.

BACCALÀ IN ZIMINO (SALT COD IN TOMATOES)

*800 g (1 lb 12 oz) salt cod, soaked in water for 2 days
• 800 g (1 lb 12 oz) beet leaves • 500 g (1 lb 2 oz)
tomatoes • extra virgin olive oil • 3 spring onions,
chopped • 2 cloves garlic, chopped • salt • pepper*

Rinse the cod, remove the skin and cut it into pieces.
Wash the beet leaves and put them in a pan with just
the water that adheres to the leaves. Cover and cook
over a low heat for about 10 minutes. Drain, squeeze out
the water and chop coarsely. Scald the
tomatoes in boiling water, peel while
still warm and cut into pieces. Heat
some oil in a pan and gently fry
the spring onions, garlic and
cod for 5 minutes. Using a
slotted spoon, remove the
cod and set aside. Add the
tomatoes to the pan, season
with salt and pepper and
simmer gently for 30 minutes.
Add the greens and the pieces
of cod and stir gently for about
10 minutes. Serve piping hot.

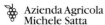

TELLINE ALLA LIVORNESE (LIVORNO COCKLES)

extra virgin olive oil • 1 onion, chopped • 350 g (12 oz) tomatoes, peeled and chopped • 1 fresh chilli, seeded and chopped • 1.2 kg (2 lb 10 oz) cockles (telline) • 3 eggs • chopped fresh parsley • salt • pepper

Heat some oil in a pan, add the onion and fry until slightly softened. Add the tomatoes and chilli and season with salt and pepper. Cook over a moderate heat for 10 minutes. Add the cockles in their shells and cook until they have all opened. Beat the eggs in a bowl, then add them to the pan with the parsley. Stir to mix all the ingredients and serve at once.

A medium-high quality selection of Tuscan, Italian and foreign wines, especially DOCG wines from central Tuscany are sold here. Wines can be tasted accompanied by salumi *and excellent cheeses in a relaxed atmosphere with background music.*

GHIZZANO (PI)

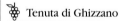

🍇 Tenuta di Ghizzano

Piccioli, via della Chiesa, 1
📞 0587 630096.

The main effort of this estate is focused on the extra virgin olive oil from its 15,000 olive trees. It is a very active estate which has enhanced the wine production of the Pisan hills with a very respectable Chianti and Veneroso, a red wine from Sangiovese, Cabernet and Merlot grapes.

LARI (PI)

Agriturismo Le Macchie

località Usigliano
via delle Macchie, 2
📞 0587 685327.

Cinta Senese pigs graze half-wild on this farm. The meat and salumi the farm produces are less salty and spicy to suit the taste of non-Tuscans. It

has lardo *(lard), which is processed at Colonnata in marble moulds,* fegatelli *(pig's liver wrapped in caul fat) and sausages in oil, as well as jams, preserves and fresh vegetables. There is also a restaurant and farmhouse holiday accommodation.*

Martelli Artigiani Pastai

via S. Martino, 3
📞 0587 684238.

This family firm welcomes visitors (it is popular with Americans) and readily answers questions about its working methods. The Martelli family's pasta (in a wide range of shapes, all dried at low temperatures and extruded through bronze) is excellent, and though output is limited, it is found in leading stores on every continent.

LIVORNO

🍇 D.O.C. Parole e Cibi

via Goldoni, 40/44
📞 0586 887583.
⬤ Mon. 🚫 Sun.

An exceptional range of wines – over 2,000 from all over the world – can be found at this wine shop. There is also a wide selection of grappas, whisky and other spirits. The store has a very lively wine bar offering tasty snacks to accompany the wines, and there is a restaurant (serving in the evenings only) which is open until the small hours.

🍇 Cantina Nardi

via Leonardo Cambini, 6/8
📞 0586 808006.
⬤ Sun.

A good selection of both Italian and Tuscan wines is sold here, with the emphasis on Val di Cornia and Bolgheri, plus the latest vintages of the "Super Tuscans". They also sell olive oil and a range of spirits. During the day they run a small osteria (hostelry) in the wine cellar with a limited number of traditional Tuscan dishes prepared to perfection. The cacciucco, *(fish soup) is very popular and you need to order it in advance.*

Fishing boats in Livorno harbour

Azienda Agricola Cecilia at Marina di Campo on Elba

MARCIANA – ELBA (LI)

🍁 Walter Ciangherotti

località La Zanca
☎ 0565 908281.

Here there are excellent organic honeys, such as lavender, rosemary, blackberry, heather, chestnut and field honey.

BAVETTINE
SUL PESCE

300 g (10½ oz) scampi • 6 small mullet • 300 g (10½ oz) clams • 6 mantis shrimps • extra virgin olive oil • 200 g (7 oz) monkfish • 200 g (7 oz) small cuttlefish • 500 g (1 lb 2 oz) bavettine *(ribbon pasta)* **• 2 cloves garlic, chopped • 400 g (14 oz) tomatoes, chopped • chopped fresh** parsley **• salt • pepper**

Peel the scampi and fillet the mullet. Use the heads to make stock and cook the shrimps and clams in it for 5 minutes. Strain the stock; reserve the clams and shrimps. Stir-fry the monkfish, cuttlefish, fillets, scampi and garlic in some oil. Add the tomatoes, salt, pepper and parsley and simmer. Cook the pasta in the stock. Add the shrimps and clams to the sauce and serve.

MARINA DI CAMPO – ELBA (LI)

🍇 Azienda Agricola Cecilia

località La Pila
☎ 0565 977322.

The complete range of this firm's Elba DOC wines includes an outstanding Ansonica, Rosso and a sweet Aleatico wine. Skins and pips of grapes from wine-making produce two kinds of grappa, one from Ansonica grapes, the other from a blend of Ansonica, Moscato and Aleatico.

MONTECATINI VAL DI CECINA (PI)

🍇 Fattoria Sorbaiano

località Sorbaiano
☎ 0588 30243.

Two types of grape typical of central Italy, Sangiovese

and Montepulciano d'Abruzzo, and two foreigners, Cabernet and Syrah (not common in Italy but recently introduced to various regions) are carefully balanced in the estate's Montescudaio Rosso delle Miniere. Equally well-balanced is the blend of Trebbiano, Vermentino, Chardonnay and Riesling for the Montescudaio Bianco Lucestraia matured in barriques. *The Vin Santo wine is made the old way. The estate makes an excellent organically produced extra virgin olive oil. It has a lively programme of* agriturismo *(farm and estate holidays).*

MONTESCUDAIO (PI)

🥫 Azienda Agricola da Morazzano

via di Morazzano, 28
☎ 0586 650015.

Quality conserves, fruit, vegetables and extra virgin olive oil are all produced by this firm. The many items include shallots in oil, tomato purée and low-sugar jams.

PISA

© Cioccolateria De Bondt

via Turati, 22
☎ 050 501896.
🌑 Mon; from June to September.

Delicacies from the Cioccolateria De Bondt

Azienda Agricola Acquabona

About 30 types of praline, chocolates – some made in moulds while others are hand-crafted like real works of art (there are even Christmas trees and Easter eggs in season) – and 15 kinds of chocolate bars are all the work of Paul De Bondt, a skilled Dutch confectioner who settled in Pisa for love.

 Pasticceria Salza

via Borgo Stretto, 46
C 050 580144.
● Mon. **☐** Sun.

A confectionery shop renowned for the freshness of its raw materials and top-of-the-range products, from chocolates to biscuits, cakes, ice-creams, chilled cream desserts, and traditional Sienese fruit cakes including panforte *and* ricciarelli.

PONTEDERA (PI)

 Pastificio Caponi

via Verdi, 16
C 0587 52532.
● Sat.

This small, family-run pasta-maker is one of the leading firms still using traditional methods to produce limited quantities of an excellent egg pasta, which is dried at low temperatures. It has been famous throughout Italy and Europe for 40 years for its good quality

ingredients and the care devoted to all phases of production. In addition to dried pasta, it sells various other gastronomic specialities.

 Pescheria Toti

via Marconcini, 72
C 0587 53921.
● Wed and Sat pm.

Here you have a wide selection of excellent fresh fish, which comes mainly from Livorno and Viareggio harbours.

PORTOFERRAIO – ELBA (LI)

 Azienda Agricola Acquabona

località Acquabona
C 0565 933013.

This is one of the largest vineyards and wineries on the island, with 15 hectares (37 acres) of the traditional Elba vines including Ansonica,

which it produces in more limited quantities. The Aleatico is interesting, with about 1,000 half-litre (500 ml) bottles produced a year. It also produces small quantities of grappa.

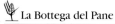 **La Bottega del Pane**

viale Elba, 13
C 0565 914165.
● Wed pm.

Well-known locally for its fine focaccia *reflecting the sunny flavours of the Mediterranean and a wide variety of modern filled rolls, this bakery also sells excellent standard white and brown bread.*

Azienda Agricola La Chiusa

località Magazzini, 93
C 0565 933046.

Long-established on Elba, this estate's fine vineyards slope down to within a few metres of the sea. It principally makes Elba Bianco, but its most interesting products are two dessert wines, Elba Ansonica (made from partly dried grapes) and Elba Aleatico. The extra virgin olive oil produced by the estate merits separate mention because it is excellent quality and, unhappily, there is not enough to satisfy the very high demand for it.

CÉE ALLA LIVORNESE (LIVORNO-STYLE EELS)

1 kg (2 lb 4 oz) elvers • extra virgin olive oil • 1 sprig of sage, chopped • 3 cloves garlic, chopped • 250 g (9 oz) tomatoes, peeled • chopped fresh chilli • salt • pepper

Wash the elvers carefully and pat dry. Heat some oil.in a pan, add the sage and garlic and fry gently until the garlic has softened. Add the elvers to the pan and cook for 5 minutes over a moderate heat. Add the tomatoes and a small amount of chopped chilli. Season with salt and pepper. Simmer for another 10 minutes before serving.

TRIPPA ALLA LIVORNESE

extra virgin olive oil
• *3 cloves garlic , chopped*
• *1 kg (2 lb 4 oz) tripe,*
cut into strips • *4*
dessertspoons vinegar
• *chopped fresh parsley*
• *salt* • *pepper*

Heat some oil in a pan, add the garlic and fry gently for a few minutes. Add the tripe and cook for 3–4 minutes. Pour in the vinegar and a glass of hot water. Cook until the liquid has evaporated and then remove from the heat. Taste and adjust the seasoning. Sprinkle with the chopped parsley and serve at once.

PROCCHIO – ELBA (LI)

 Macelleria Mazzarri

via Centrale
℃ 0565 907289.
◉ Wed pm.

In the open season, Mazzarri butchers local wild boar; the rest of the year he has excellent meat, mostly Tuscan (including Chianina beef), otherwise Piedmontese.

SALIVOLI DI PIOMBINO (LI)

 Romeo Formaggi

via dei Cavalleggeri, 5
℃ 0565 44455.

The region's best salumi, *as well as authentic* culatello di Zibello *and* Norcia hams, *are sold by this shop, which specializes in* salumi. *It also has a rich selection of cheeses from central and northern Italy:* formaggi ubriachi *from the Veneto, various types of* robiola *from the Langhe,* pecorino di fossa *from Soliano al* Rubicone, *and the famous Piedmontese* Castelmagno.

SAN GIOVANNI ALLA VENA (PI)

 Macelleria Bernardini

via Garibaldi
℃ 050 799375.
◉ Wed pm.

Prosciutto crudo *and* salumi *made from pork or game are produced here. The* Boccone del buttero *is an intriguing speciality made from strips of boar meat seasoned with olives.*

SAN MINIATO (PI)

 Frantoio Sanminiatese

via Maremmana, 8
℃ 0571 460528

This estate produces excellent extra virgin olive oil and spicy table olives. It is open daily except during the olive-pressing season (this is usually from mid-October to mid-January).

SUVERETO (LI)

 Azienda Agricola Gualdo del Re

località Notri, 77
℃ 0565 829888.

The unusual DOC Val di Cornia range of wines – Bianco, Rosso and Rosso Riserva – are the staples of this estate. They are backed up by other notable wines, like the red Federico Primo (Sangiovese and Merlot in equal parts) and the white Vermentino Vigna Valentina.

TRIGLIE ALLA LIVORNESE

1.5 kg (3 lb 5 oz) red mullet, cleaned • *4 cloves garlic, finely chopped* • *extra virgin olive oil* • *1 kg (2 lb 4 oz) tomatoes, peeled and chopped* • *1 fresh chilli (misleadingly called* zenzero *- ginger - in Tuscany), seeded and finely chopped* • *handful of parsley, chopped* • *salt* • *pepper*

Arrange the red mullet in a single layer in a greased pan. In a second pan, sauté the garlic in a little oil, add the tomatoes and simmer. When the tomatoes are half-cooked, add the chilli and season to taste with salt and pepper. Once the sauce is well cooked, pour it over the mullet and simmer over a low heat, taking care that the sauce does not dry out (add a little hot water to the pan, if necessary). When the fish are cooked, sprinkle in the chopped parsley and serve.

Oil jars at the Azienda Agricola Orlando Pazzagli

Azienda Agricola Orlando Pazzagli

via Cavour, 40
📞 0565 829333.

With its own olive groves and press, this estate covers the whole cycle of production. Its La Piastrina extra virgin olive oil is typical of the area and is outstanding.

Azienda Agricola Tua Rita

località Notri, 81
📞 0565 829237.

On the borders of the provinces of Livorno and Grosseto, this estate's wines are designed to highlight both traditional local vines and imported ones. Especially notable are the reds Giusto di Notri (from Merlot and Cabernet) and Perlato del Bosco Rosso from Sangiovese alone. There are three whites: Perlato del Bosco Bianco (Ansonica and Clarette), Sileno (Gewürztraminer, Riesling, Chardonnay), and Val di Cornia.

Azienda Agricola Ambrosini Lorella

località Tabarò, 96
📞 0565 829301.

This estate's Riflesso Antico demonstrates how to make a great wine from a local vine, Montepulciano d'Abruzzo. The Val di Cornia Rosso and Bianco are also very good.

VOLTERRA (PI)

Agriturismo Lischeto

località San Giusto
📞 0586 670346.

The owner of this estate is one of many Sardinians who have moved to this region; his wife is Tuscan. The estate has a milking herd of 1,000 ewes and

PICCHIANTE

800 g (1 lb 14 oz) lights (pork or lamb lungs), cleaned • extra virgin olive oil • 2 cloves garlic, chopped • 1 onion, chopped • 2 carrots, chopped • 1 sprig of rosemary, chopped • 1 sprig of sage, chopped • basil leaves, torn • 1 glass white wine • 150 g (5½ oz) tomatoes, peeled and chopped • salt

Cut the lights into pieces. Heat some oil in a pan and lightly fry the garlic, vegetables and herbs. Add the lights and fry until browned. Pour in the wine and tomatoes. Season with salt, cover and simmer for about 45 minutes, then uncover the pan and cook until the sauce has thickened.

their milk is used to produce excellent pecorino cheeses, both fresh and mature, and also fresh and baked ricotta cheeses. A second family estate not far from the sea produces very good extra virgin olive oil and the honey is excellent. The agriturismo facilities on the estate include apartments to rent with meals of typical Sardinian and Tuscan dishes available.

View of the countryside from the heights of Volterra

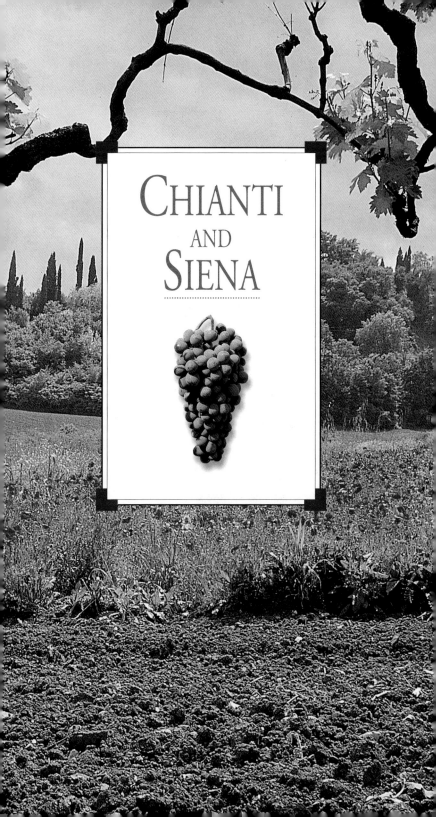

CHIANTI
AND
SIENA

Chianti and Siena

ITALY'S BEST KNOWN WINE comes from this region. The geographical region of Chianti, which had the name long before the wine, is only one part of the wine-growing area of the same name. Chianti wine is produced over a huge area of central Tuscany. The area that gave birth to Chianti wine now sports the Chianti Classico label on its bottles of wine, to indicate that it comes from the classic heartland of Chianti. This heartland, a hilly district stretching across the provinces of Florence and Siena, does not look like a wine-producing area. The woodlands are studded with ancient towns and villages, whose long history is visible at every gateway. On the hilltops, often screened from the main roads, stand country houses set in estates where the olive groves and vineyards are separated by extensive woodland. These villas and castles bear witness to the splendours of past nobility and prosperity, but also to bloody wars.

The old rivalry between Florence and Siena still smoulders, and, in fact, has helped to spur on the revival of wines that were produced in the past, and which have now regained much of their original character and vitality.

0 kilometres   10

0 miles   10

Cinta Senese pigs, which are easily distinguished by their dramatic markings, browse freely with herds of other pigs in the oak woods and meadows in Val di Pesa. In Tuscany the breed dates back to antiquity and you can spot them in celebrated Renaissance paintings, including those of Luca Signorelli.

STAR ATTRACTIONS

- MONTERIGGIONI (SI): Town wall, **C** 0577 280551
- SIENA: Palazzo Pubblico, **C** 0577 292263 Cathedral, **C** 0577 47321 Piazza del Campo
- SAN GIMIGNANO (SI): Cathedral, Palazzo del Podestà, **C** 0577 940340 Museo Civico, **C** 0577 940008

◁ **Spring landscape at Incisa Val d'Arno**

CHIANTI
The famous red wine was once identified by its distinctive straw-padded bottle. Nowadays, this bottle has fallen out of favour because of the high cost of production and difficulties of transport and storage.

The vineyards in this area are often estates with large old country houses. The Cusona estate belongs to the noble Guicciardini Strozzi family and produces an excellent Vernaccia di San Gimignano.

Incisa in Val d'Arno

Figline Valdarno

Greve in Chianti

San Giovanni Valdarno

anzano Chianti

Montevarchi

Radda in Chianti

Arno

Gaiole in Chianti

Bucine

Pergine Valdarno

Chianti

Castelnuovo Berardenga

IENA

Monte San Savino

Panforte, the rich fruit cake, is a symbol of Siena's gastronomic pleasures. Its origins lie in the honey breads of the Middle Ages (*see p106*).

TRANSPORT

FS RAILWAY STATION
- SIENA – STAZIONE FS
  C 0577 280551
- COLLE DI VAL D'ELSA
  C 0577 922791

BUS STATION
- SAN GIMIGNANO
  C 0577 940008
- CASTELFIORENTINO
  C 0571 629049

Chianti extra virgin olive oil is the most famous and celebrated of Tuscany's oils in other parts of the world. The quality is excellent, but it is not produced in the same quantities as the oil from other regions, and it is expensive.

Places of Interest pp112–123
Restaurants pp185–187

Wines

THE CHIANTI AREA is very extensive, covering six of the region's provinces, all with very different terrains and microclimates. Its beauty is reminiscent of a magical Renaissance atmosphere and the area has attracted many foreign investors and businessmen from northern Italy who have settled here, invested in vineyards and made an essential contribution to reviving the region's wine. This is the realm of the Sangiovese vine, which seems to have originated here. It is used for making numerous wines, often in large quantities, especially the Chianti DOCG.

Other important red grapes are Canaiolo Nero and Colorino. The main whites are Trebbiano Toscano and Malvasia del Chianti or Malvasia Bianca, used in small amounts in Chianti but more important for wines such as Vin Santo. Vernaccia di San Gimignano, a very compact thin-skinned white grape is an important grape which gives its name to the wine it is used for.

The properties of the soil and climate in this area make it possible to get good results from Cabernet Franc, Chardonnay, Merlot, Syrah and Pinot Nero red grapes, and Chardonnay and Sauvignon white grapes. Formerly, grapes were dried on racks and then added to the must while it was still young to make Chianti mellow (a practice known as *"governo"*), but this technique is very rare nowadays.

Sangiovese, also called Sangioveto, is the most important red grape vine not only of the Chianti area but of all Tuscany.

CHIANTI

The label on a bottle of this wine may say Chianti or it may have the name of one of seven sub-denominations: Colli Aretini, Colli Fiorentini, Montalbano and Rùfina *(see pp24-6)*, Colline Pisane *(see p81)*, Colli Senesi and Montespertoli. This last one goes back only to '97 and has just reached the market. Chiantis from the various sub-zones differ in body, bouquet and the length of the ageing time.

With Chianti Superiore there is a lower yield per hectare; Chianti Superiore Riserva is aged for at least 2 years and is stored in the bottle for 3 months.

CHIANTI COLLI SENESI

This wine has many of the qualities
of Chianti Classico but is not as
full-bodied and mellow. It can be
served with the same dishes as
a young Chianti Classico.

CHIANTI CLASSICO

The Chianti Classico area was defined
in 1932 as the "most ancient area of
origin" whose boundaries were laid
down by the Grand Duke Cosimo II in
1716. The label Chianti Classico
distinguishes the Chianti
made in this historical
area from the Chianti
produced elsewhere in
Tuscany. The wines
made here are full-
bodied and suited to
lengthy ageing.

*Young Chianti
Classico goes well
with the
traditional local
antipasti, and
with pollo alla
diavola (spicy
chicken) and
spit-roasted pork.*

*The Riserva complements
red meat dishes such as
bistecca alla fiorentina
and the strong flavour of
mature pecorino cheese.*

THE GALLO NERO COMMUNES

The Chianti Classico area stretches
between Florence and Siena and
comprises the communes of Castellina,
Gaiole, Greve, and Radda, and part of
Castelnuovo Berardenga, Barberino Val
d'Elsa, Poggibonsi, San Casciano and
Tavernelle Val di Pesa. Only 10 per cent of this
area is earmarked for Chianti Classico
DOCG. In 1924 the producers of Chianti
Classico founded a consortium and chose
as its emblem a black cockerel (gallo
nero), the historic badge of the Chianti
military league. In 1966 Chianti
Classico received independent
DOCG status.

GALESTRO
This is a fairly recent white wine, born from the marriage of Tuscan vines such as Trebbiano and Malvasia and foreign varieties that may include Chardonnay and Pinot Blanc.

VERNACCIA RISERVA
This wine has to age for at least a year, with 4 months' storage in the bottle. Some producers age the wine in wood, others do not. This results in a wide variety of different and very interesting styles. It is good served with baked fish and white meats.

VERNACCIA DI SAN GIMIGNANO
One of Tuscany's most famous wines, this white DOCG is produced on the hills of San Gimignano. It has a dry, harmonious flavour which has been greatly enhanced by modern techniques of processing at low temperatures. The young wine is ideal with first courses and shellfish dishes.

Grapes for Vernaccia di San Gimignano wine

CINGHIALE AL VINO BIANCO

1 kg (2 lb 4 oz) leg of wild boar • 1 glass red wine vinegar • 1 glass white wine • 3 cloves garlic • 1 lemon • chilli pepper • extra virgin olive oil • salt • pepper

Crush one of the cloves of garlic and mix it with the vinegar. Season with pepper. Marinate the meat in this mixture overnight. The next day, heat the oven to 160°C (325°F/gas mark 3). Dry the meat and sprinkle with the remaining garlic, chopped, and the chilli pepper and salt. Place the meat in an earthenware dish greased with olive oil and baste with the white wine. Cook in the oven until it begins to sizzle, then add the lemon cut in slices. Roast for 3 hours, adding a little more white wine if necessary. Serve the leg cut in slices. Skim the fat off the cooking juices and serve the juices as gravy.

SAN GIMIGNANO ROSATO
This is one of the seven new varieties of DOC San Gimignano, comprising three reds (Riserva and Novello), two rosés (one from Sangiovese alone) and two types of Vin Santo (white and rosé).

Grapes hung to dry for making Vin Santo

VIN SANTO

Vin Santo almost certainly originated in Tuscany and possibly in Chianti, although it is produced in other regions as well – there are about 20 different types. It owes its distinctive flavour to grapes that are hung up or set on racks to dry. Vin Santo is sold either as a dry wine (though it is never perfectly dry) or as a dessert wine, for which demand is falling. It is particularly well suited to the dry confections of the Siena area, such as *biscotti* or *cantuccini (see p34)*.

VIN SANTO DEL CHIANTI

The Vin Santo of Chianti Classico has earned its own DOC label, and from the '97 vintage also that of Chianti. However the leading estates avoid using the DOC appellation and continue to label their products as "Vino da tavola" (table wine).

WINE TYPE	GOOD VINTAGES	GOOD PRODUCERS
Red Wine		
Chianti Classico	98, 97, 95, 93, 90	Fonterutoli di Castellina in Chianti, La Massa di Panzano in Chianti
Super Tuscans *(see p130)*	98, 97, 95 90	Felsina di Castelnuovo Berardenga, S. Giusto & Rentennano di Gaiole in Chianti, Fattoria di Nozzole di Greve in Chianti, Vicchiomaggio di Greve in Chianti
White Wine		
Vernaccia di San Gimignano	99, 97, 95	Montenidoli di San Gimignano, Panizzi di San Gimignano

OTHER WINES WORTH TRYING

Combining the traditional local vines with foreign varieties has produced a profusion of original wines. They include the so-called Super Tuscans *(see p130)*, many of which are very expensive. The DOC **Colli dell'Etruria Centrale** is a range of wines, labelled Bianco, Rosato, Rosso, Novello, Vin Santo. A less successful initiative is the creation of four new-style Tuscan wines identified by the term **Capitolato**: **Muschio** (Chardonnay and Pinot Bianco) and **Selvante** (Sauvignon) for the white wines, **Biturica** (Cabernet and Sangiovese) and **Cardisco** (Sangiovese) for the reds.

Cinta Senese Pork

CINTA SENESE PIGS are a very old local breed with a long history in the area's art as well as its cuisine. They appear in paintings dating back to the 14th century, including Ambrogio Lorenzetti's celebrated fresco of the *Effetti del Buongoverno* (Results of Good Government) in Siena. Cinta Senese pigs have a dark coat with a white belt round their forequarters. They are not, as most people will tell you, a cross between a wild boar and a pig. Some years ago the breed was almost extinct due to the fact that the pigs can only be reared semi-wild in lightly wooded areas, but now local breeders are working hard to save it. The pigs graze freely on tubers, roots, truffles and acorns. Although they look leaner than other breeds, they have a thick layer of fat and their flesh is very firm with a delicate flavour. Inevitably, the quality of the meat, both fresh and cured, combined with the high cost of breeding the pigs, makes Cinta pork products much more expensive than those from other types of pig.

BURISTO DI CINTA

This pork speciality is made from the flesh of the pig's head, including the tongue and some of the skin. The meat is boiled and minced, then spices, pig's blood and boiled fat are added. The mixture is stuffed into a natural casing made from the pig's small intestine and slowly boiled.

Two Cinta pigs grazing in an oak wood

GRIFI

1 kg (2 lb 4 oz) meat from the muzzle of a Cinta pig, cubed • 2 cloves • 1 onion, chopped • 1 clove garlic, chopped • 1 sprig of thyme, chopped • 1 sprig of rosemary, chopped • 2 glasses Chianti • 1 dessertspoon tomato purée • 1 sprig of tarragon, chopped • salt • pepper

Put the meat in a flameproof earthenware casserole, add the cloves and cover with water. Bring to the boil, then simmer until the water has evaporated. Add the onion, garlic, thyme and rosemary. Stir in the wine mixed with the tomato purée and season with salt and pepper. Cover and simmer gently, adding a little hot water if it starts to dry out. When the meat is almost tender, add the tarragon and cook for a further 5 minutes.

The hoof of the Cinta hindquarter is black.

CINTA PROSCIUTTO

Prosciutto crudo from Cinta pigs is seasoned with plenty of pepper in the traditional Tuscan way. It is then left to mature for at least 18 months, resulting in a very tasty ham. Unlike other hams, the foot and hoof are always left on this one.

The hoof of the forequarter is usually a light colour.

SPALLA (SHOULDER)
Cured shoulder is drier and saltier than the ham made from a leg of pork and tastes more peppery. It costs much less than *prosciutto crudo*.

ARISTA (CHINE OF PORK)
Salted *arista* has a thick layer of fat, which makes it look almost like pig's cheek.

RIGATINO
This is a very peppery *pancetta* (bacon) used a great deal in Tuscan cooking. It is excellent also in *antipasti* and Tuscan unsalted bread.

SOPPRESSATA DI CINTA
This salami is much the same as ordinary *soppressata* except for the fact that the meat used to make it is high-quality Cinta.

CINTA SALAME
Drier and firmer than normal Tuscan *salame*, but seasoned in the same generous way, this type is generally a medium–small size.

Coarsely minced meat is mixed with fat chopped with a knife.

OTHER CINTA PORK PRODUCTS WORTH TRYING
The **fresh meat**, which is sold in the usual pork cuts, can be found only at a few specialist butchers. The tasty meat is very fashionable in Tuscany and much in demand among restaurateurs. Apart from the *salumi* illustrated above, the meat is used to make **capocollo** (dry-cured sausage), **lardo** and **fresh and cured sausages**.

Sienese Fruit Cakes

Sienese cakes are made with dried and candied fruit – candied pumpkin is especially popular – and sometimes contain nuts. They are bound together with egg whites and sweetened, at least originally, with honey. Nuts and dried figs were once high-energy food for the poor, and these cakes were nourishing as well as being a good way of using up egg whites when the yolks had been used in other dishes. The cakes have the added advantage of keeping well, so they can be made in advance. Recipes date back to the Middle Ages: *panforte* dates from the 13th century, when it was originally a variant of *pan pepato* (pepper cake) and *dolceforte,* made with spices and honey, was a medieval staple. Arab influences are also evident in some of the spices and other flavourings. These cakes are worth sampling freshly made, if possible: fresh *panforte,* in particular, tastes quite different from the commercial product.

PANFORTE DI SIENA
This is Siena's most famous cake, made from flour, almonds, egg whites, sugar and honey. It is flavoured with dried and candied fruit – especially pumpkin and citrus fruits – and scented with vanilla, cloves, cinnamon, nutmeg and, occasionally, a little cocoa powder.

The flat cake is dusted with icing sugar, sometimes mixed with a little ground cinnamon.

PAN PEPATO
This cake is older than *panforte* and there are many different recipes in existence from various parts of Italy. In the Siena area it is often called *panforte scuro.* It contains larger quantities of cocoa powder and more spices, including pepper, than *panforte.*

CAVALLUCCI
These pale biscuits are made with almonds, dried fruit, flour and egg whites, and are sweetened with sugar and honey.

TORTA NATALIZIA RUSTICA

6 eggs, separated • 200 g (7 oz) flour • 500 g (1 lb 2 oz) dried figs, finely chopped • 500 g (1 lb 2 oz) walnuts, crushed • 200 g (7 oz) caster sugar • 100 g (3½ oz) lard, melted

Preheat the oven to 160°C (325°F/ gas mark 3). Whisk the egg whites until stiff. Sift the flour and gradually add to the egg whites. Beat the yolks, sugar and lard and fold into the whites. Stir in the figs and nuts. Spoon into a greased cake tin and bake the cake for 30 minutes.

CANTUCCI OR TOZZETTI

These crisp biscuits are almost identical to the *biscottini* or *cantuccini di Prato (see p34)*, except these biscuits sometimes contain aniseed, in which case they are called *anicini*. They are made with flour, eggs, almonds, sugar and pine nuts. The dough is shaped into a long loaf, baked and cut into slices. The slices are returned to the oven to dry. They are eaten dipped in Vin Santo.

PANE CON I SANTI

This large, shallow loaf is made from sweetened bread dough flavoured with raisins, nuts and pepper.

The biscuits are sprinkled with icing sugar.

RICCIARELLI

These biscuits are made from a simple almond paste mixed with sugar and egg whites to soften them. They are flavoured with vanilla, lemon zest and honey, then baked on a wafer base made from rice flour.

The dough is cut into lozenge shapes.

SCHIACCIATA CON L'UVA OR CIACCINO CON L'UVA

This sweet *focaccia* covered with raisins probably came originally from Gaiole in Chianti.

OTHER FRUIT CAKES WORTH TRYING

Schiacciata di Pasqua is a raised sweetened loaf flavoured with aniseed that is made for Easter. **Torta di Cecco** or **torta al cioccolato** is taller than *pan pepato*, has more candied than dried fruit and is covered with chocolate icing. A popular recent innovation is **ricciarelli**, covered with chocolate. Also typical of Siena is **torrone** (nougat) in jaw-breaking or softer versions, both covered in chocolate. The **torta natalizia rustica** (rustic Christmas cake) made by peasant families from nuts and dried figs is probably the origin of most modern-day Sienese fruit cakes.

Traditional Produce

IN FLORENCE EVER SINCE the Middle Ages there has been the saying: "You're as rich as if you had a farm in Chianti" because this was the wealthiest area of the countryside around Florence. Here, the old, established families of Florence and Siena still have their farms and estates, together with people from all over the world. In the shops, restaurants and the *agriturismi* of Chianti you hear dozens of languages spoken, not just because of the visiting tourists but because many foreigners live and work here, most of them from other parts of Europe and the United States. They share a great love of Tuscan history and traditions. And, paradoxically, it is these newcomers, together with some of the younger members of the old families, who struggle to preserve the area's traditional products. As long as farms avoid specializing and continue to produce a wide range of foodstuffs, they will enable small local firms to obtain genuine local produce, from pork and vegetables to cheese, oil and vinegar.

BLACK CABBAGE

Cavolo nero is the prince of Tuscan vegetables, cultivated throughout Tuscany. With its long, dark, crinkly leaves and delicate, sweetish flavour, it is essential for *ribollita* (vegetable soup) and many of the more celebrated regional soups.

PICI

The typical Sienese pasta is a kind of thick *spaghetti* made of ordinary wheat flour (not the hard durum wheat) and water. The dough is cut into long strips which are then rolled with the flat of the hand to make them thinner and rounded. *Pici* are sold both fresh and dried in the shops.

MARZOLINO

At one time this cheese was made only in the spring from the milk of ewes who had been grazing on the first fresh grass of the year.

This cheese is oval.

PESTO TOSCANO

500 g (1 lb 2 oz) *black cabbage* • *young extra virgin olive oil (produced in November and December)* • **3** *cloves garlic* • **2** *dessertspoons mature grated* pecorino • **1** *dessertspoon pine nuts* • *salt* • *pepper*

Plunge the cabbage into a pan of boiling water and leave until the water boils again. Drain, cool, then process in a blender with the garlic and pine nuts until finely chopped. Stir in the *pecorino* and add salt and pepper. Stir in enough oil to give a creamy consistency. Spread on bread croutons.

VINEGAR
Many celebrated wine-making estates offer excellent single-grape or Chianti vinegars, often aromatized with herbs.

CHIANTI OLIVE OIL
This comes from the territory south of Florence comprising Greve, Radda, Gaiole, Castellina, Figline, Cavriglia, San Giovanni. These oils are very fruity with a fresh scent, full-bodied and astringent. They have medium fluidity, with a slightly bitter and intensely pungent aftertaste, some herbal notes and a faint tinge of sour tomato.

BREAD FROM WOOD-FIRED OVENS
In Chianti you still find Tuscan bread baked the traditional way in wood-fired ovens.

GRAPPA
The skins and pips of grapes left from making Chianti wine are used to produce very fashionable, modern grappas.

TONNO DEL CHIANTI
Despite its fancy name of "Chianti tuna", this is steam-cooked, brine-cured pork, produced by Cecchini, an unusual butcher's shop in Panzano in Chianti (see p119).

WHAT TO SAMPLE
Though rare, you can still find **pecorino** made the local way from a fresh paste curdled with the flower tufts of the wild artichoke. It is rich in milk fat and usually matured before eating. This area also has the most authentic producers of Tuscan *salumi*: they make excellent traditional **guanciale**, **finocchiona**, **prosciutto crudo**, **salame** and **sausage**, as well as some innovative variations. The meat is excellent, especially **pork** from **Grigio** pigs, **lamb** and **Chianina beef** (more likely to be found in shops here than the rest of Tuscany, but nearly all imported from the Arezzo area). San Gimignano has **white truffles**. Val di Pesa has fine fruit, above all **peaches**.

Wild Produce

GRISETTE
(Amanita vaginata)
Grisette *(fungo gentile)* is one of the commonest amanita mushrooms found in woods from May to November. The colours vary, but it can be identified by the furrowed edge of the cap and the absence of a ring on the stalk; however, it should always be shown to an expert before eating. It is a very delicate mushroom and is excellent cooked with garlic and parsley.

MAN-ON-HORSEBACK MUSHROOM
(Tricholoma equestre)
Common in mixed pine woods in the autumn, this yellow mushroom *(equestre)* adds a delicious flavour to sauces, or savoury pies, and goes well with garlic and parsley. It can also be preserved in oil. There is a poisonous mushroom that looks very similar, so this one must be checked by an expert before it is eaten.

GREY WAX-CAP MUSHROOM
(Hygrophorus limacinus)
This handsome mushroom *(limaccioso)* has a grey cap with thick, fleshy white gills and a white stalk covered in grey viscous gluten. It is common in pine woods in the autumn. The white flesh, with its rich aroma, is excellent in pies and stuffings, or preserved in oil.

DOVE-COLOURED TRICHOLOMA
(Tricholoma columbetta)
It takes experience to recognize these fleshy white mushrooms *(columbetta)*, which sometimes have green patches at the foot of the stalk. They are common in chestnut and oak woods in autumn. They are excellent with meat or bottled in oil, and go well with man-on-horseback mushrooms and the related grey tricholoma mushroom *(see opposite)*.

TAGLIATELLE AI FUNGHI

extra virgin olive oil • 1 bunch of parsley • 3 cloves garlic • small piece of chilli, chopped • 600 g (1 lb 5 oz) mixed mushrooms, sliced • 100 g (3½ oz) fresh sausages, chopped • 500 g (1 lb 2 oz) tomatoes, peeled • 500 g (1 lb 2 oz) tagliatelle • *salt*

Heat some oil in a pan and add the mushrooms, parsley, garlic, chilli and sausage. Season. Cook over a high heat until the mushrooms have shed their water. Lower the heat and cook until the liquid has evaporated. Add the tomatoes and simmer until cooked. Meanwhile, cook the *tagliatelle*. Serve the sauce with the pasta.

MARMELLATA DI ROSA CANINA (ROSE HIP JAM)

• *dog rose hips* • *sugar*

Cut open the hips and remove the seeds and bristles inside. Wash the hips well in running water. Pour enough water into a preserving pan to come 2.5–5 cm (1–2 inches) up the side. Weigh the rose hips and put them in the pan with half their weight in sugar. Cook until all the water has evaporated and the fruit is soft. Sieve the fruit, return it to the pan and continue cooking until it reaches the desired density. Bottle at once.

DOG ROSE
(Rosa canina)
Dog rose *(rosa di macchia)* hips, picked after the first frosts, are excellent in jams, sweet sauces, fortified wines and liqueurs. The bristles around the seeds need to be removed before using them.

BLACKTHORN
(Prunus spinosa)
The blackthorn *(marruche)* is a common tree on the edges of woods and fields. Its very astringent fruit, sloes, can be eaten after the first frosts. They are very good in liqueurs and syrups.

GREY TRICHOLOMA MUSHROOM
(Tricholoma terreum)
Little grey tricholoma mushrooms *(moretta)* spread through pine woods in their thousands in autumn. The mushroom cap is covered in what looks like mouse fur and the gills and stalks are a greyish white. Always have them checked by an expert before eating as they are similar to poisonous tricholomas. They are exquisite in sauces, savoury pies and with fish. They can also be preserved in oil.

BUTCHER'S BROOM
(Ruscus aculeatus)
In springtime the young shoots of this attractive bush *(pungitopo)* are delicious, though slightly bitter. They can be preserved in oil, or simmered and served with egg sauces. Here, they are shown growing with the true wild asparagus *(Asparagus acutifolius)* – both are picked and eaten.

Places of Interest

THE RUSTIC ORIGINS of many of the gastronomic suppliers listed here are preserved intact. The farmhouses, for instance, are nearly all historic mansions crammed with colourful works of art. When shopping you can hear a mixture of many languages from all the French, American, German and Japanese visitors mingling with the local Italian population. Despite the high numbers of tourists, the quality of the regional food produce has hardly suffered at all – unlike the situation in some of the big cities. Often, in fact, the foreigners shopping in Chianti are even more discerning than the local customers.

BARBERINO DI VAL D'ELSA (FI)

 Casa Emma

località Cortine
☎ 055 8072859.

The Merlot Soloìo produced on this estate is very fine, with unusual body and bouquet. There is also a mellow Chianti Classico Riserva, which is very good drinking.

 Fattoria Isole & Olena

località Isole, 1
☎ 055 8072763.

From a truly skilled professional comes a series of wines of the greatest interest: Chianti Classico, Cepparello (based on Sangiovese), Eremo (on Syrah) and Cabernet Sauvignon Collezione De Marchi. The extra virgin olive oil is very fine.

 Castello di Monsanto

via Monsanto, 8
☎ 055 8059000.

This estate can justly claim to have played an important role in the region's wine-making revival by its foresight and enterprise. Its wines are excellent: the Chianti Classico, elegant and full-bodied, plus the reds Fabrizio Bianchi (Sangiovese) and Nemo, based on Cabernet.

Fattoria Pasolini Dall'Onda

piazza Martini, 10
☎ 055 8075019.

Extra virgin olive oil with an intense fruity flavour is produced from olives grown and pressed on the estate. Olive oil production goes back a long way here – it has been made on the estate since 1573.

Wine ageing in barrels at the Cecchi winery at Castellina in Chianti

---

CASTELLINA IN CHIANTI (SI)

 Casa Vinicola Cecchi

località Casina dei Ponti
☎ 0577 743024.

Wines made from a range of grapes are on offer here. Of particular interest is the Chianti Classico Messer Pietro di Teuzzo and Spargolo made from Sangiovese grapes. A recent addition is Arcano made from organic Sangiovese grapes. The group has other estates, including Castello di Montauto which makes a good Vernaccia di San Gimignano.

Castello di Fonterutoli

località Fonterutoli
☎ 0577 73571.

This is an old-established wine estate with a great

tradition behind its
Chianti Classico: it retains
all its vigour in the
regular version and in
the Riserva Castello di
Fonterutoli, and the
Riserva Ser Lapo. Note the
two other excellent wines
in Concerto (Sangiovese
and Cabernet Sauvignon)
and Siepi (Sangiovese
and Merlot).

Azienda Agricola Villa Cerna at Castellina in Chianti

 Gagliole

località Gagliole, 42
0577 740369.

The favourable position of
these vineyards, and their
organic cultivation, have
produced excellent results
in both the Gagliole Rosso
(Sangiovese with Cabernet
Sauvignon) and Gagliole
Bianco (Trebbiano with a
little Chardonnay).

Apicoltura Lecchini

località La Piazza
0577 733560.

Local honey, especially
from chestnut, acacia
and wild flowers, as well
as honey-based energy-
boosters and beauty
products are sold here.

 Castello di Lilliano

località Lilliano
0577 743070.

The Chianti Classico
and Riserva, both wines
of distinctive, forceful
character, are backed up
by Anagallis, a red wine
from Sangiovese and
Colorino grapes matured
in oak barriques.

Rocca delle Macìe

località Le Macìe
0577 7321.

An attractive, dynamic
estate with a carefully
gauged production
centred on the red wines
of the region. The Chianti
Classico is vinified from
various crus, including
La Tenuta Sant'Alfonso.
The Fizzano Riserva is
notable. Also interesting is

the Roccato (Sangiovese
and Cabernet) and Ser
Gioveto (Sangiovese). It
also has a mellow grappa
and extra virgin olive oil.

Macelleria Stiaccini

via Ferruccio, 33
0577 740558.
Wed pm.

This butcher's shop sells
its own fresh sausages,
as well as a good selection
of Tuscan salumi with
some Sienese specialities
as well. It has Chianina
beef plus various other
cuts of meat, all from
animals which have
been carefully selected
by the owners from herds
in the province. It also
offers ready-to-eat
spiedini (kebabs),
fegatelli and other
seasoned meats.

Azienda Agricola Villa Cerna

località Villa Cerna
0577 743024.

This estate is owned
by the Cecchi family.
It offers a Chianti
Classico with a
good structure,
and a
Riserva
matured
in wood,
both in
large
barrels
and oak
barriques.
The
estate also
makes a
Vin Santo
which is allowed to
ferment in casks.

PANFORTE

**150 g (5½ oz) caster sugar • 150 g (5½ oz) honey
• 1 dessertspoon cocoa powder • 150 g (5½ oz) each of
peeled almonds and hazelnuts, roasted and halved
• 50 g (1¾ oz) chopped nuts • pinch each of ground
cinnamon, cloves and nutmeg • vanilla essence
• 70 g (2½ oz) flour • 250 g (9 oz) diced candied fruit
• icing sugar • rice flour wafer or rice paper**

Preheat the oven to 160°C (325°F/gas mark 3).
In a pan (preferably copper), heat the sugar
and honey over a gentle heat until a drop
of the mixture forms a soft ball when
dropped into cold water. Remove from
the heat and add the cocoa, nuts, fruit,
spices, few drops of essence and 60 g
(2 oz) of the flour; stir carefully. Pour the
mixture into a shallow cake tin lined with
the wafer or rice paper. Mix the remaining
flour with 2 dessertspoons icing sugar and a
little cinnamon. Sprinkle it over the mixture,
then bake in the oven for 30 minutes. Cool, turn
out and sprinkle with icing sugar mixed with cinnamon.

CASTELNUOVO
BERARDENGA (SI)

 Azienda Agricola
Castell'in Villa

località Castell'in Villa
0577 359074.

*The wine here is of
a consistently high
quality, thanks to
the skilled hand
of a wine-maker
on this estate
who excels at the
production of Chianti
Classico as a young
wine and a Riserva. Also
worth noting are the
Poggio delle Rose, made
from Sangiovese alone,
and the Vin Santo.*

Fattoria di Felsina

strada Chiantigiana, 484
0577 355117.

*This is one of the most
interesting cellars in
Tuscany, containing a
wide range of fine wines,
from Chianti Classico to
the Berardenga and
Rancia selections (at
their best in the Riserva
version). The Fontalloro
(from pure Sangiovese)
and Maestro Raro
(Cabernet) are equally
excellent. The estate also
produces a very good Vin
Santo and two whites: I
Sistri (Chardonnay) and
Pepestrino (made from
Trebbiano, Sauvignon
and Chardonnay grapes).*

FAGIOLI ALL'UCCELLETTO

*2 cloves garlic, chopped • sprigs of sage, chopped
• extra virgin olive oil • 1.5 kg (3 lb 5 oz) fresh beans or
450 g (1 lb) dried beans, soaked overnight
• 600 g (1 lb 5 oz) tomatoes, sliced
• salt • pepper*

Lightly fry the garlic and sage in
the oil. Add the beans, tomatoes
and about 400 ml (14 fl oz)
water. Season to taste with salt
and pepper and simmer for
about 30 minutes.

Pasticceria
Lodi Pasini

via Fiorita, 6
0577 355638.
● Mon.
◯ Sun am.

*Traditional Sienese cakes
and fresh stuffed pasta
are the two specialities
here – try their lemon-
scented ravioli filled with
a mixture of ricotta and
other cheese.*

Fattoria di Petroio

località Querciagrossa
0577 328045.

*The two classic wines of
this part of Tuscany are
produced on the richly
endowed land of this
small estate – Chianti
Classico and Chianti
Classico Riserva.*

Agricola San Felice

località San Felice
0577 359087.

*This estate has produced
good results with some of
its wines, such as the
Riserve di Chianti Classico
Poggio Rosso, Il Grigio
and the Vigorello red,
which is made from
Sangiovese plus small
amounts of Cabernet
Sauvignon grapes. The
olive oil is very good.*

COLLE VAL D'ELSA (SI)

Frantoio Roncucci

località Mensanello
0577 971080.

*The oil comes exclusively
from the estate's own
groves (70% Correggiolo
olives) and is sold by
measure straight from the
press while it is operating.
As the oil is not bottled,*

The Castello di Brolio of the Tenuta Ricasoli

you need to take a suitable container with you to carry your oil home.

GAIOLE IN CHIANTI (SI)

 Agricoltori del Chianti Geografico

via Mulinaccio, 10
0577 749489.

This cooperative winery, run by a great wine-maker, is based on two estates. The Gaiole estate produces the red wines, especially Chianti Classico with the Contessa di Radda selection, the Riserva Montegiachi, and the Capitolare di Biturica (based on Cabernet Sauvignon and Sangiovese). The San Gimignano estate principally produces whites, including Vernaccia.

 Apiari Floridea

località Badia a Coltibuono L'Osteria, 27
0577 746110.

This apiarist is rigorous about the production of honey by natural methods. Honeys include ones made from pollen from chestnut trees, woodland flowers, broad-leaved trees, acacia and heather.

 Badia a Coltibuono

località Badia a Coltibuono
0577 749498.

This estate, with its old monastery buildings dating from the 11th century, favours a traditional approach to production with particular emphasis on Sangiovese vines. Its star product is Sangioveto, made from Sangiovese alone. Another noteworthy wine is the Chianti Classico Riserva.

Badia a Coltibuono

 Barone Ricasoli – Castello di Brolio

località Brolio
0577 7301.

This is one of the oldest and most renowned of the Chianti Classico wineries. Much of the production is Chianti Classico Brolio, which also comes in a Riserva version. This is followed by Casalferro, a Sangiovese from a particular clone with the Merlot grape. In recent years the Sangiovese vine used for producing the Casalferro has been used to make Formulae, a young wine that offers very good value for money.

 Castello di Ama

località Ama
0577 746031.

Only a small number of vines are grown on this particular estate but all of them are of the highest quality, from Chianti Classico onwards. In addition, in the best years, the estate also produces Vigneto La Casuccia and Bellavista selections. The most applauded wine is Vigna l'Apparita, based on Merlot grapes. The extra virgin olive oil is also excellent. For purchases, apply to the Enoteca Rinaldi, Lecchi in Chianti (0577 746021).

Castello di Cacchiano

località Cacchiano, frazione Monti in Chianti
0577 747018.

The Ricasoli Firidolfi family have drawn on expert help to enhance the Sangiovese grapes in the Chianti Classico, the Riserva and the Rosso R.F. from Merlot, Sangiovese and Canaiolo, matured in small casks. The Vin Santo is very good.

Macelleria Chini

via Roma, 3
0577 749457.
Mon and Wed pm.

The Chini family have worked in the meat trade since the 17th century. Their products are of the highest quality – there is salumi *made from pure-bred Cinta Senese pigs, plus meat from other local animals.*

POLLO ALLA DIAVOLA

1 free-range chicken
• *marinade of sliced garlic, rosemary leaves and extra virgin olive oil*

Cut the chicken down the backbone, open it out and flatten with a meat mallet. Pour over the marinade and leave for 1 hour. Grill over hot embers, turning it every 6–7 minutes until tender.

Fattoria Pile e Lamole and Fattoria di Vistarenni

località Vistarenni
 0577 738186.

These two estates produce a Chianti Classico Lamole di Lamole and Villa Vistarenni, both very good value for money, and an interesting Lamole di Lamole selection, again Chianti Classico. Other notable products are an excellent extra virgin olive oil; Lamole di Lamole, an aqua-vitae; and Codirosso, from Sangiovese and Cabernet Sauvignon matured for six months in barriques.

 Azienda Agricola Riecine

località Riecine
 0577 749098.

This property has changed hands and at present it seems that the previous style is continuing with just a few excellent wines: Chianti Classico, Chianti

---

POLLO CON LE OLIVE

3 spring chickens, each cut into 8 pieces • 300 g (10½ oz) pitted green olives • flour • 3 bay leaves • 3 cloves garlic • extra virgin olive oil • about 400 ml (14 fl oz) dry white wine • chicken stock • salt • pepper

Dredge the chicken pieces in flour. Heat some oil in a frying pan, add the chicken and fry over a brisk heat to seal on all sides. Add the bay leaves, garlic and wine and cook until the wine has evaporated. Add the olives and a little stock. Cover and continue cooking until the chicken is tender, adding more stock if required. Adjust the seasoning and serve.

Vineyards of the Fattoria Pile e Lamole at Vistarenni

Classico Riserva and La Gioia di Riecine, from Sangiovese alone.

 Rocca di Castagnoli

località Castagnoli
 0577 731004.

Two vineyards belong to this estate, one at Gaiole and the other at Castellina. The wine most representative of the "Super Tuscan" style is Stielle, made from Sangiovese and Cabernet grapes, followed by Buriano, made from Cabernet Sauvignon alone. Chianti Classico Riserva, Poggio a' Frati and Capraia are all produced in the traditional style.

 Fattoria di San Giusto a Rentennano

località Monti in Chianti
 0577 747121.

This estate limits its wines to three different types, all of them of very high quality. The Chianti Classico is a powerful wine with complex perfumes, especially the Riserva. Percarlo, from Sangiovese alone, has good character and the estate's Vin Santo is held to be one of the best in the whole of Tuscany.

Le Antiche Delizie del Bianchi

via Ricasoli, 72
 0577 749501.
Tues pm.

This bakery offers a very varied range of specialities, which reflect its basic principle: to keep a close rapport with the surrounding district and use natural ingredients. It has bread made with fresh yeast and kneaded by hand, especially the classic Tuscan loaf and what is called "Etruscan bread", made with spelt and a mixture of flours. It also sells traditional cakes and some of the firm's own creations, like the Torta Chiantigiana, made with extra virgin olive oil. Their ice-cream is made with good quality natural ingredients. The delicatessen has a select range of local specialities and the small restaurant, Lo Sfizio del Bianchi, offers real local cuisine.

GREVE IN CHIANTI (FI)

 Gelateria Cabana

località Strada in Chianti
via Mazzini, 32
 055 8588659.
Wed pm.

Very fine cream and fruit ice-creams in a variety of

flavours, all from natural ingredients, are sold in this ice-cream parlour. It also has ice-cream cakes and pastries – the zuccotto *and the* millefoglie *both merit a special mention.*

Casa Vinicola Carpineto

località Dudda
 055 8549062.

A good Chianti Classico, also in a Riserva version, is produced here as well as Cabernet Sauvignon Farnito.

Antica Macelleria Falorni

piazza Matteotti, 69
 055 853029.
☐ daily, including Sunday.

This large store has a wine cellar and wine-tasting shop. It sells a wide range of salumi *which can be sampled with the wine. The family firm has long been closely associated with traditional Tuscan products, including Chianina beef, Cinta pork, wild boar and local* salumi. *It also has a modern outlook, producing best-selling items like* zampone *(stuffed pig's trotter) and packaging its own sliced hams and other meats in sealed containers. However, the traditional spirit and methods remain, evident in the excellent fresh meat and local game, and* salumi *from both Cinta and ordinary pigs and wild boar.*

Tenuta di Nozzole

località Passo dei Pecorai
 055 2385901.

The Folinari family own this splendid villa and the vineyards, which produce

great wines. Especially try the Chianti Classico Nozzole and the Riserva La Forra. The estate also makes a Cabernet Sauvignon, Il Pareto and Chardonnay, Le Bruniche. The Fattoria di Nozzole is the sales point for all the Folonari estate's various products.

Castello di Querceto

località Dudda
 055 85921.

This family firm produces Chianti – the younger version and the Riserva il Picchio are noteworthy – and draws on Sangiovese vines for its La Corte red.

Azienda Agricola Querciabella

località Ruffoli
via S. Lucia a Barbiano, 17
 055 853834.

A professional and far-sighted approach to the

estate's objectives is the key to the success of its outstanding wines. The Chianti Classico produced here is one of the finest in the area and also comes in a Riserva version. Equally fine are the Camartina, made from Sangiovese and Cabernet Sauvignon grapes, and the Batàr produced from equal parts of Pinot Bianco and Chardonnay grapes.

Azienda Agricola Poggio Scalette

località Ruffoli
via Barbiano, 7
 055 8546108.

Vittorio Fiore, one of Tuscany's best-known wine-makers, owns this small estate. It has old vines and its production is select and of the very highest level. At present it offers only one wine, Carbonaione, produced from Sangiovese grapes alone, and a fine extra virgin olive oil.

RIBOLLITA (VEGETABLE SOUP)

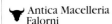

300 g (10½ oz) dried cannellini beans • 3 courgettes • 3 carrots • 1 stalk celery • 300 g (10½ oz) potatoes • 3 tomatoes • 350 g (12 oz) onions • 100 g (3½ oz) guanciale (pig's cheek) • extra virgin olive oil • 200 g (7 oz) peas • ½ black cabbage, cut into strips • a few sprigs of parsley • meat stock • stale Tuscan bread, sliced • salt • pepper

Rinse the beans, soak overnight and then cook them in the same water over a very low heat. Meanwhile, chop the courgettes, carrots, celery, potatoes, tomatoes, half the onions and the *guanciale* and fry them in oil in a large pan until softened. Add the peas, cabbage and parsley, moisten with the bean cooking water and some stock. Add salt and pepper. Simmer for 1 hour. Purée some of the beans in a vegetable mill and add to the soup with the whole beans. Arrange the bread slices in an ovenproof dish. Pour the soup over the bread and leave to cool. Preheat the oven to 180°C (350°F/gas mark 4). Finely slice the remaining onions and add them to the soup with more oil. Bake in the oven until the oil simmers and the onion forms a golden crust.

Azienda Agricola Vecchie Terre di Montefili

via San Cresci, 47
 055 853739.

Refined Chianti Classico matched by the Sangiovese Colli della Toscana Centrale Anfiteatro is produced by this estate. Also of great interest is the Colli della Toscana Centrale Bruno di Rocca, from Cabernet Sauvignon and Sangiovese, and Vigna Regis, a white wine from Chardonnay, Sauvignon and Traminer.

Tenuta Vicchiomaggio

via Vicchiomaggio, 4
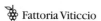 055 854079.

A splendid, intensely fruity extra virgin olive oil, one of the best in the whole region, is produced by this estate. It also makes Chianti Classico and grappa.

Fattoria Viticcio

via San Cresci, 12/A
055 854210.

This small estate in Chianti is interesting because it adds Nebbiolo grapes to the Cabernet Sauvignon and

Sangiovese in its Monile red. Its other very good reds are Prunato from Sangiovese grapes and Chiantis.

MERCATALE VALDARNO (AR)

 Fattoria Petrolo

località Galatrona
055 9911322.

The range of extra virgin olive oil is excellent and can be purchased directly at the estate together with its Vin Santo. The wines (Torrione from Sangiovese alone, Galatrona from Merlot alone, Terre di Galatrona from Sangiovese with a little Merlot) are found only in wine shops, and they are expensive.

MERCATALE VAL DI PESA (FI)

Castelli del Grevepesa

località Ponte di Gabbiano
via Grevigiana, 34
055 821101.

This large cooperative winery has a wide range of good wines. Notable among them is the Chianti Classico Clemente VII

because of its very reasonable price for the quality of the wine. There are numerous estate wines: among the range of Chianti Classici, the Vigna Elisa and Sant'Angiolo Vico l'Abate are noteworthy.

MONTESPERTOLI (FI)

 Fattoria Le Calvane

via Castiglioni, 1/5
0571 671073.

A Chianti Colli Fiorentini Il Quercione, a Riserva Il Trecione and Vin Santo Zipolo d'Oro are all on offer here. There are also wines made from vines not traditional to the area, including Borro del Boscone, from Cabernet Sauvignon matured in new oak barriques, Sorbino from Chardonnay grapes, and Colle Cimoli made from Chardonnay, Sauvignon Blanc and Traminer.

Azienda Agricola Poggio Tizzaoli

via Barrucciano, 1/2
0571 671379.

A good extra virgin olive oil, very typical of the area, is produced at this estate.

The splendid hill panorama of Montespertoli

PANZANO IN CHIANTI (FI)

 ## Enoteca Baldi

piazza Bucciarelli, 25
 055 852843.
daily, including Sunday.

This is a first-rate wine bar, offering an excellent selection of Italian and international wines and, above all, a wide range of the delicacies of central Tuscany. There are good gourmet savouries to sample with the wines.

 ## Antica Macelleria Cecchini

via XX Luglio, 11
055 852020.
Wed.
Sun am.

At first glance you seem to have entered an ordinary butcher's when you go into this shop. Then you notice the classical background music playing softly

CARNE IN GALERA

1.2 kg (2 lb 10 oz) sirloin or fillet of beef • 1 sprig of sage, finely chopped • 2 or 3 sprigs of rosemary, finely chopped • 1 clove garlic • 100 ml (3½ fl oz) white wine vinegar • 200 ml (7 fl oz) hot beef stock, plus extra, if necessary • extra virgin olive oil • salt

Heat some oil in a pan, add the beef and fry until well browned and sealed on both sides. Add the garlic and herbs and fry for 1–2 minutes. Lower the heat, add the vinegar and stock. Cover and cook over a low heat until the liquid has evaporated. Add salt when the meat is half cooked. Add more stock if it evaporates before the meat is tender.

The Antica Macelleria Cecchini

and behind the counter a second room opens out with a fine table for sampling wine and hams, with other local and traditional specialities hanging from the ceiling. Then you start to browse through the large, elegant 16-page menu (at present reduced for renovation), which looks more like a restaurant menu than a butcher's price list. It offers 22 cuts of Tuscan lamb ready to cook (seasoned, dressed and packaged); 9 types of meat for roasting (from Chianina beef to pigeons); 12 stuffed-meat dishes; 13 different meats for grilling; 12 sorts of sausages, 12 meat preparations for cooking in a saucepan; 10 for cooking in a frying pan; 18 unusual sauces and delicacies, all of them made by the firm; 9 pork products; 12 terrines and pâtés; 8 different cuts of cold meats (tongue, boned calf's head, galantines). In addition, there are chestnuts, traditional pulses, extra virgin olive oil, Vin Santo, herbs and fresh produce from the firm's farm. These quality products are presented with an almost maniacal devotion to tradition, a careful search for the oldest recipes (some are reprinted on the menu) and a careful choice of authentic ingredients. All these factors add a cultural dimension to the gourmet extravaganza, making it an unmissable experience for meat lovers.

 ## Azienda Agricola Cennatoio

via San Leolino, 35
055 852134.

The star product from this estate is its Vino Etrusco from Sangiovese grapes. The Chianti Classico Riserva and the Rosso Fiorentino, made from Cabernet Sauvignon, are also good.

Tenuta Fontodi

via San Leolino, 89
055 852005.

This carefully managed estate produces high quality wines, starting with its Chianti Classico Riserva Vigna del Sorbo, which is among the finest in its class. Outstanding among the varietals are the Colli della Toscana Centrale Flaccianello della Pieve, from Sangiovese, and a great Colli della Toscana Centrale Pinot Nero Case Vie. It also makes a good extra virgin olive oil.

La Massa

via Case Sparse, 9
055 852701.

This estate has focused on only two wines, with the aim of giving Chianti the same dignity as the great international wines, and it has succeeded with its Chianti Classico and the Giorgio Primo selection.

RICCIARELLI (ALMOND BISCUITS)

250 g (9 oz) *peeled almonds* • **300 g (10½ oz)** *caster sugar* • *1 egg white* • *1 dessertspoon honey* • *pinch of ground cinnamon* • *grated zest of 1 lemon* • *icing sugar* • *1 rice flour wafer or rice paper*

Preheat the oven to 140°C (275°F/gas mark 1). Crush the almonds in a blender and mix them with the sugar. Beat the egg white and mix it into the almonds with the honey, cinnamon and lemon zest. Mix well. Roll out the dough on a work surface sprinkled with icing sugar until it is 2 cm (¾ inch) thick. Cut out lozenge shapes 7.5 cm (3 inches) in length. Place each on a slightly larger piece of wafer or on rice paper. Bake in the oven for about 15 minutes, taking care not to let the biscuits brown.

Fattoria Villa Cafaggio

via San Martino in Cecione, 5
055 8549094.

Besides an interesting Chianti Classico, this estate makes two wines of unique character from the area's most important red grapes, blended in different proportions: Sangiovese dominates in the San Martino and Cabernet Sauvignon in the Cortaccio.

POGGIBONSI (SI)

Melini

località Gaggiano
0577 989001.

On one of the largest Chianti Classico estates, half the estate provides the grapes for its Chianti Classico La Selvanella Riserva, possibly its most renowned product. There is also a good white wine, Vernaccia di San Gimignano Le Grillaie. The estate also produces an interesting olive oil.

RADDA IN CHIANTI (SI)

Castello d'Albola

via Pian d'Albola, 31
0577 738019.

Belonging to the Zonin family, this estate is known for two innovative classics – the Acciaiolo from Sangiovese and Cabernet Sauvignon grapes, and Le Fagge from Chardonnay. The Chianti Classico Riserva and the Novello Sant'Ilario are both very good.

Enoteca Arte Vino

viale XI Febbraio, 21
0577 738605.
Tues. Sun.

This wine bar specialises in local wines and serves hot and cold dishes with them, including crostini, local salumi and pecorino.

Azienda Agricola Il Poggerino

via Poggerino, 6
0577 738232.

The professional skill and passion with which this fairly small vineyard is managed have produced interesting results in the Chianti Classico and the Riserva Bugialla.

Casa Porciatti

via IV Novembre, 1
0577 738055.
Wed pm.
Sun am May to October.

All sorts of good things can be found in this food store-cum-butcher's-cum wine shop and much else besides. Apart from the fine wares on display, the staff will procure all kinds of specialities on request. It has real Chianina beef, Sienese cakes bearing the shop's own hallmark, local marzolino cheese matured in the store's cellars, and its own salumi, including their own creation "tonno di Radda" (dried lean pork) and sausage flavoured with black truffles (not the synthetic aroma). It also has a rich selection of the region's olive oils, wines and local honey.

Azienda Agricola Terrabianca

località San Fedele a Paterno
0577 738544.

The star wine here is definitely Campaccio, which also comes in a Riserva version, from Sangiovese and Cabernet Sauvignon. It is backed up by one of the finest Tuscan whites, Piano della Cappella. Try the Chianti Classico Vigna della Croce and the estate's other white, Fior di Fino, from Malvasia and Trebbiano.

Castello di Volpaia

località Volpaia
0577 738066.

The village of Castello di Volpaia

One of the finest estates in Tuscany, this has excellent agriturismo (farm holiday) facilities and quality products. The Chianti Classico Riserva, the Coltassala from Sangiovese grapes, and the Balifico from Sangiovese and Cabernet are all noteworthy. The estate has excellent extra virgin olive oil and a whole range of vinegars.

SAN CASCIANO IN VAL DI PESA (FI)

Tenuta Castello il Corno

via Malafrasca, 64
055 8248009.

This is an ancient farm, producing wines and, above all, an excellent extra virgin olive oil.

Fattoria Corzano e Paterno

località San Vito
055 8249114.

Located close to the boundary of the Chianti Classico area, this firm produces a fine Terre di Corzano Chianti and a very good Vin Santo, one of the best in the region.

Oleificio Giachi

località Mercatale in Val di Pesa via Campoli, 31
055 821082.

This firm bottles excellent extra virgin olive oil, mostly from local olive presses, including their own blend, Colle dei Giachi.

Azienda Agricola Massanera

via di Faltignano, 76
055 8242360.

Free-range Cinta Senese pigs are raised here and turned into fine salumi, but prices are high. The estate also makes very good, but expensive, oil and wine.

Antica Fattoria Niccolò Machiavelli

località San Andrea in Percussina
0577 989001.

This estate is owned by the Gruppo Italiano Vini (group of wineries in key regions), which has recently attracted praise for its wine. One example is the Chianti Classico Riserva Vigna di Fontalle, but the best known is Ser Niccolò, from Cabernet Sauvignon grapes.

SAN GIMIGNANO (SI)

Azienda Agricola Il Casale-Falchini

via di Casale, 40
0577 941305.

This estate was one of the first to revive production of Vernaccia, a policy that has produced the excellent wines Vigna al Solatio, enriched with a little Chardonnay, and Vinea Doni. Among its other wines, Càmpora, a red from pure Cabernet Sauvignon, is very good.

Fattoria di Cusona

località Cusona, 5
0577 950028.

The Guicciardini Strozzi firm owns this centuries-old property. They make a good Vernaccia, which also comes in a Riserva version, made from grapes gathered late in the harvest and then fermented in barriques. There is also a spumante version. Among the red wines, is Sodole, which is produced from Sangiovese grapes.

The towers of San Gimignano

PAPPARDELLE SULLA LEPRE (PASTA WITH HARE)

4 dessertspoons olive oil • 1 onion, chopped • 1 carrot, chopped • 1 stalk celery, chopped • a few sage leaves • a handful of parsley, chopped • 150 g (5½ oz) guanciale (pig's cheek), chopped • shoulder, neck and breast of a hare, cut into pieces • hare giblets (lights, heart, liver) and blood • 2 glasses Chianti • vinegar • beef stock • 100 ml (3½ fl oz) milk • 600 g (1 lb 5 oz) fresh pappardelle • grated Parmesan cheese • salt • pepper

Heat the oil in a pan (preferably earthenware) and fry the onion, carrot, celery, sage, parsley and *guanciale* lightly. Gradually add pieces of hare and the lights and stir-fry until browned. Add the red wine and allow it to evaporate. Moisten with the blood and a little vinegar. Simmer gently for 10 minutes. Add salt and pepper. Warm the milk and add to the pan, cover and simmer for 1 hour, adding a little stock if it starts to dry out. Bone the pieces of hare and return them to the pan with the chopped heart and liver. Simmer for another 5 minutes. Meanwhile, cook the *pappardelle*. Drain the pasta and serve it with the sauce and Parmesan cheese.

 ### Azienda Agricola Fontaleoni

località Santa Maria, 39
0577 950193.

With its 15 hectares (37 acres) of vines and 3 hectares (7 acres) of olives, this estate focuses on the area's classic wines. There are two styles of Vernaccia, the normal and the Vigna Casanuova.

 ### Montenidoli

località Montenidoli
0577 941565.

A small estate with a very good Vernaccia. The traditional version is good value for money, and there are two choices, Carato and Fiore.

 ### Fattoria di Pietrafitta

località Cortennano
0577 943200.

Four kinds of Vernaccia: normal, Riserva and two selections are produced

here. The firm has 400 hectares (988 acres) of vines and produces Chianti Colli Senesi and has recently begun making DOC San Gimignano wines, with an interesting Rosato. Its 22 hectares (54 acres) of olives yield excellent, fruity extra virgin olive oil.

Azienda Agricola Panizzi

località Santa Margherita, 34
0577 941576.

The estate's care for its vines and the quality of its wines is apparent in the Vernaccia with a Riserva version partly fined in

barriques. *The Chianti Colli Senesi is more full-bodied and structured than the others.*

 ### Teruzzi & Puthod – Ponte a Rondolino

località Casale, 19
0577 940143.

This is the domain of Enrico Teruzzi, who reinvented Vernaccia di San Gimignano. The estate is a leading producer of the very finest Vernaccia, in a normal version and in the Terre dei Tufi selection matured in barriques. *The table wines include an excellent Carmen, a Sangiovese vinified as a white wine.*

 ### Fattoria San Quirico

località Panicole, 39
0577 955007.

From an area ideally sited for vineyards comes a pure Vernaccia and the Riserva I Campi Santi, a notable wine not aged in wood. The Chianti Colli Senesi is also very good.

SIENA

Pasticceria Buti

via Vittorio Emanuele II, 53
0577 40464.
Mon. Sun.

Sienese cakes, including an authentic spicy pan pepato, *are sold here.*

The Teruzzi & Puthod estate at Ponte a Rondolino

Enoteca Italiana

Fortezza Medicea, 1
0577 288497.
Sun.
12noon–10pm.

This interesting wine shop has an enormous range of Italian wines – there are over 900 names from all regions plus 400 Tuscans, chosen by an expert committee. A dozen wines are opened in turn daily for tasting with assorted snacks.

Forno dei Galli

via dei Termini, 45
0577 289073.

Bread, fresh pasta and traditional Sienese cakes are sold here.

Bar Impero

via Vittorio Emanuele, 10/12
0577 47424.
Mon.
Sun.

Excellent ice-cream is made and sold here all year round.

Drogheria Manganelli

via di Città, 71/73
0577 280002.
Wed pm.

The original furnishings date back 120 years in this real old-fashioned grocer's shop. It makes its own traditional Sienese cakes and has a choice selection of products from all over Italy, as well as some imported delicacies, all from high quality producers. There is a good range of wines.

Gastronomia Morbidi

via Banchi di Sopra, 75
0577 280268.
Wed pm.

This is a delicatessen for gourmets, selling a small, select range of wines with choice grappas, plus the firm's own traditional salumi *and an array of hams and sausages from other regions. It also has an assortment of cheeses from its own dairy and other parts of Italy, and a range of international dishes, both fresh and ready-cooked.*

Bar Nannini

Banchi di Sopra, 97
0577 247013.
daily, including Sunday.

At this long-established café it is possible to sample nearly all the traditional Sienese cakes.

La Nuova Pasticceria di Iasevoli

via Dupré, 37
0577 41319.
Mon.
Sun am.

Fine traditional Sienese confections, including cantucci *(biscuits) and* pane con i santi *(sweet bread containing fruit), can be found here.*

Pasticceria Pierini

via Mencatelli, 2
0577 283159.
Mon.
Sun am.

This confectionery shop makes excellent Sienese cakes to sell.

Enoteca San Domenico

via del Paradiso, 56
0577 271181.
daily, including Sunday.

A selection of Italian wines is sold here – not just the big names but also fine wine from smaller producers – plus a choice of spirits, champagne, Tuscan olive oil and the firm's own traditional cakes.

TAVARNELLE VAL DI PESA (SI)

Azienda Agricola Poggio al Sole

località Badia
a Passignano
055 8071504.

The area's classic red grapes can be found in the juicy Seraselva, *produced from Merlot and Cabernet, and the full-bodied Chianti Classico Casasilia, which is from Sangiovese.*

AGNELLO IN FRICASSEA (LAMB FRICASSÉE)

1 leg and 1 shoulder of lamb • 2 onions • 1 carrot, chopped • 1 stalk celery, sliced • 2 dessertspoons flour • 4 egg yolks • juice of 1 lemon • a few calamint (or mint) leaves • extra virgin olive oil • salt • pepper

Bone the lamb. Slice 1 onion. Put the bones, sliced onion, carrot and celery in a pan of water and cook for 2 hours to make stock. Cut the meat into pieces 5–6 cm (2–2½ inches) long. Finely chop the remaining onion. Flour the pieces of meat and brown them in the oil with the onion. Add salt and pepper and moisten with the stock. Cover and simmer until the meat is cooked. Add enough stock to make a sauce. Beat the egg with the lemon juice, pepper and calamint. Remove the pan from the heat, add the egg and stir briskly. The sauce should have the consistency of mayonnaise. Serve hot or cold, but do not reheat.

MONTALCINO
AND THE
SIENESE CRETE

Montalcino and the Sienese Crete

IN THIS GOURMET GUIDE, the southern part of the province of Siena has been separated from the north because the zone of Chianti Classico wine and the zone of Brunello and Vino Nobile deserve separate treatment. A corner of the province of Arezzo has been added to this section because Lucignano and Monte San Savino are influenced more by Sienese gastronomic habits than by their own.

The clay hills known as the Crete have fine truffles, rounded and regular, without knobbly bits or cracks, especially San Giovanni d'Asso, Trequanda, Buonconvento and Asciano. In fact, the commune of San Giovanni d'Asso has the highest production of truffles in Italy. There is nothing smooth and regular about the eroded hillocks that give the Crete its name. The sunny rolling hills have tremendous, jagged gashes in them, spectacular gulleys denuded of topsoil by heavy rain so they are bare of vegetation. Great slashes suddenly open in wheat fields, vineyards, olive groves and young oak scrub. The Crete, like the wooded areas of Montalcino, the valley of the Merse and the Val d'Orcia, is studded with ancient farms set in woods rich with mushrooms, herbs and fruits. The farms often have a complete food production cycle (cereals, cattle, sheep and pigs, cheese-making, olive groves and presses).

Colle di Val d'Elsa

FS

Monteriggio

Casole d'Elsa

Sovicille

Colline Metallifere

Chiusdino

Monticiano

STAR ATTRACTIONS

- CHIUSI (SI): National Etruscan Museum, **C** 0578 227667
- MONTE OLIVETO MAGGIORE (SI): Abbey, **G** 0577 707017
- MONTEPULCIANO (SI): Cathedral, Madonna di San Biagio, **G** 0578 75887
- MONTE S. SAVINO (AR): Loggia dei Mercanti, **G** 0575 843098
- PIENZA (SI): Cathedral, **G** 0578 749071
- SANT'ANTIMO (SI): Abbey, **G** 0577 835659

Pecorino cheese made in the Crete – especially the mature *pecorino* of Pienza – is world-famous *(see pp132–3).*

Bee-keeping at Montalcino has reached very high quality levels with a whole range of unusual honey-based products *(see pp134–5).*

WHITE TRUFFLES
The Sienese Crete area is blessed as far as truffle lovers are concerned because it has a rich supply of the white truffle *(Tuber magnatum).* San Giovanni d'Asso is the truffle centre and holds a truffle fair every November.

◁ **The Tuscan hills dominated with cypresses**

Large old estates in this area often produce the celebrated Brunello di Montalcino DOCG, one of the great internationally famous wines. These farms were once bustling villages: around the main landowner's house were a wine cellar, an olive press, shops and workshops, a herbalist, dairy, butcher, and church. In many cases, such as Fattoria dei Barbi at Montalcino, the estate pictured here, these activities still continue.

Cakes and biscuits are another well-known Montalcino product.

TRANSPORT

FS RAILWAY STATION
- CHIANCIANO TERME AND CHIUSI – STAZIONE FS
- C 0578 63648
- C 0578 227667

BUS STATION
- MONTEPULCIANO
- C 0578 757341
- PIENZA
- C 0578 749071

0 kilometres 10
0 miles 10

SIENA

Rapalano Terme

Lucignano

Monteroni d'Arbia

Asciano

Monte San Savino

Sinalunga

Monte Oliveto Maggiore

Trequanda

Murlo

Buonconvento

San Giovanni d'Asso

Torrita di Siena

A.1

Ombrone

Montefollonico

MONTEPULCIANO

Lago di Montepulciano

Montalcino

San Quirico d'Orcia

Pienza

Bagno Vignoni

Chianciano Terme

Lago di Chiusi

Sant'Antimo

Castiglione d'Orcia

Chiusi

Monte Amiata

Sarteano

Cetona

Abbadia San Salvatore

Radicofani

Rosso di Montalcino is a recent appellation, created to safeguard those wines not aged sufficiently to be called Brunello *(see p129).*

San Casciano dei Bagni

Piancastagnaio

Places of Interest pp140–51
Restaurants pp187–190

Wines of Montalcino

THE MAJESTIC RED WINE grown around Montalcino, south of Siena, is one of Italy's greatest wines. Brunello di Montalcino DOCG dates from the late 19th century, which is relatively recent compared with other noble wines. Its fortune and that of all Sienese wine-making lies with the Sangiovese Grosso vine, the only grapes used to make this wine. The same is true of the Rosso di Montalcino. The great Sienese reds were born out of patient effort and a careful eye to market, and the work of Tuscan and foreign vine-growers who have preserved the link with the local tradition.

There are subtle variations in the bouquet and flavour of Montalcino wines, depending on where they come from. The area around the city is like a large pyramid with four sides sloping to the valleys. On the north side, the wines are elegant and have good body; to the east, the cooler climate confers a more austere structure and great potential for ageing; to the south, the body is sustained but the perfume is less elegant; to the west, the wines are especially well balanced and pleasant to drink.

MOSCADELLO DI MONTALCINO

Few estates produce this wine, so it is not easy to find on the market. In the commonest versions it is liqueur-like, but it can also be sweet and sparkling. It is a pale yellow or golden colour and has the typical muscatel scent. It is perfect with the sweet dry biscuits of Siena and with fruit. It should be made from the ancient Moscadello vine, which has largely disappeared; attempts are being made to nurture some of the original vines. Moscato Bianco is widely used in its place.

The Sangiovese grape grown in Montalcino is called Brunello.

The oldest wines are sometimes called "wines for meditation".

BRUNELLO DI MONTALCINO

Described in Tuscany as the king of wines, this wine has found world-wide fame. It is aged for at least 4 years before it is sold; 5 years if it bears the Riserva label. The high price is justified by this lengthy ageing process. The wine's ruby red colour takes on a garnet red hue as it ages. The elegant bouquet is intense and the taste very well balanced. It is a great wine to drink with roasted or braised meats and strong, mature cheeses.

WINE TYPE	GOOD VINTAGES	GOOD PRODUCERS
Red Wine		
Brunello di Montalcino	97, 95, 94, 90	Siro Pacenti, Capanna, Salvioni La Cerbaiola, Lisini, Fattoria del Casato, Caparzo di Montalcino
Rosso di Montalcino	97, 95, 90	Altesino di Montalcino Argiano di Montalcino
Super Tuscans (*see p130*)		Argiano di Montalcino

PICI CON L'ANATRA MUTA

1 muscovy duck • 1 carrot • 1 red onion • 1 bunch of parsley • extra virgin olive oil • 1 glass red wine • 1 kg (2 lb 4 oz) tomatoes, peeled and chopped • 2 tablespoons tomato purée • salt • pepper

Bone the duck, leaving the neck, legs and wings complete. Use the bones and the neck to make stock. Mince the rest of the duck meat, giblets, carrot, onion and parsley. Fry this mixture slowly in the olive oil with the whole parts of the duck. Season to taste with salt and pepper. Continue cooking slowly, moistening with the red wine. When the wine has all evaporated, add the fresh tomatoes and the tomato purée, then simmer gently for 3 hours. Check from time to time and add some of the duck stock if it looks as if it is becoming dry. Serve the duck sauce on the local *pici* pasta. (at Trequanda this pasta is also known as *pinci* or *lunghetti*).

ROSSO DI MONTALCINO

Brunello grapes are used to make this younger, less austere wine. Quite dry with an intense ruby-red colour, it is a versatile table wine which goes with Sienese cuisine's many savoury dishes, such as first courses with meat sauces and second courses of pork, stewed meats and meat with sauces.

NOVELLO

Many estates are successfully making this young wine, which has earned a place for itself in the market. Produced by the *macération carbonique* method, where grapes are fermented whole in a closed vat, it is richly perfumed and suited to drinking with all courses. However, it can be expensive for the quality and does not age.

The Azienda Col d'Orcia at Montalcino

Other Wines from South of Siena

The province of Siena boasts the richest and most diverse wine production in the whole of Tuscany. The area south of Siena produces not only Brunello but also two great DOCG wines, Vino Nobile di Montepulciano and Chianti Colli Senesi made from Sangiovese Grosso grapes. In the Montepulciano area the Sangiovese Grosso vine is called Prugnolo Gentile, because of the elongated shape of its grapes and their plummy blue colour and scent. This vine attains its full potential in the Colli Senesi, either with the grapes used alone or in combination with other reds such as Cabernet Sauvignon, Cabernet Franc, Pinot Nero and Merlot. Sangiovese Grosso forms up to 80 per cent of Chianti while it varies from 60 per cent to 80 per cent in Vino Nobile and Rosso di Montepulciano. Other red grapes are also added to these wines, including Canaiolo for mellowness and Mammolo for its bouquet.

The Sienese region also has a long tradition of white grape vines. The commonest is Trebbiano Toscano, but the present trend is to reduce the quantity of this grape and gradually replace it with other grapes such as Chardonnay, Pinot Bianco, Sauvignon, Traminer Aromatico, Rhineland Riesling, Pinot Grigio, and Muller Thurgau, which have long been grown here. The second traditional white grape is Malvasia Toscana, then there are other lesser varieties like Grechetto Bianco, also called Pulcinculo because of the dark spot found on the tip of the grape.

VIN SANTO DI MONTEPULCIANO

This highly prized traditional Vin Santo is made with Pulcinculo in addition to the other traditional grapes. It can be labelled Riserva after it has aged for at least 5 years in wood. Served as a dessert wine, it goes well with sweet dry biscuits. The price varies, but it can be very expensive. Some estates produce it in a *"Vendemmia Tardiva"* version, from grapes left to dry on the vines instead of picking them and drying them on racks.

The white version from white grapes.

This attractive amber-coloured Vin Santo, called Occhio di Pernice, is made from at least 50 per cent Sangiovese grapes.

THE SUPER TUSCANS

Many Tuscan estates have long been engaged in producing wines outside the rules of the DOC or DOCG wines. The choice of vines and methods of production aim at the very highest quality. The techniques vary from one estate to another – they may be based on traditional Tuscan vines alone or combined with noble vines like Cabernet Sauvignon and Merlot. Some excellent wines have been produced and they are much in demand internationally. These wines are called Super Tuscans, an appellation which indicates prized wines much sought-after abroad.

CHIANTI E CHIANTI DEI COLLI SENESI

Chianti is made from Tuscan grapes vinified in the Siena area; Chianti dei Colli Senesi is made from grapes that have been grown and vinified locally.

VINO NOBILE DI MONTEPULCIANO

This DOCG wine can be one of Italy's most impressive reds. The area of production for the wine stretches west from Valdichiana and east into another small area. Specific areas that produce superior wine include Argiano, Caggiole, Canneto, Casalte and Valiano. The wine is aged for 2 years in casks, or 3 years in the case of the Riserva. It is a deep red colour, with an intense, balanced bouquet, excellent with *bistecca alla fiorentina*, grilled meats and mature cheeses.

ROSSO DI MONTEPULCIANO

This red wine, which has practically no ageing, was created to bring Montepulciano wine closer to the general public. It is a bright ruby red with an intense bouquet and a pleasant dry flavour. It is ideal as a general table wine with full-bodied dishes, such as grilled meats.

VAL D'ARBIA

Made mainly from Trebbiano Toscano and Malvasia grapes, this dry white wine is a pale yellowish colour with a hint of green. Fruity and fresh-tasting, it makes a good aperitif or it can be served with fried or baked fish.

Wine Type	Good Vintages	Good Producers	Wine Type	Good Vintages	Good Producers
Red Wine			Super Tuscans *(see p130)*	98, 97, 95, 90	Avignonesi di Montepulciano
Rosso di Montepulciano	97, 90	Avignonesi, Poliziano, Dei di Montepulciano	**White Wine**		
Chianti *and* Chianti dei Colli Senesi	98, 97, 95, 93, 90	Farnetella di Sinalunga, Fattoria del Colle di Trequanda	Vino Nobile di Montepulciano	97, 95, 90	Avignonesi, Fattoria del Cerro, Poliziano di Montepulciano

Pecorino from the Sienese Crete

SOUTH OF SIENA, in the primeval landscape of the Crete, shepherds tend sheep whose milk is used to make *pecorino* cheese. The ancient craft of cheese-making is now largely practised by Sardinian shepherds who have settled here in recent decades, but this has not altered the traditional quality of the cheese – the Sardinians have preserved their own sheep-tending skills, while absorbing the habits and tastes of the Sienese people. The Crete and the southern part of the province of Siena produce the most prized *pecorino* in Tuscany.

MATURE PECORINO DI PIENZA
This is the most prized and famous of Tuscan *pecorini*, prepared with milk solely from the Crete and Montalcino areas. The secret of its quality lies in the use of fresh, unpasteurized milk and a covering of olive oil lees (skins after the olives have been pressed) to keep the inside soft and slightly mellow. (Avoid cheeses covered with plastic film, which ruins the cheese.) These cheeses are matured for anything from 5 to 18 months.

The whitish colour of the crust is due to the olive oil lees.

MATURE PECORINO
The area of production for this cheese is the same as for the traditional Pienza cheese and the two are quite similar, except that this cheese does not have the olive oil crust, so the inside has a drier texture and a stronger flavour.

This cheese has a hard, deep yellow crust.

SEMI-MATURE PECORINO
After 90–120 days of maturing, *pecorino* is still beautifully mellow, ideal for eating with *salumi*, with pears, or in thin slices on meat, *crostini* or baked vegetables. Sometimes chillies, black pepper or black truffles are incorporated into the cheese. It is rare, however, to find a cheese-maker who uses pieces of fresh truffle; most use semi-processed truffles or the synthetic aroma, resulting in an inferior product.

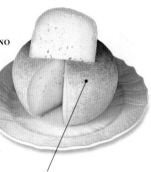

A coating of extra virgin olive oil on this white cheese keeps the inside soft.

This cheese is covered in tomato purée which keeps the inside soft and enhances its scent, giving it a red crust.

FRESH PECORINO

Sweet and creamy, with a markedly milky flavour, fresh *pecorino* is eaten within 90–120 days of being made. It is popular with all age groups and can be eaten at the end of the meal or as an *antipasto* dressed with extra virgin olive oil from the Crete region and seasoned with salt and black pepper.

CIPOLLE IN FORNO

12 red onions • extra virgin olive oil • white wine vinegar • 50 g (1¾ oz) pecorino, grated • 100 g (3½ oz) breadcrumbs • salt • pepper

Preheat the oven to 200°C (400°F/gas mark 6). Peel the onions, cut two slits to form a cross at the top of each and put them in a baking tin. Brush with oil and season with salt and pepper. Roast in the oven until well cooked. Moisten with the vinegar and return to the oven to evaporate the liquid. Mix the cheese and crumbs, sprinkle them over the onions and serve.

FRESH PECORINO WITH HERBS OR NUTS

Fresh *pecorino* may have herbs or nuts added to it. The cheese should be eaten within a week and is excellent as an *antipasto* or as a snack with a little extra virgin olive oil from the Crete drizzled over it.

Chopped rocket in fresh pecorino is a recent innovation.

Adding small pieces of walnut to the cheese is an old tradition.

PECORINO SOTT'OLIO

In some families and farmhouses there is a tradition of preserving mature *pecorino* in olive oil mixed with herbs or spices.

OTHER EWE'S MILK PRODUCTS WORTH TRYING

Raviggiolo is a fresh curd cheese eaten within 4 days of making. Traditionally it is salted and eaten as an antipasto or sugared as a dessert. It is very delicate and should be kept in a sealed container in the refrigerator. The **ricotta** in this area is delectable, especially when made from raw milk: it is eaten on ribbon pasta or made into fillings for stuffed pasta such as ravioli. Another product of this area is **marzolino** *(see p108)*.

Honey

Throughout tuscany – from the mountains to the coast, where the Mediterranean landscape is dotted with wonderfully aromatic plants – honey *(miele)* is produced. Renowned for its therapeutic properties, honey is thought to help with disorders in all parts of the body, from liver to lungs to circulation. At Montalcino bee-keeping (apiculture) has a long history, originating with the skill of the foresters who used to gather wild honey from hollow trees, and are still capable of hiving swarms of wild bees. Traditional honey production in Montalcino and the surrounding area is based on the flowering chestnut woods on the Apennine slopes. Many local firms take hives to other parts of Italy, so they can extend the honey-producing season.

*Chestnut honey is a
rich, dark brown colour.*

CHESTNUT HONEY
The aroma and slightly bitter taste of chestnut honey *(miele di castagno)* make it good for cooking and confectionery. It is believed to be useful for intestinal disorders and helpful in regulating the nervous system and in cases of anaemia.

SUNFLOWER HONEY
This honey *(miele di girasole)* is thought to be mildly effective at soothing pain or fever and is a mild diuretic.

*Sunflower honey is very
dense with an opaque
yellowish colour.*

*Woodland honey is a
deep golden colour.*

CANTUCCI DI MONTALCINO

200 g (7 oz) unpeeled almonds • 500 g (1 lb 2 oz) plain flour • 4 eggs • 1 teaspoon baking powder • 350 g (12 oz) sugar • 100 g (3½ oz) chestnut honey • few drops of vanilla essence • butter • salt

Preheat the oven to 180°C (350°F/gas mark 4). Roast the almonds for 4 minutes. Heap the flour on a work surface and make a well in the centre. Beat the eggs and pour into the well with the baking powder, sugar, honey, essence and a pinch of salt. Knead until the dough is smooth, then add the almonds. Roll out the dough and shape into long fingers. Transfer to a buttered and floured baking sheet and bake for about 20 minutes. Cut the fingers diagonally into 2 cm (¾ inch) slices and leave to dry.

WOODLAND HONEY
Rich in mineral salts and iron, woodland honey *(melata do bosco)* is very fortifying.

SULLA CLOVER HONEY
Because it has a faint aroma, this honey *(miele di sulla)* can be used for sweetening foods without affecting their flavour. It is thought to help purify the liver and keep the intestines in good order.

This clear honey is a light golden colour.

HEATHER HONEY
Delicately scented heather honey *(miele di erica)* is good for coughs and colds, as it helps to soothe sore respiratory organs.

ARBUTUS HONEY
Arbutus honey *(miele di corbezzolo)*, from the wild strawberry tree, is quite bitter. It is thought to be good for the circulation and blood.

Jelly-like heather honey is brownish-orange.

Arbutus honey is mustard colour, or milky white if very pure. It is very thick and granular.

PRESERVES IN HONEY
The classics – hazelnuts, almonds or walnuts in honey *(vasetti "sotto miele")* – are found in most parts of Tuscany. There is also the unusual delicacy of boiled chestnuts flavoured with vanilla and conserved in acacia honey.

OTHER VARIETIES OF HONEY WORTH TRYING
Acacia honey, clear and very fluid, is probably the variety most commonly seen. It is not strong and suits a range of tastes. Rich in energy, it is fortifying and has mild laxative properties which are thought to help purify the liver. **Tiglio** (linden) honey, excellent for problems with the respiratory tract, is also useful for inducing sleep. **Millefioro** (wild flower) is versatile and very nourishing. **Eucalipto** (eucalyptus), helpful in disorders of the respiratory tract, is a decongestant and emollient for smokers. **Lavanda** (lavender) is richly scented and helps to calm the nervous system. **Rosmarino** (rosemary) has a strong flavour and is a mild diuretic. **Timo** (thyme), rich in fructose, is believed to be good for the circulation, as is **trifoglio** (clover) honey. At Montalcino, other honey specialities include grappa, sweets, fruit cakes and preserves.

Traditional Produce

THERE ARE PLENTY of genuine Tuscan specialities for the gourmet in this area, and they are nearly always produced with due respect for the environment. The *prosciutti* and *salumi*, cep mushrooms and truffles, extra virgin olive oil, game birds and animals, Chianina beef, lamb and fine vegetables produced in this part of Tuscany all have their own very distinctive character.

OSSI DI MORTO
These very hard biscuits, made from egg whites and chopped almonds, are typical of Montalcino.

GRAPPA
In recent years a lot of work has gone into improving the grappa made by distilling the grape skins and pips left over from the wine-making process. Leading wine-makers have staked their names on these grappas, some of interest to true connoisseurs.

COLLI SENESI OLIVE OIL
The Colli Senesi is a broad, homogeneous area south of Siena, from Montalcino toward the northeast, comprising Asciano, San Quirico d'Orcia, San Giovanni d'Asso, Pienza, Montepulciano, Trequanda, Rapolano Terme, Lucignano and Sinalunga. The olive oils produced here are of medium to high fruitiness, and generally full-bodied. They vary in taste, but all are peppery when young, usually with a slightly bitter aftertaste.

POLLASTRELLA AL DRAGONCELLO

1 young free-range pullet • 1 apple • a large bunch of tarragon • 1 knob of butter • 1 dessertspoon plain flour

Preheat the oven to 180°C (350°F/gas mark 4). Flame the pullet, then stuff it with the apple and tarragon. Sew up the bird with kitchen twine, wrap in baking parchment and roast in the oven for about 40 minutes. Remove the paper and pour off the cooking juices. Roast the bird for another 5 minutes until it is a golden colour, then remove from the pan. Thicken the juices in the pan with the butter and flour; serve with the bird.

TARRAGON
One of the classic herbs of international cuisine, tarragon (*persia* in Tuscany, elsewhere *dragoncello* or *estragone*) is a common aromatic in the Siena area, where it is widely used in sauces and meat dishes.

PLAGA DI MONTALCINO OLIVE OIL
This intensely fruity olive oil is produced throughout the whole Montalcino area. It has a fresh scent of herbs and a rounded taste, rather astringent and pungent. The strong flavour has a markedly bitter, peppery aftertaste.

*For this salami the meat is
coarsely minced and the fat
is chopped with a knife.*

MORTADELLA
The local name for Tuscan salami
encased in pig's large intestine
is *mortadella* (while the smaller
size is usually called *salame*).
This salami is slightly less fatty
than some types and its
medium-high quality is due
to the good local pork.

*This meat is
finely minced
and rather fatty.*

FINOCCHIONA
This salami, which is cured for eating raw,
contains aromatic fennel seeds or flowers.
It is similar to Florentine *sbriciolona*, but
usually cured for longer.

Wrapped in straw paper,
lombo *can breathe.*

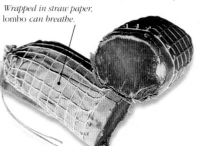

LOMBO
Chine of pork is boned and salted and
scented with fennel seed to add even
more flavour to the good quality meat.
If fresh, *lombo* is served dressed with
olive oil and lemon.

BURISTO
Typical of the Siena area, *buristo* (blood
pudding) is made from the flesh of the pig's
head – including the tongue and some of the
skin – minced finely and mixed with spices,
pig's blood and boiled fat. The meat is encased
in the pig's stomach and slowly boiled. It is
traditionally eaten strewn with chopped raw onion.

WHAT TO SAMPLE
Rigatino, salted belly of pork, is indispensable in local cooking. There are numerous
traditional cakes, especially at Montalcino, where you can find Sienese classics such
as **ricciarelli** and **panforte**. Specialities peculiar to Montalcino and the Crete are
pane coi santi, bread dough with nuts, raisins and aniseed mixed into it; **torta di
Montalcino**, a soft cake containing raisins and covered with chocolate, hazelnuts and
almonds; **morselletti**, aniseed biscuits (the original recipe also calls for olive oil);
pinolata, made of pastry with cream and raisins, covered with pine nuts to look like
a pine cone; **schiacciata di Pasqua**, a bread flavoured with mint, rosewater, saffron,
aniseed and citrus peel. The local pasta, **pinci**, is like large spaghetti. **Saffron** grows
wild in this area, and the medieval village of Murlo has grown **rice** for centuries.

Wild Produce

WHITE WAX CAP
(Hygrophorus penarius)
Late in the season this mushroom *(lardaiolo bianco)* is abundant in thick stands of evergreen and deciduous oaks. It remains white and fleshy after cooking and is good in sauces with white meats.

LESSER BOLETUS
(Boletus duriusculus)
The sturdiest and most prized of this group of *porcini*, the lesser boletus *(oppiarello)* grows under poplars along the coast. It is good cooked with garlic and parsley (it darkens when cooked). When young, these mushrooms are preserved in oil; mature ones are dried.

CHANTERELLE
(Cantharellus cibarius)
This mushroom *(giallarello)* has adapted to pretty well all cuisines and is popular in many countries. Chanterelles grow in all kinds of woodland but in this area are found mainly under holm oaks. Less perfumed than the Alpine chanterelles that grow under beech and spruce, they are excellent fried with garlic and parsley, in cream and sauces.

PARASOL MUSHROOM
(Lepiota procera)
Common in both the coastal scrub and on grassy hillsides, this popular mushroom *(bubbola)* is very conspicuous because of its height – up to 50 cm (20 inches) – and the drumstick shape of its cap. It is excellent raw in salads or preserved in oil when young. When ripe, the cap is very good grilled, fried or devilled. The woody stalk is dried and made into an aromatic powder.

FUNGHI CON LA NEPITELLA (MUSHROOMS WITH CALAMINT)

800 g (1 lb 12 oz) mixed mushrooms, sliced • 3 cloves garlic, chopped • 1 sprig of calamint (or mint) • 1 dessertspoon tomato purée • extra virgin olive oil • salt • pepper

Put the mushrooms in a pan with the garlic, sprig of calamint, plenty of oil, and salt and pepper. Cook over a high heat until the mushrooms shed their water, then lower and cook till the liquid evaporates (the oil should be clear again). Add the tomato purée and cook over a moderate heat for 10 minutes.

COMMON SOW THISTLE
(Sonchus oleraceus)
One of the best-known edible wild plants, sow thistle *(crespigno)* grows abundantly on the edges of vegetable patches and paths, on waste ground and in orchards. Sweet and tasty when young, it is good raw. As it matures, it is eaten in mixed salads, stuffings and omelettes.

WILD ASPARAGUS
(Asparagus acutifolius)
Plentiful early in spring growing by hedgerows, ditches and on the edge of woods, picking wild asparagus *(asparago selvatico)* is a pleasant pastime. It is used in the same way as the cultivated variety.

PENNE IN SALSA D'ERBETTE DI PRIMAVERA

1 young wild fennel plant • a few calamint (or mint) leaves • 1 rosette of common poppy leaves • 1 young borage plant • 1 small bunch of parsley • 20 basil leaves • 1 handful nettle tips • 1 handful of field eryngo • 1 head of wild chicory leaves • 2 heads of wild lettuce leaves • 3 young sow thistle plants • 1 sprig tarragon • 10 leaves lemon balm • 1 sprig marjoram • 6 walnuts • extra virgin olive oil • 1 chilli • 2 cloves garlic • 500 g (1 lb 2 oz) tomatoes, peeled • 500 g (1 lb 2 oz) penne • salt

Make sure the herbs are dry. Mince them in a blender or food processor with the walnuts. Put them in a jar, cover with olive oil and leave for at least 2 days. Heat a little oil in a pan, add the chilli and garlic and fry until softened slightly. Add the tomatoes and season with salt. Cook over a brisk heat. Add the herbs and walnuts and cook for a further 5 minutes. Meanwhile, cook the pasta. Drain well and serve with the tomato and herb sauce, mixing thoroughly.

WILD LETTUCE
(Lactuca serriola)
This salad vegetable *(lattuga di campo)* is well known to country people in Tuscany, who go looking for it. Check with an expert before you pick it: the rosettes at the base of many spring plants can look similar and not all are edible. Wild lettuce is very good raw or cooked and dressed with oil, lemon juice or vinegar.

STRAWBERRY TREE (ARBUTUS)
(Arbutus unedo)
The strawberry tree *(corbezzolo)* is common in Mediterranean thickets, where its colourful appearance – green leaves, white flowers and red fruit – enlivens the scenery. When ripe, the fruit is creamy rather than juicy, and is very sweet. It can be eaten fresh (in moderation) or used in preserves.

Places of Interest

As with the Chianti region, the well-informed, polyglot clientele of this area want the genuine flavours of the past, thus helping to ensure the survival of these foods. There are fewer shops here, but there are many interesting farms, as well as some of the finest wine producers. The farms have such a wide range of products that they are almost self-sufficient: they offer not only olive oil and wine but also *salumi*, cheese, fresh vegetables and local honey, all of them excellent.

ASCIANO (SI)

Tenuta Monte Sante Marie

località Monte Sante Marie
☎ 055 700020.

This farm, which offers agriturismo facilities, makes a marvellous extra virgin olive oil. In years when they have a bumper crop of fruit, they make and sell excellent cakes and jams as well.

BUONCONVENTO (SI)

La Bottega del Pane

via del Taia, 21
☎ 0577 806800.

The Tuscan bread made the old traditional way with fresh yeast by this shop keeps well for several days. The shop also sells a wide range of Sienese cakes and its illustrious clientele includes the Queen of the Netherlands.

CASTIGLIONE D'ORCIA (SI)

Podere Forte

località Petrucci
☎ 0577 887488.

At present this young estate produces an outstanding extra virgin olive oil. However, it is preparing to begin wine production with the help of an international staff of experts.

CHIUSI (SI)

Azienda Agricola Colle di Santa Mustiola

via delle Torri, 86/A
☎ 0578 63462.

A single wine, Poggio di Chiari from Sangiovese grapes alone, matured in French and Slavonian oak, is produced here. The owner, a supporter of local products, has reintroduced the cultivation of spelt and breeds Cinta Senese pigs.

LUCIGNANO (AR)

Apicoltura Nocciolini

località Selva, 50a
☎ 0575 836097.

All types of honey, from this and other areas, gathered by itinerant bee-keepers is sold here.

Panificio Redi

località Croce
☎ 0575 837037.
● Sat pm.

CINGHIALE IN AGRODOLCE (BOAR IN SWEET AND SOUR SAUCE)

1.5 kg (3 lb 5 oz) lean boar's meat • 1.5 litres (2¾ pints) red wine • 250 ml (9 fl oz) wine vinegar • juniper berries • 3 bay leaves • 1 dessertspoon plain flour seasoned with salt and pepper • extra virgin olive oil • 2 carrots, finely chopped • 1 onion, finely chopped • 1 stalk of celery, finely chopped • meat stock • 100 g (3½ oz) chopped panforte • 3 cavallucci (sweets) • 100 g (3½ oz) dark chocolate • 25 g (1 oz) butter • 50 g (1¾ oz) raisins • 50 g (1¾ oz) pine nuts • 50 g (1¾ oz) chopped walnuts • salt • black peppercorns and ground pepper

Marinate the boar's flesh for 24 hours in the wine, half the vinegar, the juniper berries, bay leaves and a few peppercorns. Remove the meat, reserving the marinade. Cut the meat into small cubes and coat with the seasoned flour. Heat some oil in a pan, add the meat and brown on all sides. Add the vegetables and cook until they are tender, then moisten with a little stock. Simmer gently adding the marinade a little at a time. Meanwhile soak the *panforte* and *cavallucci* in the stock until they crumble, add the chocolate, butter, dried fruit, nuts and the rest of the vinegar. When the boar is cooked, remove it from the pan and keep warm. Add the *panforte* mixture to the cooking juices and heat, stirring until it forms a thick, smooth sauce. Pour the sauce over the meat and serve.

The Azienda Agricola Argiano at Montalcino

Here Tuscan bread is made the old-fashioned way, kneading by hand before leaving it to rise.

Franco Scarpelli

via Matteotti, 121
0575 836016.
Mon, Wed, Thurs.

The owner of this butcher's is an expert on Chianina beef and is guided by an innate passion for the breed. He raises and butchers mostly Chianina beef following traditional methods. He also makes his own excellent hams and sausages from local pigs. The poultry comes from nearby farms.

MONTALCINO (SI)

Azienda Agricola Altesino

località Altesino
0577 806208.

This is one of the very few estates to produce brandy from Brunello. It takes courage to distil a wine destined to become Brunello. All the same, in less generous years, this is a good way to obtain something different. Production is limited and the brandy is aged in barrels for a minimum of 10 years. Outstanding among the wines is the Brunello di Montalcino Alte d'Altesi, based on

Sangiovese grapes with a small amount of Cabernet Sauvignon, and Quarto d'Altesi, a pure Merlot.

Azienda Agricola Argiano

località Sant'Angelo in Colle, 54
0577 844037.

On one of the most attractive estates in Montalcino, a staff of wine-making experts have produced a widely praised Brunello and a Riserva version. Other wines with harmonious aromas and flavours produced here are the Rosso di Montalcino and the Solengo, from Cabernet Sauvignon, Merlot, Syrah and Sangiovese grapes.

Banfi Spa

Castello di Poggio alle Mura
0577 840111.

A very varied range of wines is produced on this estate – not surprising, as it is probably the largest estate in the district. The castle has been restored by the large American corporation, Banfi, and it houses a valuable collection of antique wine bottles and glasses, which is open to the public.

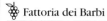 Fattoria dei Barbi

località Barbi
0577 848277.

Not so much a farm as a village for gourmets: this ancient hamlet southeast of Montalcino produces one of the most famous Brunello wines. There is a cheese dairy and a building where salumi are made. In the best years, as well as Brunello DOCG, an excellent special selection is produced: Brunello di Montalcino DOCG Vigna del Fiore. Other notable products are Rosso di Montalcino, Chianti dei Colli Senesi, Brusco dei Barbi, Grappa di Brunello and extra virgin olive oil.

Batignani Roberto

via Delle Caserme, 7
0577 848444.

This family bee-keeping business has honey from sulla clover, sunflowers, wild flowers, chestnut and many others.

Barrels in the cellar of the Fattoria dei Barbi at Montalcino

Biondi Santi Spa

via Panfilo dell'Oca, 3
0577 847121.

A single firm distributes the wines produced by the Biondi Santi family's various estates. From the Greppo estate come the Brunello and Rosso di Montalcino, wines that reflect a traditional style, a tribute to Tancredi, son of Ferruccio who, a century ago, made Brunello world famous. From Villa Poggio Salvi comes the Lavischio (Merlot) and some of the grapes used for the "Super Tuscans", including Sassoalloro (Sangiovese). The Tenuta Greppo olive oil is very good.

Azienda Agricola Capanna

località Capanna, 333
0577 848298.

This small family-run vineyard has made a name with its Brunello di Montalcino Riserva and Rosso di Montalcino.

Azienda Caparzo

località Torrenieri,
0577 848390.

The decision to make wine with Brunello grapes only in the best years has been rewarded by significant results, especially in the Brunello

La Casa selection. Also excellent is the Rosso La Caduta and Ca' del Pazzo, from Sangiovese and Cabernet Sauvignon, a success since it was first made in 1982. Among the new generation of wines there is an outstanding Val d'Arbia Le Crete, made from Trebbiano, Malvasia and Chardonnay.

Fattoria del Casato

località Podernovi
0577 849421.

An integral part of Fattoria dei Barbi (see p141) until 1998, the Fattoria del Casato, now run by Donatella Cinelli, has become independent and is connected with the Fattoria del Colle di Trequanda (see p151) where the Rosso and Brunello di Montalcino produced here can be purchased. Its cellar will remain combined with the Barbi estate's until its own facilities are finished. The star wine is Brunello Prime Donne made by an all-female staff.

Azienda agricola Case Basse

località Villa
Santa Restituta
0577 848567.

Only three wines are produced here and all of them are excellent. They

COLLO RIPIENO

50 g (1¾ oz) parsley • 4 cloves garlic • 100 g (3½ oz) chicken livers • 100 g (3½ oz) breadcrumbs • 1 glass vegetable stock • 3 eggs • 100 g (3½ oz) grated pecorino • 6 chicken necks • 1 carrot, chopped • 1 stalk celery, chopped • 1 onion, chopped • 1 clove • 1 tomato, chopped • salt • pepper

Make a stuffing by mincing the parsley, garlic, chicken livers, breadcrumbs softened in the stock, eggs and cheese. Season with salt and pepper. Clean and bone the chicken necks and fill with the stuffing. Tie them at the ends. Make a stock with the carrot, celery, onion, clove and tomato. Put the chicken necks in the stock and simmer for about 45 minutes. When cooked, allow to cool and serve cut into pieces with boiled potatoes and a green sauce.

are the Brunello di Montalcino, Brunello di Montalcino Riserva and Intistieti, made from Brunello grapes in less favourable years. The wines can be purchased from Drogheria Franci (see p144).

Castel Giocondo

località Castelgiocondo
0577 848492.

New vineyards facing south in a breezy climate are a productive bonus which the Marchesi de' Frescobaldi firm manages with great care. The Brunello di Montalcino Riserva is one of the most sought-after, followed by the Rosso di Montalcino and the Lamaione, based on Merlot. Recently, in a joint venture with the

Harvesting Brunello grapes at the Azienda Caparzo

Some of Hubert Ciacci's hives

American wine-maker Robert Mondavi, it has produced two "Super Tuscans": Luce and Lucente from Sangiovese and Merlot grapes in different proportions. The wines can be purchased from Enoteca La Fortezza and Drogheria Franci (see p144).

and the practice of travelling to other parts of the country with the hives, has resulted in a wide variety of honeys (including bitter arbutus honey). Other delicacies include jams made with honey, chestnuts preserved in honey, liqueurs and traditional confectionery.

PICCHIO PACCHIO

extra virgin olive oil
• 1 small onion, chopped
• 1.5 kg (3 lb 5 oz) ripe tomatoes, peeled
• vegetable or meat stock
• 6 eggs • Tuscan bread, sliced • salt

Heat the oil in a pan, add the chopped onion and cook until softened. Add the tomatoes, lower the heat and simmer for 30 minutes. Cover the mixture with plenty of stock. As soon as it boils, beat the eggs and add them to the soup, stirring briskly. Arrange the sliced bread in soup plates and ladle the soup on top of it. Drizzle a little extra virgin olive oil over each dish and serve at once.

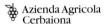 Azienda Agricola Cerbaiona

località Cerbaiona
☎ 0577 848660.

Diego Molinari, a former airline pilot, has successfully turned to the production of wines. His star wine is Brunello, at an above-average price, and Cerbaiona, based on Sangiovese grapes.

🍴 Hubert Ciacci

via Traversa dei Monti, 227a
☎ 0577 848640.

Here there is bee-keeping of the highest quality; great respect for the natural qualities of honey,

Azienda Agricola Col d'Orcia

località Sant'Angelo in Colle
☎ 0577 808001.

Many of the vines here are Brunello and the estate's Poggio al Vento vineyard produces its finest Brunello. Equally good are the classic Brunello di Montalcino and the Rosso di Montalcino. This estate is one of the few to produce Moscadello di Montalcino, offered in the "Vendemmia Tardiva" (late harvest) version of the Pascena selection. Olmaia, from Cabernet Sauvignon, is a "Super

Tuscan". The Novello Novembrino is made from traditional Sangiovese.

Azienda Agricola Collemattoni

località Sant' Angelo in Colle
via del Capannino
☎ 0577 844127.

Father and son share the work on this estate, one of the smallest in the area, the former working in the vineyard and the latter in the wine cellar. They produce excellent Brunello and an even finer Rosso di Montalcino.

The Azienda Agricola Col d'Orcia at Montalcino

Costanti

località Colle
al Matrichese
☎ 0577 848195.

*The vines on this estate
are carefully tended,
down to the rose bushes
planted at the ends of the
rows as a useful indicator
of any possible disease in
the vines. The results are
attractive: the Brunello
di Montalcino is excellent
in the two versions,
regular and Riserva.*

Enoteca La Fortezza

piazzale Fortezza
☎ 0577 849211.
● Mon.
○ Sun.

*Inside the fortress of
Montalcino, in what was
once the garrison tower,
there is a wine shop that,
together with the local
council, stocks produce
from all the local
producers. Hundreds of
firms are represented,
almost all wineries,
together with the few
major producers of
cheese and various*
pecorini, salumi *and*
finocchiona, salami *and*
cured ham suppliers. The
oil comes from the few
producers who guarantee
consistent quality. There
is a charge for tasting.

Drogheria Franci

piazzale Fortezza, 5
☎ 0577 848191.
● Wed pm.
○ Sun.

*This firm's apiary has
been one of the area's best
known for over three
generations. It has 10
types of honey, including
bitter arbutus honey,
dried fruit preserved in
honey and honey sweets.
The shop also has a wine
section that specializes
in Montalcino wines but
has a pleasing selection
of other wines, not all of*

*them Tuscan. It also sells
various local gastronomic
specialities, with* salumi
*and cheeses to accompany
the wine tasting.*

Forno Lambardi

via Soccorso Saloni, 24
☎ 0577 848084.
● Wed pm.

*On sale here are fresh
bread and traditional
biscuits –* ossi di morto,
morselletti, brutti e buoni
*and many others – made
from natural ingredients,
sold loose or pre-packed.*

Lisini

località Sant'Angelo in
Colle
☎ 0577 844040.

*Its favourable position
and the richness of the
soil make this estate one
of the finest in the area.
It produces a Brunello di
Montalcino of great body
and elegance. The Ugolaia
selection is interesting.*

Pasticceria Mariuccia

piazza del Popolo, 29
☎ 0577 849319.
● Mon. ○ Sun.

*Pasticceria Mariuccia
produces traditional
Montalcino cakes such
as* torta di Montalcino,
bacio di Montalcino *(a
cold dessert made from
a very old recipe) and*
pane coi santi.

Mastrojanni

località Castelnuovo
dell'Abate
Podere Loreto
☎ 0577 835681.

*Despite the fact that this
estate is unable to satisfy
the growing demand for
its wine, it continues the
policy of producing
Brunello only in the best
years. The result is an
excellent Brunello, which
has been appreciated
for many years. The
table wines combine
Sangiovese and Cabernet
Sauvignon grapes to
make Rosso San Pio.*

Siro Pacenti

località Pelagrilli, 1
☎ 0577 848662.

Vineyards around Montalcino

A highly interesting
Brunello and Rosso di
Montalcino are being
made by an estate that
is growing significantly
through careful renewal
of the vines and the cellar.

 La Poderina

località La Poderina
Castelnuovo dell'Abate
℡ 0577 835737.

This is the second estate
owned by the Saiagricola
company (they also own
the Fattoria del Cerro
at Montepulciano). Here
the company's energies
are concentrated on
trying to get the very best
out of the Sangiovese
grape in the form of its
most tantalizing product,
Brunello di Montalcino.

 Poggio Antico

località Poggio Antico
℡ 0577 848044.

The output is focused on
Brunello, which in its best
years achieves a notable
level and also comes in a
Riserva version. The
estate's small wine shop
contains a selection of its
finest vintages, which are
difficult to find even in
specialist shops.

Il Poggione

località Sant'Angelo in
Colle
℡ 0577 844029.

The estate's best wine is
definitely Brunello, but
the Rosso di Montalcino
is also of great interest.
In addition, the estate
produces a small amount
of Moscadello in a
sparkling version and
traditional Vin Santo.

 **Salvioni Azienda
Agraria Cerbaiola**

piazza Cavour, 19
℡ 0577 848499.

This estate produces a
great Brunello and an
excellent Rosso di
Montalcino. The quality
of the wine is very high
but so, unfortunately,
are the prices – without
apparently discouraging
the wine connoisseurs:
there is always limited
availability of this wine.
The small amount of olive
oil they produce is also
excellent.

Talenti

località Sant'Angelo in
Colle-Pian del Conte
℡ 0577 844043.

Pierluigi Talenti has
worked hard on his
Sangiovese vines and,
after years of careful
selection in the vineyard,
he has created a great
Brunello. There was
nothing immodest in his
dedication of a wine
to himself: the Rosso
Talenti, which is made
from Sangiovese grapes
combined with the

Tuscan Colorino and
the French Syrah, is a
great success.

Pasticceria Ticci

località Torrenieri,
via Romana, 47
℡ 0577 834146.
◯ Sun am.

This is a great café and
confectioner's with a
wide range of excellent
traditional cakes,
including panforte and
ciambelline made with
red Montalcino wine.

MONTEFOLLONICO (SI)

Caseificio Putzulu

località Fattoria in Posto, 1
℡ 0577 669744.

Sheep are raised here and
there is a dairy producing
ricotta and a selection of
other excellent ewe's milk
cheeses which are aged
for varying periods.

LESSO RIFATTO

500 g (1 lb 2 oz) leftover boiled meat (beef, veal and
chicken) • extra virgin olive oil • 1 onion, chopped
• 1 carrot , diced • 1 stalk celery, diced • **50 g (1³⁄₄ oz)**
pancetta, diced • 1 glass red wine • **300 g (10¹⁄₂ oz)**
tomatoes, pulped • **25 g (1 oz)** dried porcini (ceps)
• salt • pepper

Cut the beef and veal into slices and the chicken into
strips. Heat the oil in a pan, add the onion, carrot, celery
and **pancetta** and fry gently until browned, then add the
meat and wine. Add the tomatoes and season to taste
with salt and pepper. Cover and simmer for 15 minutes.
Meanwhile, soak the **porcini** in warm water for 15
minutes, then add to the pan. Continue to cook gently
for 20 minutes. Arrange the meat on a serving dish, pour
the sauce over it and serve.

MONTEPULCIANO (SI)

Avignonesi

Via di Gracciano
del Corso, 91
☎ 0578 757872.

*This company has four
estates producing wine:
two at Montepulciano
and two at Cortona.
Their flagship wine is
the Vino Nobile di
Montepulciano but
another wine that has
made a name for itself
is Toro Desiderio, from
pure Merlot, Cabernet
Sauvignon and Prugnolo
Gentile grapes. Other
pearls are the Vin Santo,
from white grapes, and
the Occhio di Pernice
from Prugnolo Gentile.
The careful selection of
grapes and the lengthy
ageing of these dessert
wines inevitably means
that they will never be
cheap to buy. The extra
virgin olive oil produced
by the company is also
excellent.*

La Braccesca

strada statale, 326
località Gracciano
di Montepulciano
☎ 0578 707058.

The Azienda Avignonesi at Montepulciano

*Since most of their vines
are Sangiovese, this
estate's output has been
limited to two wines, the
Vino Nobile and Rosso di
Montepulciano Sabazio,
but they have recently
added an important
Merlot variety. They have
only recently become
known on the market but
they have attracted much
interest. The credit is
due to the staff and the
philosophy of Antinori,
who took over the estate
in 1990. Purchases can
be made at Enoteca Borgo
Buio, Montepulciano
(0578 717497) and
Enoteca di Ghino, Pienza
(0575 748057) (see p149).*

Fattoria del Cerro

località Acquaviva
via Grazianella, 5
☎ 0578 767722.

*This is probably the biggest
private producer of Vino
Nobile di Montepulciano.
Most of the vines, owned
by the Saiagricola group,
are reserved for the Vino
Nobile, on which the estate
is staking a lot, especially
on the Riserva, but it also
has a splendid Rosso di
Montepulciano. The white
wines are Braviolo, based
on Trebbiano, and Cerro
Bianco from Chardonnay.*

Azienda Agricola Contucci

via del Teatro, 1
☎ 0578 757006.

*The centuries-old cellars,
which have belonged to
the family since the 13th
century, contain large
and small casks in which
the Vino Nobile ages for
the Pietra Rossa label. The
Vin Santo is produced in
the traditional manner in
very small casks that hold
from 50–100 litres (11–22
gallons) and the wine is
allowed to settle naturally,
without being filtered.*

Caseificio Cugusi Silvana

strada statale per Pienza
via della Boccia, 8
☎ 0578 757558.

*Outstanding pecorino
cheeses matured for
varying periods, including
the dark kind typical of
Pienza, can be found
here. The fresh pecorino
is delectable, almost juicy
in texture, somewhere
between a caciotta and a
mozzarella. Also unusual
are the more mature types
for grating which are
always mellow and never
dry. There are also
excellent fresh cheeses
with rocket or walnuts.*

Dei

località Villa Martiena
☎ 0578 716878.

*At this small property, very
respectable Vino Nobile
di Montepulciano and
Rosso di Montepulciano
wines have been created.
Recently it has introduced
French vines which are
used in its Sancta
Catharina, a red made
from Syrah, Cabernet
Sauvignon and Petit
Verdot together with
Prugnolo Gentile.
Purchases can be made
from Terra Toscana
(see p148).*

ZUPPA DI LENTICCHIE CON FAGIANO

500 g (1 lb 2 oz) lentils • 1 carrot • 1 onion, halved • 1 stalk celery, halved • 2 cloves garlic • 1 sprig of winter savory • 2 bay leaves • 1 pheasant • 100 g (3 ½ oz) lardo (pork fat), finely sliced • 1 sprig of rosemary • 1 sprig of sage • extra virgin olive oil • chicken stock • salt • pepper

Preheat the oven to 250°C (475°F/gas mark 9). Put the lentils in a pan of water with the carrot, onion, celery, garlic, winter savory, bay leaves, a little oil and salt. Cover and simmer over a moderate heat until the lentils are soft, adding more boiling water if necessary. Grease the inside of the pheasant with olive oil, tuck the sage and rosemary into the cavity and season with salt and pepper. Bard it with the pork fat and tie with kitchen twine. Place in a greased roasting tin and roast for 30 minutes, turning and basting with the cooking juices from time to time. Remove the fat, return the pheasant to the oven, baste with the juices and cook until golden. Remove the pheasant and chop the flesh. Deglaze the pan juices with a little oil and chicken stock. Drain the lentils, remove the vegetables, garlic and bay leaves. Return the meat to the pan with the lentils. Warm through and serve.

🍇 Fassati

località Gracciano
via di Gracciannello, 3/A
☎ 0578 708708.

Enhancing Vino Nobile was the objective of the Sparaco family, owners of the Fazi Battaglia firm that purchased this estate in 1969. Today the range includes red wines from traditional grape varieties. Of note is the Vino Nobile di Montepulciano Riserva Salarco, the Rosso di Montepulciano Selciaia, the Novello Fontago (from Prugnolo Gentile, Canaiolo Nero and Mammolo grapes), the Chianti Le Gaggiole and Torre al Fante, this last one from Prugnolo Gentile alone, presented on various occasions as a "Super Tuscan."

🏺 Il Frantoio di Montepulciano

piazza Pasquino
☎ 0578 758732.

This is a cooperative olive mill producing fine extra virgin olive oil, in particular the product denominated IGP

Toscano, which is produced exclusively in this area from the output of the cooperative's 600 members.

🍇 Il Macchione

località Caggiole
via Provinciale, 12
☎ 0578 758595.

The Swiss owner of this small estate, formerly a dentist, has done things properly. With meticulous care and attention he has produced a Vino Nobile di Montepulciano, Le Caggiole (also in a Riserva version), which has great texture and elegance. The main problem is laying one's hands on it, since the output never meets the

demand. Also excellent is the young Rosso di Montepulciano.

🍇 Enoteca Oinochoè

via Voltaia del Corso, 82
☎ 0578 757524.

A wide range of the best Tuscan wines is sold in this wine shop, with nearly all the estates of the Montepulciano area represented. In addition to a range of regional products, including dessert wines such as Moscadello and Vin Santo, there are classics from Piedmont, Friuli, the Veneto and Lombardy. A selection of Tuscan oils and vinegars is also sold.

🍇 Poliziano

località Montepulciano Stazione, via Fontago, 11
☎ 0578 738171.

Only in the best years is Vino Nobile di Montepulciano Vigna Asinone made. This wine shows its fine qualities early but also ages well. The same Sangiovese vines but from selected grapes from different vineyards are used to make Elegia, while Cabernet Sauvignon is used with a small amount of Merlot to make the much prized Le Stanze di Poliziano, a tribute to the famous poet and humanist. You can buy the wines from Enoteca Borgo Buio (0578 717497) and Enoteca Oinochoè, Montepulciano.

The winery at Fattoria Poliziano

The countryside around Pienza

 Azienda Agricola San Benedetto

strada per Chianciano, 25
[0578 757649.

This estate, set amid very beautiful hills, sells fruit (peaches, apricots, quinces and grapes) and organically grown plums and figs, natural jams (some made without sugar) and wild flower honey.

🍇 **Terra Toscana**

via Ricci, 14/A
[0578 757708.

Situated just 50 metres (55 yards) from Piazza Grande is this winery, representing 35 estates in the Montepulciano area. Many of them are essentially vineyards making only wine and grappa. The others have been chosen for the traditional quality of their regional produce: organically produced pasta, honey, truffles and mushrooms from Monte Amiata, and excellent pecorino cheese. A daily selection of wines is offered for tasting.

🍇 **Vecchia Cantina di Montepulciano**

via Provinciale, 7
[0578 716092.

This winery is responsible for over half the volume of wine produced in the area. The extent of the vineyards, spread over a wide area, has made it possible to make some interesting wines, five or six altogether, that form a line of products marketed under the Cantina del Redi trademark. They include Vino Nobile di Montepulciano, Rosso di Montepulciano and a Vin Santo, while the greatest success of the Vecchia Cantina trademark is its Vino Nobile di Montepulciano.

MONTERONI D'ARBIA (SI)

🌳 **Azienda Agricola Santa Margherita**

località Ville di Corsano
via del Colle,711
[0577 377101.

This farm makes fresh and matured goat's milk cheese, packaged French-style in various forms. The cheeses are produced organically and some of them are flavoured with fresh herbs.

MURLO (SI)

🔺 **Apicoltura Quercioli Sonia**

piazza Benocci,
frazione Vescovado
[0577 814255.

All the local Sienese varieties of honey, including wild flower, arbutus and sunflower are produced by this apiarist.

PIENZA (SI)

🍇 **La Cornucopia**

piazza Martiri
della Libertà, 2
[0578 748150.
🕐 daily.

This wine store and gourmet shop sells all kinds of preserves from Tuscany and other Italian regions. It has a wide range of wines, mostly Tuscan labels but with a good selection from other regions. There are also grappas, mainly Tuscan, and various other national and international spirits. The store also sells a variety of vinegars.

SUGO DI CHIOCCIOLE (SNAILS IN SAUCE)

extra virgin olive oil • 1 stalk celery, sliced • 1 carrot, chopped • 1 onion, chopped • 2 cloves garlic, sliced • 1 chilli, deseeded and chopped • sprig of rosemary • 500 g (1 lb 2 oz) snails, prepared for cooking, boiled and removed from shells • 1.5 kg (3 lb 5 oz) tomatoes, peeled • 300 g (10½ oz) minced beef • chopped parsley • white wine • vegetable stock • salt

Heat some oil in a pan, add the vegetables, chilli, garlic and rosemary, then add the beef and fry until the meat is browned. Add the tomatoes and salt and cook for 30 minutes. Add the snails and parsley and cook for another hour, adding a little wine and stock from time to time.

L'Enoteca di Ghino

via del Leone, 16
0578 748057.
Sun.

*Since customers coming
from abroad would be
disappointed if they found
this wine shop closed
when they arrived, Ghino
Poggianini decided to
live over his shop so he
could always be on call
for his customers. He
concentrates on wine
and has over 2,000 labels,
with wines ranging in
price from a few euros
up to several hundred a
bottle. He even has fine
old wines and collectors'
items. The shop also has a
selection of extra virgin
olive oils, which come
from about 15 producers.*

Forno Sacchi Danilo

via delle Mura, 16/18
0578 748545.
Wed pm.

*This baker and pastry
cook is renowned for
tasty Tuscan bread and
traditional cakes,
especially* ricciarelli, *made
from coarsely ground
almonds. He also makes*
ossi di morto *from
almonds and egg whites,
and other confections
based on almond paste
enriched with various
dried fruits and chocolate,
such as* pinolati, pizzicotti
and serpe. *Tarts and*
ciambelloni *(ring-shaped
cakes) complete the range.*

 ## Caseificio Solp

località Poggio
Colombo, 40
0578 748645.

Pecorino *matured for
various periods is sold
here, plus* caciotta *from
a mix of cow's and ewe's
milk, and* raviggiolo *(see
page 133) made to order.*

RADICOFANI (SI)

 ### Cooperativa Agricola Produttori latte Val d'Orcia

località Contignano
strada dell'Orcia, 15
0578 52012.
Wed pm.

*This cooperative makes
pecorino and ricotta
cheeses from the milk
produced by its 80
members. It makes
small* caciotte *from a
mixture of cow's and
ewe's milk.*

SAN QUIRICO D'ORCIA (SI)

Macelleria Bassi Raffaello

piazza della Libertà, 1
0577 895077.
Wed pm.

*Raffaello Bassi chooses
his beef from small farms
which devote special care
to the feeding of their
animals. He sells
Chianina beef and lamb*

CAVALLUCCI

*300 g (10½ oz) sugar
• 300 g (10½ oz) plain
flour • 50 g (1¾ oz)
candied orange peel
• 100 g (3½ oz) walnuts,
crushed • 15 g (½ oz)
ground aniseed • a pinch
of ground cinnamon*

Preheat the oven to
150°C (300°F/gas mark
2). Put the sugar in a
pan with a glass of water
and heat until it forms a
thick, clear liquid. Off
the heat, stir in the flour,
candied orange peel,
walnuts, aniseed and
cinnamon. Roll out the
dough to the thickness
of a finger. Cut into
lozenge shapes and
bake in the oven for
about 30 minutes.

*from local farms. His
poultry and pork come
from trusted breeders. He
makes a variety of* salumi,
sausages and hams.

SARTEANO (SI)

 ### Prodotti Tipici

via Di Fuori, 73
0578 267020.
Wed pm.

*The traditional food
specialities of the area
are stocked here – in
particular, a wide range
of* pecorino *cheese.*

SINALUNGA (SI)

Barbieri

via Trieste, 102
0577 678256.
Wed pm.

*Fresh meat, prosciutti
and pork sausages all
from the firm's own pigs
are sold here.*

The Enoteca di Ghino at Pienza

RIVOLTI CON RICOTTA

extra virgin olive oil • 2 cloves garlic • 1 handful parsley, chopped • 1 carrot, chopped • 1 onion, chopped • 1 stalk celery, chopped • 300 g (10½ oz) minced beef • 2 fresh sausages, chopped • 100 g (3½ oz) prosciutto crudo, chopped • 2 glasses white wine • 500 g (1 lb 2 oz) tomatoes, peeled • 1 egg • 300 g (10½ oz) plain flour • 300 g (10½ oz) cooked spinach, chopped • 200 g (7 oz) ricotta • 100 g (3½ oz) grated Parmesan cheese • ground nutmeg • salt • pepper

In a large pan, heat some oil and fry the garlic, parsley, vegetables and meat over a moderate heat until the meat is browned. Add the wine, cook until it evaporates, then add the tomatoes. Simmer gently for about 3 hours; stir frequently. Meanwhile, beat the egg and mix with 500 ml (18 fl oz) water and the flour to make a batter. Season with salt. Warm a pan lightly greased with oil. Pour in a ladleful of batter and smooth out to make a pancake. Cook on both sides until golden, then remove from the pan. Repeat until all the batter is used. Stir the spinach into the pan with some more oil, the ricotta, half the Parmesan and the nutmeg. Season. Use to fill the pancakes. Arrange in an ovenproof dish, cover with the meat sauce, sprinkle with the rest of the Parmesan and cook in the oven at 180°C (350°F/gas mark 4) until the cheese melts.

Tenuta Farneta

località Farneta
0577 631025.

Although it has a significant range of Chianti, this estate's most successful wines are its Bentivoglio and Bongoverno, two finer wines from Sangiovese grapes aged by different methods. The Bentivoglio is matured for 16–18 months, partly in large casks and partly in small ones, while Bongoverno is matured for 21 months in small oak casks (barriques) alone. The difference in maturing methods and the use of barriques for maturing makes the Bongoverno the more expensive of the two wines.

Azienda Agricola Castello di Farnetella

località Farnetella
0577 663520.

This firm's star product is its Chianti Colli Senesi, a quality wine which is very good value for money. They also produce wines made from non-Tuscan vines that give their best here, such as the Pinot Nero, vinified in red to create Nero di Nubi, and Sauvignon Blanc, used in a richly perfumed and very elegant wine. The Castello trademark is marketed by the Fattoria di Felsina (see p114), Giovanni Poggiali's other estate at Castelnuovo Berardenga.

Purchases can be made at La Cornucopia di Pienza (see p148).

Frantoio Mazzarrini

frazione Rigomagno
0577 663624.

Excellent extra virgin olive oil, typical of the Colline Senesi, is produced here. Their olive press works on a continuous system, keeping temperatures low, to the benefit of the oil.

Pa. Ri. V.

frazione Guazzino
via XXV luglio, 4
0577 624061.
Sun pm.

There is a retail sales point for Tuscan bread and traditional Sienese cakes at this wholesale bakery .

TREQUANDA (SI)

Azienda Agricola Belsedere

località Belsedere
0577 662307.

Agriturismo facilities are on offer at this farm. The lamb is certified organically produced,

The Fattoria del Colle at Trequanda

as is the ricotta *and* pecorino, *made by hand from fresh milk. It has excellent pork and* salumi *which, though not certified organic, are produced completely naturally. In addition to Tuscan* prosciutto *and* spalla, *there is excellent* buristo, mortadella, soppressata, lombo, finocchiona *and other meat specialities which can be purchased in small quantities.*

🌳 **Azienda Agricola San Polo**

Podere San Polo
📞 0577 665321.

Pecorino of Pienza is matured for different lengths of time here. Some of the cheese is wrapped in walnut leaves and left to mature.

🐝 **Fattoria del Colle**

via Torta, 7
📞 0577 662108.

The remarkable vivacity of one of Italy's leading oenologists (wine-makers), Donatella Cinelli, guarantees quality and superior hospitality on this farm with its expanding agriturismo facilities. She devised the Movimento Turismo del Vino, which organizes Open Cellars – days when hundreds of the leading cellars all over Italy welcome visitors like guests to a party, with tastings, guided tours and general pageantry. The brand-new osteria (inn) has tastings and sells excellent extra virgin olive oil, pecorino cheeses, truffles, Chianti DOCG, Vin Santo, a white wine from Traminer grapes, and other wines. Donatella Cinelli's policy is to produce everything in an environmentally friendly manner.

ZUPPA DI CECI (CHICKPEA SOUP)

300 g (10½ oz) chickpeas, soaked overnight • extra virgin olive oil • 2 cloves garlic • rosemary • 1 dessertspoon tomato purée • 300 g (10½ oz) Tuscan bread • salt

Preheat the oven to 200°C (400°F/gas mark 6). Cook the chickpeas in a pan of water until tender, then press through a sieve to purée them, adding the cooking water. In an earthenware pan, heat some oil and lightly fry the garlic, rosemary and the tomato purée diluted in half a glass of warm water. Add the chickpeas to the pan, season with salt and stir for some minutes to absorb the flavours. Slice the bread into croutons and brown them in the oven. Put them into soup plates and pour in the chickpea purée. Drizzle with a little olive oil and serve.

🍾 **Cooperativa Agricola Il Lecceto**

via della Trove
località Castelmuzio
📞 0577 665358.

This cooperative brings together 65 small olive growers from the village of Trequanda and the neighbouring communes who produce an extra virgin olive oil that is very typical of this area. The olive oil can also be purchased at the Pro Loco in Piazza di Trequanda.

 Il Panaio di Cinzia e Roberto Mancini

via di Diaccecto, 16
📞 0577 662288.
🔴 Wed pm.

Traditional Tuscan bread and cakes typical of this region are sold here. The cantucci, pinolata, panforte *and* schiacciata di Pasqua *are all well worth trying.*

🐂 **Macelleria Ricci**

viale Rimembranze
📞 0577 662252.
🔴 Mon, Tues, Wed pm.
⚪ Sun in summer.

A fine butcher's shop with scrupulous hygiene methods, this is run by the Azienda Agricola Trequanda. It sells the estate's Chianina beef. The complete cycle for producing meat from birth to butchering is covered, faithfully following traditional methods. Also on sale are pecorino cheeses from the estate of Sorano (GR) which raises sheep and has its own dairy.

FRITTATA FINTA

1 kg (2 lb 4 oz) potatoes, cut into cubes • 1 sprig of sage • 3 cloves garlic • extra virgin olive oil • salt

Cook the potato cubes in salted boiling water until tender. Drain the potatoes, then purée by passing them through a vegetable mill. Mince the sage and garlic in the vegetable mill. Heat some oil in a non-stick frying pan, add the sage and garlic and fry briefly over a gentle heat. Add the puréed potatoes, stirring constantly to blend them with the sage and garlic. Using a fork, press the mixture to shape it into a flat, compact cake. Continue cooking, carefully turning the cake over a number of times until it is golden brown on both sides. The potato cake can be eaten hot or cold.

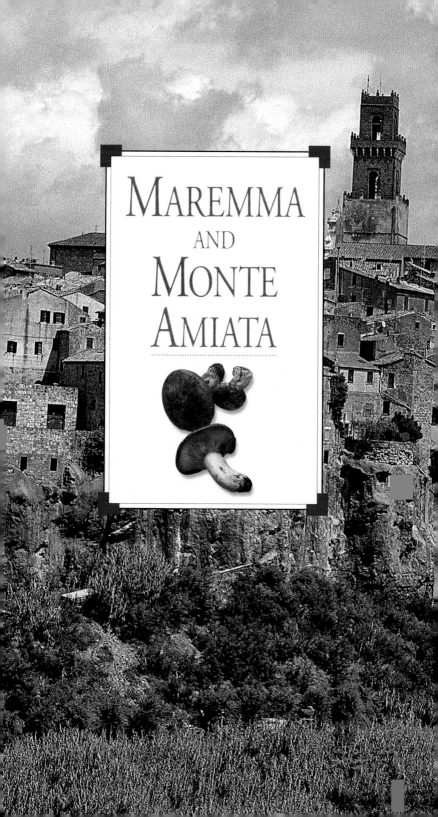

MAREMMA
AND
MONTE
AMIATA

Maremma and Monte Amiata

THE MAREMMA AND MONTE AMIATA region is the wildest part of Tuscany. Impenetrable scrub, criss-crossed by foresters following the wild boar tracks, alternates with the majestic forests of Monte Amiata and coastal pine woods studded with rosemary – especially those in the breathtaking park, Monti dell'Uccellina. The area covers the province of Grosseto, including Monte Amiata which is the highest mountain peak in southern Tuscany, and some communes from the province of Siena. For centuries human activities have been adapted to Nature, which has bestowed rich gifts but equally been quite hostile in the marshlands. Maremma cattle are raised here, looking like buffaloes with their wide horns.

This is a land of strong flavours, with game a speciality on every restaurant menu and plenty of fresh fish in the fishing harbours of Porto San Stefano and Castiglione della Pescaia and the prolific lagoon of Orbetello. Old traditions endure and it is a region of organic farming and farmhouse hospitality, in a land where there are still open spaces for men and animals.

Maremma cattle were mainly bred as draught animals, as they gave little milk or meat, though their meat tastes good. Some herds, tended by *butteri* (cowherds), graze half-wild on the edge of the stunningly beautiful Parco dell'Uccellina.

Massa Marittima

Roccastrada

Follonica

Montepescali

Vetulonia

Punta Ala

Castiglione della Pescaia

GROSSETO

FS

Marina di Grosseto

Ombrone

Monti dell'Uccellina

Marina di Alberese

Talamone

0 kilometres   10

0 miles   10

Alb

Monte Argentario, once an island, is now a promontory, rich in vegetation, with two ancient fishing ports, Porto Ercole and Porto San Stefano. It is joined to the coast by two strips of land enclosing the lagoon of Orbetello.

Giglio

Giglio Castello

Giglio Campese

Giglio Porto

ORBETELLO

Porto San Stefano

Monte Argentario

Po Erc

◁ **The medieval city of Pitigliano**

STAR ATTRACTIONS

- MASSA MARITTIMA (GR): Cathedral, **C** 0566 902766
- PITIGLIANO (GR): Museo Palazzo Orsini, **C** 0564 615568
- SOVANA (GR): Etruscan necropolis, **C** 0564 414303
- ANSEDONIA (GR): Museo di Cosa, **C** 0564 881421
- ALBERESE (GR): Uccellina National Park, **C** 0564 407098

HERBS

The abundance of herbs, cultivated in most gardens and frequently found growing wild in thickets and along the coast, has influenced the cuisine of all Tuscany. In the Maremma, foods are nearly always flavoured with herbs, particularly game dishes.

The wild boar, which is an indigenous variety, is the symbol of the Maremma. Its flesh is much prized. A Wild Boar Festival is held at Capalbio in September *(see pp158–9)*.

Monte Amiata's rugged sides are covered in chestnut woods rich with tasty mushrooms. The area is also famous for its fauna, especially the great variety of birds seen here.

TRANSPORT

FS RAILWAY STATION
- GROSSETO – STAZIONE FS
  C 0564 414303
- ORBETELLO – STAZIONE FS
  C 0564 860447

BUS STATION
- MASSA MARITTIMA
  C 0566 902016

Hare is a much-loved ingredient in many traditional Tuscan dishes. However, nowadays Italians usually have to import them as no hunters will give up the few hares they manage to shoot.

Places of Interest pp164–169
Restaurants pp190–191

Wines

THE MAREMMA USED to be considered a difficult area which produced rather lacklustre wines. Today there is a growing appreciation of some of its wines and the Maremma now appears to be a land whose wine-growing potential needs exploring. It is claimed, in fact, that the very first Sangiovese vines grew here, though some experts favour the Chianti area. Sangiovese is the main component of the area's reds, which may contain small amounts of local red grapes, including Canaiolo, Ciliegiolo, Malvasia Nera, Alicante and even Montepulciano. White wines are nearly always based on Trebbiano Toscano mixed with Greco, Grechetto, Verdello, Malvasia del Chianti and the local Ansonica. Imported vines are now grown here: Cabernet Sauvignon and Merlot for reds and Pinot, Chardonnay, Sauvignon and Riesling for whites.

BIANCO DI PITIGLIANO

This wine is named after the picturesque town in the heart of the area of production. The wine is produced from Trebbiano Toscano plus numerous other white grapes which can make up to 50 per cent of the grape quantity. It has a pleasant, slightly bitter flavour and is ideal with artichokes and savoury vegetarian dishes. There are also Superiore and spumante versions.

The Morellino di Scansano Riserva is aged for at least 2 years and goes well with game.

MONTEREGIO DI MASSA MARITTIMA

The name refers to several different types of wine. The Bianco is made from Trebbiano Toscano with up to 50 per cent of other white grapes, including Malvasia di Candia. The Vermentino has to contain at least 90 per cent of the grape from which it gets its name. Both wines make good accompaniments for delicate fish and vegetable dishes. The Rosato, the Rosso Riserva and Rosso Novello contain at least 80 per cent Sangiovese, plus other red grapes. The Rosato goes well with white meats, the Rosso with red meats and game. The Vin Santo, in ordinary and Occhio di Pernice versions, is perfect with honey cakes and sweet dry biscuits.

MORELLINO DI SCANSANO

The vines on the hills have the advantage of being exposed to cool breezes. Sangiovese grapes (here known as Morellino) from the hills are mixed with local grapes such as Alicante to produce this red wine. Its distinctive spicy perfume, full-bodied flavour and good acidity make the wine an ideal accompaniment for food in a spicy marinade.

ANSONICA COSTA DELL'ARGENTARIO

A recent appellation for a white wine from Ansonica grapes, this has subtle fruity scents. Light and fresh, it is suited to delicate fish *antipasti* or vegetable first courses. There is a sweet Passito wine, which is excellent with sweet dry biscuits. The wine produced on the island of Giglio has a brinier taste and a higher alcohol content: ideal with fish baked or cooked in a sauce.

CORATA DI CINGHIALE

100 g (3 1/2 oz) lardo *(lard), minced* • *extra virgin olive oil* • *1 onion, chopped* • *heart, spleen, lights and liver of a wild boar* • *1 sprig of calamint* • *1 sprig of wild thyme* • *1 chilli, minced* • *600 g (1 lb 5 oz) ripe tomatoes, sliced* • *100 ml (3 1/2 fl oz) red wine* • *salt*

Put the *lardo* in a pan with some oil and the chopped onion. Cook until the onion is browned. Cut the heart, spleen and lights into pieces and add to the pan with the calamint leaves, thyme and chilli. Cook until the meat is browned on all sides. Add the tomatoes and season with salt. Simmer briskly for 10 minutes. Chop the liver into small pieces and stir into the pan. Pour in the wine and cook over a brisk heat for another 5 minutes.

PARRINA ROSSO

This wine is produced from 80 per cent Sangiovese with some Canaiolo and Montepulciano grapes. It goes well with white and red meats, roulades and medium-ripe cheeses.

The Riserva version is very good with traditional Tuscan roasted meats, especially roast guinea fowl.

PARRINA BIANCO

This white wine is made with at least 50 per cent Trebbiano Toscano grapes, with some Malvasia del Chianti and Ansonica. It is good with *antipasti* and vegetable or egg dishes.

The Rosato version, made from at least 70 per cent Sangiovese grapes, is drunk young. It is ideal with shellfish in sauce.

OTHER WINES WORTH TRYING

The **Montecucco** DOC wine was first marketed with the '98 vintage. There are four types : **Bianco**, **Vermentino**, **Rosso** and **Sangiovese**. The **Rosso di Sovana** DOC (Sangiovese or Ciliegiolo) was first marketed with the '99 vintage.

WINE TYPE	GOOD VINTAGES	GOOD PRODUCERS
Red Wine		
Morellino di Scansano	98, 97, 95, 90	Le Pupille di Magliano, Moris Farm di Massa Marittima
Monteregio di Massa Marittima	98, 97, 90	Massa Vecchia di Massa Marittima
Super Tuscans (see p130)	98, 97, 95, 90	Rascioni e Cecconello di Orbetello, La Stellata di Manciano, Moris Farm di Massa Marittima

Wild Game

ONCE THE MAREMMA was so well known as "wild boar country" that the protected native Italian breed of boar was called the "maremmana". Its meat was not just an attraction in restaurants, but was commonly eaten in homes, and there was a flourishing business of making wild boar *salumi* to sell as a souvenir of the region. Wild boar was not the only game to populate the inaccessible undergrowth of this area, either – there were also deer, hares and porcupines. The foresters, who for decades were also poachers, caught whatever came their way, cooking it over a wood or charcoal fire and creating the robust recipes that were the origins of the game cuisine of today, rich not only in flavour but also in imagination.

IL CINGHIALE (WILD BOAR)
A characteristic feature of Tuscan cooking, wild boar is now found all over Italy.

COSTOLETTE DI CINGHIALE (WILD BOAR CHOPS)
With wild boar chops, the gamey taste is not pronounced, so they appeal to those who prefer delicate flavours. They are excellent grilled and should be served rare.

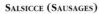

SALSICCE (SAUSAGES)
Made from a mixture of finely minced boar meat and pig fat, these sausages are dried before they are eaten.

POLPA DI CINGHIALE (CUBED BOAR MEAT)
"*In scottiglia*", a rich stew of meat in a sweet and sour sauce made with things like olives and apples, is a traditional Tuscan recipe. Leg or shoulder of wild boar, cut into cubes, is a popular ingredient for this sort of stew.

Prosciutto di Cinghiale

Cured ham made from wild boar is drier and less fatty than the local *prosciutto* made from pigs, and is usually less salty and peppery. Traditionally, the fur was left on the skin, but EU regulations no longer allow this.

Small sausages (called cacciatorini*) are made from boar in the same way as from pork.*

Salame di Cinghiale (Wild Boar Salame)

Salame made from lean boar's flesh and pig's fat (*pancetta* and *lardo*) is generally drier and has a stronger taste than pure pork salami.

Shoulder of venison is ideal for traditional Tuscan stews.

Il Capriolo (Venison)

Found all over Tuscany, venison was traditionally eaten only in a stew, *salmi* or sauces for pasta. A newer idea is to grill the chops or pan-cook them with herbs, or roast a leg until rare.

Other Game Meat Worth Trying

Wild boar is also used to make **soppressate** (matured salami), often with chilli, **salt pork** and **pork preserved in oil**. **Fallow deer** are common: they come from farms or graze in the open after being released into game reserves. The meat is usually stewed. A recent innovation is **salumi** (*salame, cacciatore, bresaoline*) made from **roe deer**, **red deer** and **fallow deer**. These meats are also found preserved in oil with olives, garlic, chilli and herbs. **Hare** is a basic ingredient of Tuscan cooking, but now, regrettably, it is impossible to find fresh hare. However, frozen ones are imported. Porcupine meat was once much prized, but it is now a protected animal.

Traditional Produce

THE LAGOON AT ORBETELLO adds wonderful variety to the foods produced in the province of Grosseto, making this region one of the richest in typical Tuscan foods. *Porcini* (cep mushrooms) can be found everywhere, especially on Monte Amiata, where picking them is a local industry. Amiata is one of the chestnut capitals of Italy. There is plentiful sea fish, with Porto San Stefano taking its catch mainly from the reefs called the Formiche di Grosseto and around the islands. With some of the Tuscany's largest olive presses in this area there is plenty of olive oil, and truffles, especially the March truffle *(see p18)*, are abundant along the coast.

MAREMMA GROSSETANA OLIVE OIL

Practically the whole province makes this type of olive oil. Communes producing significant quantities are Orbetello, Capalbio and Magliano in southern Tuscany, and Massa Marittima in the north. These are fruity oils of average intensity, with herbal and, at times, floral fragrances. They have excellent fluidity, firmly structured flavours and a pungent aftertaste, sometimes with a tinge of bitterness.

TABLE OLIVES

Tuscany is not famed for its table olives, but the Santa Caterina variety, cured in brine while green, is sold throughout Italy. All the farmhouses still salt a small part of their olive crop, dry them in the oven to reduce the bitterness and preserve them in oil, preferably Leccino oil. Olives are also an important ingredient in many of the traditional dishes of this area.

Carré (rib) of lamb is common in Tuscan restaurants. The chops are generally served in a mixed grill.

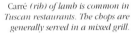

AGNELLO TOSCANO (TUSCAN LAMB)

The real Tuscan lamb comes from herds that move from pasture to pasture: they are driven from Maremma to Chianti, then Mugello and finally to Casentino. They are highly prized because the aromatic herbs they graze on flavours the meat.

WHAT TO SAMPLE

Large organically farmed estates, often offering farmhouse hospitality ("agriturismo"), make the Maremma one of the leading producers of **honey**, preserved **fruit** and **vegetables**. The **pecorino** and **ricotta cheeses** are important, both in quantity and quality. The **table grapes** are excellent, as are the **peaches**, **pears** and **yellow cherries** from Seggiano and **walnuts** from Amiata. In addition to **game animals** there are numerous **wood pigeons** and **woodcock**.

ANGUILLA (EEL)
Excellent quality eels are abundant in the lagoon of Orbetello so there is no need to farm them in this area.

SCAVECCIO

1 kg (2 lb 4 oz) eels • flour • extra virgin olive oil • 500 ml (18 fl oz) wine vinegar • 4 cloves garlic, sliced • 2 sprigs of rosemary • peppercorns • 1 chilli, deseeded and chopped • salt

Clean the eels and cut them into smallish pieces. Dredge the pieces with flour. Heat the oil, add the eel pieces and fry until tender. Dry the pieces on absorbent kitchen paper and then pack them into a clean jar. Pour the vinegar into a pan, dilute it with a glass of water and add the chilli, the pepper, salt, garlic and rosemary. Bring it to the boil, then pour it into the jar of eels, taking care to cover the pieces. Leave at room temperature for 3 or 4 days.

LE COPPIETTE (DRIED MEAT)
These are strips of meat salted, seasoned and hung up to dry on cords or slender sticks. The meat may be pork, beef, boar, mutton, donkey or horse.

CEFALO OR MUGGINE (GREY MULLET)
This fish is caught in the sea at the mouths of rivers and in lagoons. It is strongly associated with the resort of Orbetello in the middle of the Laguna di Orbetello, and is eaten both fresh and cured.

OTHER FISH WORTH TRYING

At Orbetello fish farms raise excellent **branzini** (sea bass) and **orate** (gilthead bream) in troughs fed either by warm subterranean waters or by seawater. **Latterini** (sand smelt), excellent fried or eaten raw with lemon and olive oil ("in carpione"), are caught in the sea, the lagoon of Orbetello and the Lake of Chiusi. Fishing for **cieche** (elvers – eel's fry) is traditional at river mouths. **Anguilla sfumata** (smoked eel) is a Spanish dish adapted through the centuries to local tastes: the eels are marinated and then smoked. They are sautéed in extra virgin olive oil before eating. The **cefalo** (grey mullet) raised at Orbetello is smoked to a recipe of Spanish origin. For at least 1,000 years its roe has been dried and sold as **bottarga**, a custom that may be even older here than in Sardinia.

Wild Produce

LARDAIOLO ROSSO
(Hygrophorus russula)
In late autumn this white mushroom, with its claret-coloured marbling and gills that are waxy to the touch, is very common under evergreen oak and Turkey oak. Foresters consider it one of the best mushrooms for preserving in oil.

SAMPHIRE
(Crithmum maritimum)
Samphire grows on cliffs. The narrow fleshy leaves, which have a distinct taste of iodine, are pickled before eating.

FUNGAGNELLO
(Lyophyllum fumosum)
Found in abundance in woods of broad-leaved trees, this mushroom often forms large tufts with numerous caps growing from a single base. It is much sought-after, despite the fact that it is very similar to a poisonous fungus. Firm and fleshy, it is eaten fried with garlic and parsley, in sauces and bottled in oil.

CICCIOLE
(Pleurotus eryngii and Pleurotus ferulae)
These winter mushrooms grow underneath eryngo and giant fennel. Widespread in Puglia, Sicily and Sardinia, where they are the commonest mushrooms, they are well-known to the foresters of Tuscany, who usually eat them grilled.

ACQUACOTTA CON I FUNGHI

extra virgin olive oil • 2 cloves garlic, chopped • 2 stalks celery, sliced • 600 g (1 lb 5 oz) mixed mushrooms, sliced • 400 g (14 oz) tomatoes, chopped • 1 small piece of chilli, chopped • 1 litre (1¾ pints) boiling water • 12 slices Tuscan bread • 6 eggs • grated mature pecorino • salt

Heat some oil in a pan and fry the garlic and celery until soft. Leave to cool, then add the mushrooms and season with salt. Return the pan to the heat and cook until the mushrooms have released their water and it has evaporated. Add the tomatoes and chilli. Cook for 20 minutes. Pour in the boiling water and simmer for 10 minutes. Toast the bread and put it in a pan with the eggs and *pecorino*. Pour the boiling soup over them and serve.

ARISTA DI MAIALE ARROSTO

1 kg (2 lb 4 oz) chine of pork • 2 cloves garlic, sliced • rosemary • fennel seeds • extra virgin olive oil • salt • pepper

Make incisions in the meat, especially near the bone, and insert garlic, fennel seeds and rosemary leaves. Tie sprigs of rosemary around the part opposite the bone. Season with salt and pepper and smear with oil. Leave for several hours. Preheat the oven to 160°C (325°F/gas mark 3). Put the meat in a greased roasting tin containing a little water. Cook for about 1½ hours, turning frequently and basting with the juices.

CIAVARDELLO
(Sorbus torminalis)
The fruits of this tree are called sorbs. Smaller and less well-known than those of the domestic tree, they ripen on the plant and can be picked and eaten from the tree. They are excellent for making jellies and, above all, liqueurs. They were one of the ingredients of some ancient Celtic beverages.

CASTAGNOLO
(Tricholoma acerbum)
In the autumn this mushroom can be found in the thick undergrowth and the chestnut woods of Monte Amiata. It has a distinctive yellowish cap with a flanged edge always turned downwards. Tasting of unripe fruit, it is much in demand for preserving in oil.

RAMERINO (ROSEMARY)
(Rosmarinus officinalis)
Parts of the coastal scrub are overrun with wild rosemary, loved for its heady scent and robust flavour.

OLOLO BIANCO
(Amanita ovoidea)
Among the sand dunes and pine woods by the sea you can find this mushroom, which looks a large white ball. When it opens it turns into a sturdy white mushroom with a large bulb at the base of the stalk and a ring with the texture of butter. It is good fried with garlic and parsley. Always check with an expert before eating, as the genus includes some very poisonous species.

Places of Interest

THERE IS MUCH to explore in the wild Maremma region: great areas of woodland separate the villages and conceal farms of different sizes, often offering unusual gastronomic delights. The following establishments are all tried and tested, but if visiting the region you will probably be able to make other exciting discoveries of your own. Look out for handwritten notices offering agricultural produce. In this ideal setting, there is an increasing number of small properties run by enthusiasts of organic farming and who breed cattle in the traditional way.

ALBINIA (GR)

 Tenuta La Parrina

località La Parrina
☎ 0564 862636.

This farm produces a wide range of goods. Wine is an essential part of it, with the various types of Parrina including an enjoyable Bianco Podere Tinaro and Rosso Riserva. Among the other wines, there is an interesting Ansonica Costa dell'Argentario. The olive oil, honey and cheese are very good. The farm has recently added agriturismo *to its attractions.*

 Azienda Bioagricola La Selva

località San Donato
☎ 0564/885669.

Situated near the sea, this estate has agriturismo *facilities and sells fresh*

vegetables, especially tomatoes, various kinds of preserves, and both classic sauces and a modern, creative range.

ARCIDOSSO (GR)

 Agriturismo Sorripe

frazione Montelaterone
☎ 0564 964186.

Agriturismo *facilities with a restaurant are available at this estate. It produces and sells fresh and dried chestnuts, chestnut flour and extra virgin olive oil.*

CASTEL DEL PIANO (GR)

 Corsini

via Cellane, 9
☎ 0564 956787.
◑ Sat pm.

For three generations the bread made here has been famous in southern

CALDARO

extra virgin olive oil • 1 onion, chopped • 1 chilli, chopped • 1 glass white wine • 250 g (9 oz) tomatoes, peeled • 300 g (10½ oz) octopus, ready prepared, rinsed and cut into pieces • 300 g (10½ oz) squid, cleaned and sliced • 2 scorpion fish • 1 John dory • 1 weever • 1 gurnard • 1 sea bream • a few cockles • 6 prawns • 300 g (10½ oz) sliced conger eel • 300 g (10½ oz) sliced moray eel • 1 stale loaf of bread • 2 cloves garlic, halved • chopped fresh parsley • salt

Heat some oil in a large pan, add the onion and chilli and cook until the onion has browned. Add the octopus and squid and cook until nearly tender. Stir in the wine, tomatoes and a little water, cook briefly, then add the other fish and season with salt. Slice the bread and rub the slices with the garlic. Arrange the bread in soup plates. As soon as the soup is fairly thick, pour it over the bread slices to serve.

Tuscany. Both classic Tuscan and other Italian cakes are made from natural ingredients in the traditional way.

CASTIGLIONE DELLA PESCAIA (GR)

 Enoteca Castiglionese di Luciano Lenzi

piazza Orsini, 18
☎ 0564 933572.
◑ Tues, Wed pm.
◐ Sun.

A broad, carefully chosen range of the best Tuscan DOC and DOCG wines, including 200 types of Chianti, 70 of Brunello and 20 of Vino Nobile can

The farmhouse of the Tenuta La Parrina at Albina

be found here. Practically all the producers of Bolgheri are found here, plus other significant Italian wines. There is also honey and local preserves in oil, and a selection of carefully chosen varieties of olive oil.

FOLLONICA (GR)

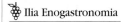

Ilia Enogastronomia

via Bicocchi, 83/85
☎ 0566 40093.
● Wed pm.

Traditional rustic soups, tortelloni maremmani and other stuffed pasta dishes are the specialities of this well-known delicatessen. It also offers a wide range of Tuscan wines and spirits. The store has an interesting selection of its own fresh and preserved produce and some imported goods. Recently it has opened a wine-tasting room.

Massai Drogheria e Pizzicheria

via Roma, 35
☎ 0566 263269.
● Wed pm.

This food shop has been in the same family certainly since 1867, when – as the proprietor likes to say – "round here it was all a swamp and the people lived in houses on stilts". Then, as now, it made its own classic Tuscan cakes and the recipes have not changed. Eugenio Massai selects the very best of the region's wines and foods. The delicatessen offers specialities made only from fresh produce and only to order.

Pescheria Pallino

Mercato coperto di piazza XXIV Maggio
☎ 0566 40322. ○ From Mon to Sat, am.

Cellar of the Azienda Agricola Val delle Rose

This fish shop sells fresh fish from the nearby ports of Argentario and Castiglione della Pescaia as well as from its own fish farms.

GROSSETO

Corsini

via Matteotti, 12/14
☎ 0564 416242.
● Only on Sun.

This is the sales point for the Corsini bakery at Casteldelpiano.

Apicoltura Rossi

viale Caravaggio, 62
☎ 0564 20459.

A most original fragrant blackthorn honey is one of various kinds of honey produced here. There are honey sweets in various flavours, including pine buds and woodland fruits.

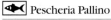 Azienda Agricola La Tartaruga-Motta

località Banditella di Alberese
☎ 0564 405105.

The estate's main wine is Morellino di Scansano, also available in a Riserva version. The other wines are based on local vines: Giove, a red made from Ciliegiolo grapes alone; and white Tartaruga from Trebbiano and Ansonica with a little Chardonnay.

Its honey, made from blackthorn, sunflowers and chestnut trees, is delicious.

Azienda Agricola Val delle Rose

località Poggio La Mozza
☎ 0564 409062. ▣

This estate has been taken over by the Cecchi family, who have widened the production range with wines from other parts of Tuscany. In this case they have added Morellino di Scansano, in both the regular and Riserva versions.

TOTANI RIPIENI

1 loaf of bread • white wine • extra virgin olive oil • 1 egg • 6 squid, cleaned • fresh thyme leaves • fresh parsley • 1 onion • 2 cloves garlic • 1 chilli • salt • pepper

Preheat the oven to 190°C (375°F/gas mark 5). Mix a little wine and oil with the egg and season with salt and pepper, then soak the bread in it. Cut off the squid tentacles and mince with the herbs and vegetables. Mix with the bread and use to stuff the squid. Close the opening with wooden cocktail sticks. Arrange in a dish, pour over a little more oil and wine and bake for 20 minutes. Cool, then slice to serve.

A view of Moris Farms

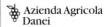 Fattoria Le Pupille

località Pereta
☎ 0564 409517.

The policy of this estate is research and innovation without neglecting the area's classic wine, Morellino di Scansano, also produced in a Riserva version. One of their innovations is Saffredi (from Cabernet Sauvignon, Merlot and Alicante). The estate's other produce includes various blends of extra virgin olive oil and preserves bottled in the estate's own oil under the "Solo Maremma" brand name.

ISOLA DEL GIGLIO (GR)

🍇 Azienda Agricola Danei

via G. Di Vittorio, 15
☎ 0564 863935.

This is the island's only estate of any size. The wines are based on Ansonica. The dry wines come in two versions: a more rustic, traditional one and a mellower version called Fior d'Ansonica. The sweet Passito is a rare wine sold in small half-litre (500 ml) bottles. The estate's headquarters are at Orbetello, via Bolgia 53.

MAGLIANO IN TOSCANA (GR)

🍇 Azienda Agricola Mantellassi

località Banditaccia
☎ 0564 592037.

The best best wine here is the Morellino di Sansano Riserva. Also worth noting is the red Querciolaia, from Alicante grapes.

MANCIANO (GR)

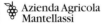 Caseificio Sociale

località Piano di Cirignano
Podere Fedeletto
☎ 0564 609137.
◉ Afternoons daily.

Here you can find pecorino at various degrees of maturity from the Maremma's biggest cheese dairy.

🍇 Azienda Agricola La Stellata

via Fornacina, 18
☎ 0564 620190.

Careful selection of the grapes guides the limited output of this small estate, which boasts one of the finest whites of the region, the Bianco di Pitigliano Lunaia. Also interesting is the Lunaia Rosso from Sangiovese, Ciliegiolo and Montepulciano d'Abruzzo, as well as the Grappa Lunaia, distilled from the leftovers after white grapes have been pressed. Its agriturismo facilities include accommodation in apartments.

MASSA MARITTIMA (GR)

🍇 Azienda Agricola Massa Vecchia

località Rocche
Podere Fornace
☎ 0566 904144.

This estate has two lines of production: one is innovative, embodied in La Fonte di Pietrarsa,

---

SCOTTIGLIA (MEAT AND TOMATO STEW)

extra virgin olive oil • 3 stalks celery, chopped • 3 carrots, chopped • 2 onions, chopped • 3 cloves garlic , chopped 1.5 kg (3 lb 5 oz) mixed meat (chicken, duck, rabbit, pigeon, lamb), cut into large pieces **• 500 g (1 lb 2 oz)** tomatoes **• 500 ml (18 fl oz)** red wine **• 1 fresh chilli,** chopped **• salt**

Heat some oil in a pan, add the celery, carrots, onions and garlic and fry lightly. Add the meat and fry until browned. Stir in the tomatoes, wine, chilli and salt. Cover the pan and simmer until the meat is tender, adding hot water if it becomes too dry.

BUGLIONE

• **1.5 kg (3 lb 5 oz) mixed cuts of lamb (such as leg, shoulder and loin), cut into pieces** • **1 onion, chopped** • **2 cloves garlic, chopped** • **1 fresh chilli, chopped** • **1 sprig of rosemary, chopped** • **1 glass Chianti** • **600 g (1 lb 5 oz) tomatoes, peeled** • **1 loaf of home-made bread** • **extra virgin olive oil** • **salt** • **pepper**

Put the meat in a pan with some oil and the chopped onion, garlic, chilli and rosemary. Brown the meat on all sides, then add the wine and cook until it evaporates. Add the tomatoes and dilute with a little hot water as the mixture cooks. When the meat is cooked, slice the bread and toast it. Dip the slices in the sauce and place them in a tureen. Pour the meat over them and serve.

from Cabernet Sauvignon; the other uses traditional vines for Le Veglie di Neri from Aleatico and a good Terziere from Alicante. Stone-ground wholemeal flour from an ancient local variety of maize is also produced.

 Moris Farms

località Curanuova
☎ 0566 919135.

One of the Maremma's most important estates by reason of its size – about 80 hectares (198 acres) of vines – and also by the praise lavished on its wines. They include a great Morellino di Sansano Riserva and an equally great younger Morellino. Also notable are the Avvoltore, from Cabernet Sauvignon and Sangiovese, and the Monteregio Rosso Moris. Its "La Mazzina" farm at Poggio Le Mozzine also produces extra virgin olive oil.

 Azienda Agraria Tesorino

località Valpiana
☎ 0566 55606.

This farm's main product and the only one on sale to visitors is an excellent, traditional extra virgin olive oil. For tourists using the agriturismo *facilities, there is no restaurant, only accommodation in houses and apartments and vegetables in season.*

MONTEMERANO (GR)

 Enoteca Perbacco

via della Chiesa, 8
☎ 0564 602817.
● Wed, Thurs am.
○ Sun.

This is the sales point for the Caino restaurant next door. It stocks the wines

on the restaurant's very fine wine list, with about 900 labels and ample space devoted to Tuscany. There are also cakes made in the restaurant kitchens, pickles and preserves in oil, coffees and olive oil.

MONTENERO D'ORCIA (GR)

 Frantoio Franci

via Grandi, 5
☎ 0564 954000.

This olive mill produces a wide and varied range of oils: a light, fruity oil for fish and delicate salads; medium fruity oil for all uses; and Villa Magra, the estate's own blend, which is intensely fruity and ideal for typical Tuscan dishes. This last one comes only from the Montenero and Montalcino olive groves, the other two come from neighbouring zones.

MONTEPESCALI SCALO (GR)

🫒 OLMA – Collegio Toscano Olivicoltori

località Madonnino, 3
☎ 0564 329090.

This mill presses the olives from its 870 member estates in the Maremma. The Madonnino, an excellent, intensely fruity oil with a distinctive bitter tinge, is bottled here.

The Azienda Agraria Tesorino at Massa Marittima

SPAGHETTI ALL'AMMIRAGLIA

2 kg (4 lb 8 oz) mussels, scrubbed • 600 g (1 lb 5 oz) spaghetti • extra virgin olive oil • 2 cloves garlic, chopped • 300 g (10½ oz) ripe tomatoes, sliced into strips • ½ fresh chilli, deseeded and chopped • 25 g (1 oz) chopped fresh parsley • salt

Put the mussels in a pan with some water, cover and cook until they all open. Remove the mussels from their shells and strain the water. Cook the pasta. Meanwhile, heat plenty of oil in a large pan and fry the garlic. Add the tomatoes, chilli, parsley and ½ glass of the mussel water. Drain the spaghetti and add to the pan with the mussels plus more of the water. Sauté briskly, stirring.

ORBETELLO (GR)

 Pescheria Covitto

via Volontari del Sangue, 15
☎ 0564 862632.
○ Sun am.

Excellent fresh fish from the Tuscan sea and the lagoon, purchased daily at local auctions, is on sale here.

✦ Pasticceria Ferrini

via Carducci, 8/10
☎ 0564 867265.
● Tues.
○ Sun.

With great bravura, Rita Ferrini continues the tradition begun by her grandfather in this quality patisserie, which sells classic fresh cakes and pastries, including fruit parcels, apple tarts and ricotta cakes. Ice-creams are also on offer.

 Orbetello Pesca lagunare

via Leopardi, 9
☎ 0564 860288.
○ Mon to Sat, mornings only.

Fresh fish from both sea and lagoon is available here, as well as various preserved delicacies, such as bottarga (grey mullet roe), smoked fillets of grey mullet and smoked eel.

 Azienda Agricola Rascioni e Cecconello

località Poggio Sugherino, frazione Fonteblanda
☎ 0564 885642.

The Poggio Capitana made from Sangiovese and Poggio Ciliegio from Ciliegiolo are wines that merit attention because of the skill of the estate's owners in bringing out the best in two traditional Tuscan vines.

PAGANICO (GR)

🍇 Distilleria Artigiana Nannoni

Fattoria Aratrice
☎ 0564 905204.
● Sat.

This distillery works for outside customers and also specializes in making its own grappa from Fragolino, a strawberry-scented grape – the estate has 25 hectares (62 acres) of vines. However, its most appealing products are fruit vinegars (plum, woodland berries, pear, orange) matured in small oak casks with the addition of small amounts of a distillate of the same fruit and beech shavings.

PITIGLIANO (GR)

🍇 Cantina Cooperativa di Pitigliano

via Nicola Ciacci, 974
☎ 0564 616133.

The Castle of Montepò near Scansano

This cooperative winery has about 700 members producing the grapes for the Bianco di Pitigliano and Duropersico, a white from an ancient local vine. It also produces a kosher wine for Jewish communities.

Macelleria Polidori

via Roma, 139
0564 616108.
Wed pm.
Sun.

Fresh local meats are sold here, as well as their own salumi – the one made from wild boar is very popular. Other specialities include dried boar's meat (coppiette), which is called "carne secca" here; schiacciata, also from boar; and turkey ham, a speciality of Jewish origin.

SATURNIA (GR)

Macelleria Vito Passalacqua

via Ciacci, 4
0564 601269.
Mon–Thurs only mornings; Fri, Sat all day.

This butcher's shop sells high quality beef and lamb exclusively from local breeders. The firm's own hams and salumi are also extremely good.

SCANSANO (GR)

Fratelli Andreini

frazione Poggioferro
via Amiatina, 25
0564 511002.

The Mignola extra virgin olive oil, exclusively from local olive groves, is an excellent oil with a medium fruity bouquet, fairly versatile and well suited to all local dishes.

POLLO ALLA CACCIATORA (HUNTER'S CHICKEN)

extra virgin olive oil • 2 onions, chopped • 3 cloves garlic, chopped • 3 spring chickens, each cut into 8 pieces • 1 glass white wine • 300 g (10½ oz) tomatoes, peeled • chopped fresh chilli to taste • salt

Heat the oil in a pan and lightly fry the onions and garlic. Add the chicken and brown on all sides. Pour in the wine and cook until it evaporates, then add the tomatoes, chilli and salt. Simmer until the chicken is cooked, adding hot water if the sauce starts to dry out.

Azienda Agraria di Montepò

Località Montepò
frazione Pancole
0564 580231.

The winery is set in a 16th-century castle perched on an imposingly rugged hill top and surrounded by vines. The estate has been actively producing wine only since the 1995 vintage. It immediately made its name due to the quality of its Morellino di Scansano and Rosso San Venanzio. It also produces fine meat from its select breed of Apennine sheep.

Erik Banti

località Fosso dei Molini
0564 508006.

This is one of the leading producers of Morellino di Scansano in the Ciabatta, a wine of excellent texture. The Aquilaia '95, made from Alicante and Morellino grapes, is also of interest.

Cantina Cooperativa Morellino di Scansano

località Saragiolo
0564 507288.

This hard-working cooperative winery makes a very fine Riserva version of the Morellino di Scansano wine. The younger versions of two special blends, Vignabenefizio and Roggiano, are extremely good.

SORANO (GR)

Azienda Agricola Sassotondo

frazione Sovana
località Pian di Conati, 52
0564 614218.

Set amid meadows and attractive woods, this organically farmed estate offers agriturismo with bedrooms and a shared kitchen. It is a new wine producer (its first wine was the 1997 vintage), but already it guarantees a product of good quality. The underground cellar, hewn out of tufa, holds a Bianco di Pitigliano, a Rosso Franze from Sangiovese grapes matured in barriques, and a Rosso which, since the 1999 vintage, qualifies for the new DOC Rosso di Sovana label. The estate also produces good extra virgin olive oil.

TRAVELLERS'
NEEDS

Restaurants

THE ADDRESSES THAT FOLLOW include the most celebrated restaurants in the region, as well as less well-known ones that are recommended for their careful presentation of the region's cuisine and its wines, in keeping with the philosophy of a gourmet guide. The list is based on such factors as the quality of the food and wine in relation to the kind of restaurant, the general standard of the food, and the exclusivity of the produce or the setting. For the price guide, €, see the inside back cover. The following criteria in each restaurant have been rated on a scale of 1 to 5.

Cellar: variety, quality and originality of the wine list.
Comfort: level of service, space between tables, the view, location, ease of parking, standard and cleanliness of the washrooms.
Tradition: conformity to local traditions and skill in choosing local ingredients.
Q/P: quality:price ratio (value for money).
☞ **Cooking pot:** a special merit for restaurants offering classic regional dishes cooked to perfection, and for the quality of the preparation and faithfulness to local traditions.
Ⓖ **Gourmet rosette:** a special merit mark for the quality of the cuisine, character of the dishes (authentically Italian), courteous staff and good service.

FLORENCE, AREZZO AND CASENTINO

ANGHIARI (AR)

Locanda Castello di Sorci

località San Lorenzo
☎ 0575 789066.
● Mon. €

This restaurant is run by Primetto, a friend of various well-known people, such as the political cartoonist Forattini, who drew the amusing wine labels. It is a must if you want to eat well and spend little. The tagliatelle are splendid, cut from enormous sheets of dough worked by the skilful chefs in a kitchen in full view of the customers.

CELLAR	●				
COMFORT	●				
TRADITION	●	●	●	●	●
Q/P	●	●	●	●	●

AREZZO

Antica Osteria L'Agania   ☞

via Mazzini, 10
☎ 0575 295381.
● Mon. €

Home-style cooking covering all the regional traditions, with the emphasis on game, can be found at this restaurant in the centre of Tuscany (don't miss the grifi con polenta*). The restaurant shows great flair in its use of wild herbs and the host is a great connoisseur of mushrooms (available from spring to winter).*

CELLAR	●	●			
COMFORT	●	●			
TRADITION	●	●	●	●	●
Q/P	●	●	●	●	

Il Saraceno

via Mazzini, 6a
☎ 0575 27644.
● Wed. €

You can enjoy authentic Arezzo cuisine at this small rustic restaurant. There is genuine Chianina beef, dishes of the local pork, game, mushrooms and classic soups. Everything is made on the premises. The cellar has a fascinating selection of all the best Tuscan wines.

CELLAR	●	●	●		
COMFORT	●	●	●		
TRADITION	●	●	●	●	●
Q/P	●	●	●	●	

BADIA TEDALDA (AR)

L'Erbhosteria del Castello

frazione Rofelle
☎ 0575 714017.
● Wed. €

This charming trattoria *is in a village high in the Apennines between Tuscany and Emilia Romagna. Its specialities are mushrooms and truffles and dishes based on wild herbs, such as omelettes with borage, or pastry cakes with alpine yarrow or thyme. There are good first and second courses of game and excellent beef from local pastures. The desserts are home-made and there are unusual wild herb and fruit liqueurs.*

CELLAR	●	●			
COMFORT	●	●	●		
TRADITION	●	●	●	●	
Q/P	●	●	●	●	

BORGO SAN LORENZO (FI)

Ristorante degli Artisti

piazza Romagnoli, 1
☎ 055 8457707.
● Wed. €€

Here, in an elegant late 19th-century ambience, Tuscan dishes feature on the richly traditional menu. There is Chianina beef from Cecchini and Cinta Senese pork from Massanera. Note the tortelli di patate al ragù, *a speciality of the Mugello. All the food is prepared on the premises.*

CELLAR	●	●	
COMFORT	●	●	●
TRADITION	●	●	●	●
Q/P	●	●	●

CAPRESE MICHELANGELO (AR)

Buca di Michelangelo

via Roma, 51
📞 0575 793921.
● Wed, Thu.
€

Real Tuscan mountain cuisine – unpretentious but with all the authentic flavours – is on offer at this simple restaurant. The desserts merit a special mention: they are very simple, but utterly delicious. The restaurant offers accommodation in a number of hotel rooms.

CELLAR	●	●	
COMFORT	●	●	
TRADITION	●	●	●	●
Q/P	●	●	●

CARMIGNANO (PO)

Biagio Pignatta

località Artimino
via Papa Giovanni XXIII
📞 055 8718086.
● Wed, Thurs midday.
€€

Fairly traditional Tuscan cooking is served at this restaurant, with the meat grilled over a wood fire. It also serves some fish

dishes. The fresh pasta and delicious pastries are all made on the spot. The restaurant's wine list is good, with a careful selection of local vintages from which to choose.

CELLAR	●	●	●
COMFORT	●	●	●
TRADITION	●	●	●
Q/P	●	●	●

Da Delfina 🍲

località Artimino
via della Chiesa, 1
📞 055 8718074.
● Mon, Sun evening.
€€€

This restaurant offers traditional Tuscan cuisine with some occasional variations on the basic theme. The classic dishes are all here, from ribollita *to pigeon. It is one of the few restaurants to make real* panzanella. *There are also good desserts. The wine list has a large selection of premium Carmignano wines. In summer you can eat outside on the attractive terrace with a wonderful view over the nearby Tuscan hills.*

CELLAR	●	●	●
COMFORT	●	●	●	●
TRADITION	●	●	●	●
Q/P	●	●	●	●

CASTELFRANCO DI SOPRA (AR)

Vicolo del Contento

via Ponte a Mandri, 38
📞 055 9149277.
● Mon, Tues, midday all weekdays.
€€€€

This restaurant is one of the jewels of the Valdarno. It serves excellent sea fish cooked in Mediterranean style and fine local meat.

Fresh seasonal produce is carefully selected for the fish and vegetable dishes (all dressed with the right oil). When they are in season, there are porcini, ovoli *and artichokes.*

CELLAR	●	●	●
COMFORT	●	●	●	●
TRADITION	●	●	
Q/P	●	●	●

FIESOLE (FI)

45 Piazzo Mino

piazza Mino da Fiesole, 45
📞 055 599854.
● Mon, midday
€€€€

This restaurant offers regional dishes and, in particular, fish dishes. There is an extensive wine list which includes useful and entertaining information. Wines are also sold by the glass.

CELLAR	●	●	●	●
COMFORT	●	●	●	●
TRADITION	●	●	
Q/P	●	●	●

CORTONA (AR)

Tonino

piazza Garibaldi, 1
📞 0575 630500.
● Wed, Mon evening (always open in summer).
€€€

Elegant in Art Nouveau style, this restaurant serves a rich range of antipasti, first courses of pasta and more or less classic second courses. The pasta, bread and desserts are all home-made.

CELLAR	●	●	●
COMFORT	●	●	●	●
TRADITION	●	●	●
Q/P	●	●	●

EMPOLI (FI)

La Panzanella ⊖

via dei Cappuccini, 10
☏ 0571 922182.
⏺ Sun, Sat.
€€

This is an old, family-run Florentine trattoria with period décor. The menu features the traditional, classic, hearty dishes of real home cooking, such as stracotto alla fiorentina. The pasta is home-made.

CELLAR	●	●		
COMFORT	●	●		
TRADITION	●	●	●	●
Q/P	●	●	●	●

FLORENCE

Caffè Concerto

lungarno Cristoforo Colombo, 7
☏ 055 677377.
⏺ Sun.
€€€

Gabriele Tarchiani's eclectic décor and the "Nouvelle Cuisine" here are a distinct innovation compared with the traditional style found in other restaurants in the area. The view of the river Arno from the veranda alone makes a visit worthwhile. Meat and fish are skilfully combined with seasonal vegetables in a choice of dishes. Their desserts are especially tempting.

CELLAR	●	●	●	●
COMFORT	●	●	●	
TRADITION	●			
Q/P	●	●	●	●

Cibreo

via Andrea del Verrocchio (corner with via dei Macci)
☏ 055 2341100.
⏺ Sun, Mon
€€€€€

This famous, elegant restaurant belongs to Fabio Picchi, who is very skilful at enhancing quite simple, traditional Tuscan dishes with his own special touch (there is no printed menu). The wide ranging and richly inventive Tuscan dishes are made on the premises from quality ingredients. Note the cuttlefish and other seafood dishes. The desserts are especially attractive. There is an international wine list with plenty of Tuscan wines. The restaurant's annex, the Vineria del Cibreino, is popular and always crowded due to its very reasonable prices (though the cooking is of the same standard).

CELLAR	●	●	●	●
COMFORT	●	●	●	●
TRADITION	●	●	●	●
Q/P	●	●	●	

Cinghiale Bianco

borgo San Jacopo, 43r
☏ 055 215706.
⏺ Wed. €€

This small restaurant is near the Ponte Vecchio on the Arno's "rive gauche". Try the first courses dressed with vegetables and good quality olive oil. The bistecca alla fiorentina and tagliata di manzo are both excellent. If you plan to go with someone special, book the table in the romantic niche on the second floor.

CELLAR	●	●		
COMFORT	●	●		
TRADITION	●	●	●	●
Q/P	●	●	●	●

Del Carmine ⊖

piazza del Carmine, 18
☏ 055 218601.
⏺ Sun. €

All the classic Florentine dishes, with occasional detours to other Italian provinces, are served here. The ribollita is notable, as are the various other soups. There are first courses of pasta, and fish is served on Friday. Don't miss the Florentine-style tripe.

CELLAR	●	●		
COMFORT	●	●	●	
TRADITION	●	●	●	●
Q/P	●	●	●	●

Il Latini

via dei Palchetti, 6r
☏ 055 210916.
⏺ Mon. €€

The setting here is a typical old-fashioned trattoria with Florentine and Chianti dishes, such as ribollita, pappa col pomodoro, spelt soup, pork, rabbit and Chianina steaks. Some of the ingredients come from local suppliers, and the wine and oil come from the owners' estate. The wine list has a selection of good Tuscan labels and there is a house wine served in flasks.

CELLAR	●	●		
COMFORT	●	●	●	
TRADITION	●	●	●	●
Q/P	●	●	●	

Le Mossacce

via del Proconsolo, 55r
☏ 055 294361.
⏺ Sat, Sun. €

The menu prices are not excessive when you think of the delicious Florentine food being served here. The restaurant has about 35 covers and its name alludes to the rapid rotation of diners as they give up their places to others waiting their turn. A good house wine (Chianti Colline Fiorentine) is served in flasks and other Chianti labels are also available.

CELLAR	●				
COMFORT	●				
TRADITION	●	●	●	●	●
Q/P	●	●	●	●	

Pane e Vino

via San Niccolò, 70, a/r
☎ 055 2476956.
🌑 Sun, midday.
€€€

As the name suggests, the wine here is particularly good. The restaurant has a wide range of very attractive regional dishes that are far from predictable. There is a choice selection of cheeses and the desserts are all prepared on the premises.

CELLAR	●	●	●	●	
COMFORT	●	●	●		
TRADITION	●	●	●		
Q/P	●	●	●		

Enoteca Pinchiorri

via Ghibellina, 87
☎ 055 242777.
🌑 Sun, Mon, Tue lunch.
€€€€€

Giorgio Pinchiorri and Annie Feolde fully deserve their world-wide fame for this restaurant. Every detail of the setting and service – its elegance, quality and sheer cachet – put it at the very top of the class in Italy and the rest of Europe. The cuisine is delectable and full of character, the ingredients are the very best the market offers, the cellar is among the finest in Europe. And the bill will reflect this.

CELLAR	●	●	●	●	●
COMFORT	●	●	●	●	●
TRADITION	●				
Q/P	●				

Ruggero

via Senese, 89r
☎ 055 220542.
🌑 Tues, Wed. €

A classic Florentine trattoria *in both the décor and the menu, which includes traditional* crostini *with regional* salumi, *various soups and* minestroni, ribollita *and* pappa col pomodoro, *with old-fashioned stews.*

CELLAR	●				
COMFORT	●	●			
TRADITION	●	●	●	●	●
Q/P	●	●	●		

FUCECCHIO (FI)

Le Vedute

frazione Ponte a Cappiano
via Romana Lucchese, 121
☎ 0571 297498.
🌑 Mon. €€€€

Quality fish dishes are the backbone of the menu, alternating with meat, and in particular game, all following the cycle of the seasons – mushrooms and truffles come in October, spring brings fresh vegetables, and so on. There is a careful selection of salumi – a wider choice in winter – and cheese. Pasta and desserts are home-made.

CELLAR	●	●	●	
COMFORT	●	●	●	
TRADITION	●			
Q/P	●	●	●	

LASTRA A SIGNA (FI)

Sanesi

via Arione, 33
☎ 055 8720234.
🌑 Mon, Sun evening.
€€

This historic restaurant in a lovely rustic setting has been in the same family for 170 years. It serves classic Tuscan home cooking, especially meat grilled over charcoal, such as bistecca alla fiorentina accompanied by beans.

MARRADI (FI)

Cucina il Camino

viale Baccarini, 38
☎ 055 8045069.
🌑 Wed. €€

Lovers of quality home cooking will enjoy this restaurant. The dishes are not always strictly Tuscan because geographically this is in Romagna. Worthy of note are the mushrooms in season, fresh pasta, meat roasted in the wood-burning oven and tasty desserts made with the celebrated local chestnuts.

CELLAR	●	●			
COMFORT	●	●	●		
TRADITION	●	●	●	●	●
Q/P	●	●	●		

PALAZZUOLO SUL SENIO (FI)

Locanda Senio

via Borgo dell'Ore, 1
☎ 055 8046019.
🌑 Tues, Wed, midday on weekdays. €€€

Sample traditional dishes of wild herbs and fruits, as well as ancient recipes handed down from memory by the old folk of the town, in this very interesting and original restaurant. Set in a 14th-century town in the Mugello, it uses local ingredients and the basic dishes are creatively assembled. There are some pleasant rooms available.

CELLAR	●	●	●		
COMFORT	●	●	●	●	
TRADITION	●	●	●	●	●
Q/P	●	●	●		

PRATO

Enoteca Barni

via Ferrucci, 22
☎ 0574 607845.
⬤ Sun, Sat midday.
€€

This pleasant, cheerful restaurant grew out of the success of a delicatessen, which at first offered meals only at midday. For several years now it has opened in the evenings as well and has retained its lively atmosphere. Three young chefs create tasty meat and fish dishes using plenty of fresh ingredients (including some unusual game). Everything is made on the premises, including the bread, fresh pasta and desserts. There is an international wine list.

CELLAR	●	●	●	●
COMFORT	●	●	●	●
TRADITION	●	●		
Q/P	●	●	●	

Osvaldo Baroncelli

via Fra Bartolomeo, 13
☎ 0574 23810.
⬤ Sun, Sat midday.
€€€€

Good food is served in elegant surroundings at this attractive restaurant. They use good quality meat and fish, some from outside the region but mostly local. Many of the dishes are inspired by traditional Tuscan ones. The desserts are delicious.

CELLAR	●	●	●	
COMFORT	●	●	●	
TRADITION	●	●		
Q/P	●	●	●	

Il Piraña

via Valentini, 11
☎ 0574 25746.
⬤ Sun, Sat midday.
€€€€

Fish dishes are the speciality of this popular restaurant. The simple Mediterranean-style dishes rely on high quality fresh ingredients for their excellent flavour. The home-made desserts are equally good.

CELLAR	●	●	●
COMFORT	●	●	●
TRADITION	●		
Q/P	●	●	●

PRATOVECCHIO (AR)

Accaniti

via Fiorentina, 14
☎ 0575 583345.
⬤ Tues. €

This is one of the rare restaurants with the courage to offer porcini *exclusively when they are found locally. The home-style cooking uses local ingredients, prepared in a way that maintains the wholesome quality.*

CELLAR	●	●			
COMFORT	●	●	●		
TRADITION	●	●	●	●	●
Q/P	●	●	●		

Quattro Cantoni

via Uffenheim, 10
☎ 0575 582696.
⬤ Mon.
€

This trattoria *serves good traditional cooking. There is a wide choice of first course dishes, including* tagliatelle, tortelli di patate *and* tortelli di carne, ravioli di magro *(ravioli stuffed with spinach and ricotta),* gnocchi *and* strozzapreti. *For a second course there are roasted and grilled meats.*

CELLAR	●	●		
COMFORT	●	●		
TRADITION	●	●	●	●
Q/P	●	●	●	

SANSEPOLCRO (AR)

Balestra

via dei Montefeltro, 29
☎ 0575 735151.
⬤ Mon, Sun evening.
€

This is a classic Tuscan restaurant in a modern setting. The restaurant gets its name from the fact that all the members of the family who own it are expert marksmen with crossbows. Creative cooking enhances the regional ingredients (plus a few from neighbouring Umbria and Marche). The pasta is hand-made and fresh Italian mushrooms and truffles are served when they are in season.

CELLAR	●	●	●	
COMFORT	●	●	●	
TRADITION	●	●	●	
Q/P	●	●	●	

Da Paola e Marco Mercati all'albergo Oroscopo

località Pieve Vecchia
via Togliatti, 68
☎ 0575 734875.
⬤ Sun, midday.
€€€€

Set in a lovely 19th-century building, this small restaurant has a rustic yet elegant quality. The fine cuisine consists partly of regional dishes and partly of innovative modern recipes. The desserts are excellent and there is a choice wine list, which includes some notable wines. The restaurant also has some attractive rooms available.

CELLAR	●	●	●	●
COMFORT	●	●	●	●
TRADITION	●	●		
Q/P	●	●	●	

Da Ventura

via Aggiunti, 30
█ 0575 742560.
● Sat.
€€

*Reflecting influences
from three different
regions – Tuscany,
Romagna and Umbria –
this restaurant serves
simple, tasty traditional
dishes from all their
cuisines. Alongside
Chianti beef there is
suckling pig and shin
of pork, freshly made
pasta (wonderful tagliolini
with truffles) and good
desserts. The restaurant
has accommodation in
six bedrooms.*

CELLAR	●	●		
COMFORT	●	●	●	
TRADITION	●	●	●	●
Q/P	●	●	●	●

TERRANUOVA BRACCIOLINI (AR)

Ristorante Pin Rose

località Cicogna
via La Pineta, 38
█ 055 9703833.
● Mon, Tues.
€€€

*The owner belongs to a
family of fish wholesalers
and this restaurant
specializes in Tuscan
fresh fish dishes. The
huge restaurant is
situated in an enormous
wood of ancient pine
and oak trees. The
fish comes mostly from
Porto Santo Stefano,
Piombino and Viareggio.
The cellar has a good
selection of wines from
the Veneto, Friuli, Alto
Adige, Tuscany and
Sardinia.*

CELLAR	●	●		
COMFORT	●	●	●	
TRADITION	●			
Q/P	●	●	●	

LUNIGIANA, GARFAGNANA AND VERSILIA

CAMAIORE (LU)

Ristorante Conca Verde da Tiziano

via Misciano, 22
█ 0584 984700.
● Tue. €€

*Following the success of
his wife's cooking for
their wine shop, Encota
Nebraska, the owner
embarked on this
restaurant. The menu
combines the authentic,
traditional specialities
of Lucca with a more
innovative cuisine.*

CELLAR	●	●	●
COMFORT	●	●	●
TRADITION	●	●	●
Q/P	●	●	●

Ristorante Emilio e Bona

località Lombrici, 22
█ 0584 989289.
● Mon. €€€

*In an old olive mill by
a mountain stream,
Tuscan and classic Italian
dishes are served. The
food is prepared with a
light touch and the meals
finish with a few carefully
chosen home-made
desserts. The wine list is
Tuscan and Italian with
some French.*

CELLAR	●	●	●
COMFORT	●	●	●
TRADITION	●	●	●
Q/P	●	●	●

Ristorante Vignaccio

località Santa Lucia
via della Chiesa
█ 0584 914200.
● Wed. €€

*Flavoursome traditional
dishes are served at this*

*restaurant in the hills.
Classic regional
specialities are combined
with other dishes made
from quality Italian and
international ingredients.
A rich selection of Italian
and French cheeses and
excellent desserts follows.
The cellar has many
delightful regional wines.*

CELLAR	●	●	●
COMFORT	●	●	●
TRADITION	●	●	●
Q/P	●	●	●

CAPANNORI (LU)

La Cecca

località Coselli
█ 0583 94130.
● Mon, Wed evening.
€€

*Here, the dishes take their
theme, in rotation, from
Garfagnana and
Lucchesia, with rustic
dishes like biroldo (blood
pudding) or a polenta of
chestnut flour and other
more elaborate dishes.
There is meat grilled over
charcoal, good salumi,
and rural desserts. The
wines are mainly
regional.*

CELLAR	●	●		
COMFORT	●	●	●	
TRADITION	●	●	●	●
Q/P	●	●	●	●

CARRARA

Da Venanzio

località Colonnata
█ 0585 758062.
● Thurs, Sun evening.
€€€

*The cuisine here is mainly
regional and confined to
seasonal produce.
Everything is made in the
kitchens, including a rich
selection of desserts. The
cellar is mostly Tuscan*

with various notable Italian or foreign wines. But Venanzio is above all undisputed king of lardo: his lardo di Colonnata, seasoned with herbs is world famous. Venanzio cures his beef for the carpaccio in brine left over from the lardo.

CELLAR	●	●	●	●
COMFORT	●	●	●	
TRADITION	●	●	●	
Q/P	●	●	●	●

CUTIGLIANO (PT)

Trattoria da Fagiolino

via Carega, 1
☎ 0573 68014.
🌑 Wed, Tues evening.
€€

Classic Tuscan mountain dishes are served here, with mushrooms and game in season, plus kid and steak. There are first courses with home-made pasta and various soups. The menu finishes with a wide range of desserts.

CELLAR	●	●		
COMFORT	●	●		
TRADITION	●	●	●	●
Q/P	●	●	●	●

FORTE DEI MARMI (LU)

Lorenzo

via Carducci, 61
☎ 0584 84030.
🌑 Mon. €€€€

This elegant restaurant, run with passion and skill by Lorenzo Viani, is a shrine to Tuscan and Italian gourmets. All the ingredients are exceptional, especially the fish which Viani gets twice daily from trusted sources. The chef, who does not lack creativity when needed, often holds back to keep things simple to

highlight the freshness and quality of the food. There are specialities like "bavette sul pesce", spaghetti with tiny squid scented with sage or bocconcini di pescatrice with slivers of artichokes. For meat-lovers there is equally good fare. The wine list is one of the finest in Italy.

CELLAR	●	●	●	●	●
COMFORT	●	●	●	●	
TRADITION	●	●	●		
Q/P	●	●	●		

LUCCA

Buca di Sant'Antonio

via della Cervia, 1/3
☎ 0583 55881.
🌑 Mon, Sun evening.
€€

There was an inn on this site as long ago as the 17th century. Nowadays it is an elegant rural restaurant featuring regional specialities with certain innovations. The meat and vegetable dishes are imaginative, and the desserts reflect the town's gastronomic traditions. There is a good choice of wines at reasonable prices.

CELLAR	●	●	●	●
COMFORT	●	●	●	●
TRADITION	●	●	●	●
Q/P	●	●	●	

Canuleia

via Canuleia, 14
☎ 0583 467470.
🌑 Sun. €

This very attractive restaurant is in an ancient vault behind piazza dell'Anfiteatro. Great care is evident in the choice of ingredients, from the vegetables to the oil, and from the breads to the meat. The dishes reflect the traditions of Lucca with some modern touches.

CELLAR	●	●		
COMFORT	●	●	●	
TRADITION	●	●	●	●
Q/P	●	●	●	●

Da Giulio - in Pelleria

via delle Conce, 45
☎ 0583 55948.
🌑 Sun, Mon. €

The menu here features the classic dishes of Lucca, starting with antipasti of crostini, salumi and other rustic specialities, and continuing with local minestre and soups, meat and game, almost all in rustic style.

CELLAR	●	●		
COMFORT	●	●		
TRADITION	●	●	●	●
Q/P	●	●	●	●

MONTIGNOSO (MS)

Il Bottaccio

via Bottaccio,1
☎ 0585 340031.
€€€€€

An enchanting Relais & Châteaux (historic hotel), set in an old oil mill, has a restaurant which is acquiring an increasingly leading role thanks to the quality and character of the cuisine. The menu includes fresh seafood, good meat (especially the game) and extremely good cakes and pastries.

CELLAR	●	●	●	●
COMFORT	●	●	●	●
TRADITION	●	●		
Q/P	●			

PESCIA (PT)

Cecco

viale Forti, 96
☎ 0572 477955.
🌑 Mon.
€€

This restaurant has always been a shrine to the green asparagus of Pescia, the most prized in all Tuscany – but only in springtime. The rest of the year try the local mushrooms, truffles, Sorana beans and whatever else the season offers. Everything is made on the premises and there is a marked preference for local produce. The house speciality is chicken "al mattone". The wine list is largely Tuscan with some whites from Friuli.

CELLAR	●	●			
COMFORT	●	●	●		
TRADITION	●	●	●	●	●
Q/P	●	●	●	●	

PIETRASANTA (LU)

L'Enoteca Marcucci

via Garibaldi, 40
℡ 0584 791962.
● Mon, midday daily.
©©©

This is somewhere halfway between a wine bar and a restaurant. It presents simple country and seafood dishes with a regional accent, chosen especially to accompany the excellent wines in the cellar.

CELLAR	●	●	●	●	●
COMFORT	●	●			
TRADITION	●	●	●		
Q/P	●	●	●	●	

PISTOIA

Trattoria dell'Abbondanza

via dell'Abbondanza, 10/14
℡ 0573 368037.
● Wed, Thu lunch. ©

Here you will find Tuscan cuisine prepared the old way – no cream or frozen foods, and only seasonal produce fresh from the kitchen garden. Among the regular dishes are bollito misto, chicken and fried vegetables with good oil, and fish (on Fridays). The desserts are home-made. There is no wine list, just the house red and white.

CELLAR	●				
COMFORT	●	●	●		
TRADITION	●	●	●	●	●
Q/P	●	●	●	●	

Il Castagno di Pier Angelo   ⓖ

località Piteccio
via del Castagno, 46/b
℡ 0573 42214. ● Mon, midday on weekdays.
©©©

Set in a glade of chestnut trees, this restaurant provides good service with its three menus, featuring meat, fish and creative dishes. They are all based on traditional cuisine, but with innovative touches. The imagination shown in the fish cuisine is truly admirable, as is the originality shown in finding ingredients from Tuscany and the rest of Italy. The wine list prices are reasonable.

CELLAR	●	●	●	●	
COMFORT	●	●	●	●	●
TRADITION	●	●	●		
Q/P	●	●	●	●	

PODENZANA (MS)

La Gavarina d'Oro   ◔

via Castello, 13
℡ 0187 410021.
● Wed. ©

This is the right place to sample the famous panigacci, once a simple dish of Lunigiana, now a traditional delicacy: focaccine cooked between two testi (earthenware pans) and flavoured with pesto or mushrooms. There is also chargrilled meat, testaroli and other fresh pasta and simple traditional dishes.

CELLAR	●				
COMFORT	●				
TRADITION	●	●	●	●	●
Q/P	●	●	●	●	●

PONTE A MORIANO (LU)

La Mora   ⓖ

via Sesto di Moriano
℡ 0583 406402.
● Wed. ©©©

La Mora means "the stopover" and this is the place to stop if you want to eat good Tuscan food or simply eat and drink well. The well-established restaurant is Sauro Brunicardi's jewel (his family has run it since 1867). He is a passionate lover of his region and of good wine. This is apparent in the excellent cellar which has everything from the Lucca area and much from the other regions of Italy and the world, as well as a distinctive choice of spirits and liqueurs. The Garfagnana cuisine – modernized where necessary – is equally good and the restaurant has an elegant, hospitable atmosphere. Try the gran farro and local porcini.

CELLAR	●	●	●	●	
COMFORT	●	●	●	●	
TRADITION	●	●	●	●	
Q/P	●	●	●		

UZZANO (PT)

Mason

via Parri, 56
℡ 0572 451363.
● Wed, midday Sat.
©©©

The chef's skill is displayed to best advantage in the fish and game bird dishes in this restaurant, which is tucked away in the hills between Pescia and Montecatini. The cuisine is traditional, local Tuscan but it has a very distinctive personal touch that serves to show off the produce at its best.

CELLAR	●	●	●		
COMFORT	●	●	●		
TRADITION	●	●	●	●	
Q/P	●	●	●		

VIAREGGIO (LU)

Gusmano

via Regia, 58
C 0584 31233.
● Tues, lunchtime on weekdays in summer.
€€€

Situated in the heart of Viareggio, this pleasant restaurant is distinguished by its excellent fish cuisine. Importantly for a seafood restaurant, fresh fish is delivered twice a day thanks to the good rapport between the restaurant owner and the fishermen who cast their nets in the waters off Viareggio.

CELLAR	●	●	●	
COMFORT	●	●	●	●
TRADITION	●	●	●	
Q/P	●	●	●	

Oca Bianca

via Coppino, 409
C 0584 388477.
● Tues, lunchtime.
€€€€

Upstairs with a view over the sea and the harbour, in a luxurious setting with a very distinctive décor, is a traditional restaurant. The cuisine is mainly seafood with a tried and tested menu. The fish is local, the

cellar huge (2,000 wines) and excellent. Downstairs at the Bistrot dell'Oca the mood changes. There are wines by the glass, great dishes of oysters and other French-style raw shellfish, steam-cooked seafood, Catalan-style lobsters, soups according to the season and a choice of over 100 international cheeses, all at very reasonable prices.

CELLAR	●	●	●	●	●
COMFORT	●	●	●	●	●
TRADITION	●	●	●		
Q/P	●	●	●		

Romano

via Mazzini, 120
C 0584 31382.
● Mon.
€€€€

This is one of the best seafood restaurants in Italy. Romano and Franca Franceschini cook wonderful dishes from high quality fresh fish. Their menu is a stunning mixture of simplicity and creativity, with harmonious colours, aromas and accompaniments. Trying to choose between stuffed baby squid, sparnocchi (mantis shrimps) with honey or cacciucco alla viareggina (Viareggio-style fish soup) is hard because all the dishes are an inspiration. The excellent extra virgin olive oil and perfectly fresh vegetables only serve to enhance the dishes. The style of the desserts is just as good, and the quality and variety of the cellar puts it on the same level. Try the Montecarlo wine from the restaurant's own vineyard, a white well above the average.

CELLAR	●	●	●	●	●
COMFORT	●	●	●	●	
TRADITION	●	●	●		
Q/P	●	●	●		

BIBBONA (LI)

La Pineta

località Marina di Bibbona
via dei Cavalleggeri, 27
C 0586 600016.
● Mon. €€€

The owners of this seafront restaurant have no fewer than three fishing boats in the family, which augurs well for the fresh fish which is its staple fare. The fish comes to the table perfectly fresh in simple dishes, accompanied by equally fresh vegetables. Other dishes on the menu are either made on the premises or by local producers – even the mayonnaise is made on the spot with extra virgin olive oil. The cellar contains a wide selection of mostly Italian wines with the odd French label.

CELLAR	●	●	●
COMFORT	●	●	
TRADITION	●	●	●
Q/P	●	●	●

CAPOLIVERI – ELBA (LI)

Il Chiasso

vicolo Sauro, 13
C 0565 968709. **●** Tues, lunchtime. **□** April-Oct.
€€€

The layout of this restaurant is unusual. Situated in a small street in the town, it has tables set outside and two rustic dining rooms at the side. The affable host, Luciano, serves octopus with potatoes (minestrone di polpo), Livorno-style mullet in a pot, spaghetti with amberjack roe or served alla Chiasso (with sea urchins, prawns and *tomatoes), and other seafood dishes, with both local and regional recipes.*

CELLAR	●	●	●	
COMFORT	●	●	●	
TRADITION	●	●	●	●	●
Q/P	●	●	●	●

Da Pilade

località Marina di Mola
📞 0565 968635.
🕐 Easter–Oct. €€

Tuscan fish and meat dishes are served here – grilled meat, game in season, fresh fish, and the island's mushrooms. Desserts include sorbets and schiacciata *(fruit bread). This is a hotel as well as a restaurant.*

CELLAR	●	●	●
COMFORT	●	●	●
TRADITION	●	●	●
Q/P	●	●	●

CASTAGNETO CARDUCCI (LI)

Ristorante Da Ugo

via Pari, 3
📞 0565 763746.
🕐 Mon. €

This restaurant offers traditional Tuscan and Maremma cooking with particular emphasis on mushrooms and game. Wood pigeon, pork and rabbit are served, plus some seafood, especially in summer. The owner also runs the Enoteca Il Borgo opposite the restaurant.

CELLAR	●	●	●	
COMFORT	●	●		
TRADITION	●	●	●	●	●
Q/P	●	●	●	

Zi' Martino

località San Giusto, 264
📞 0565 763666.
🕐 Mon. €

This inexpensive rustic trattoria is typically Tuscan. You can find wild boar, lamb and grilled meats and tortelli on the menu.

CELLAR	●	●		
COMFORT	●	●		
TRADITION	●	●	●	●	●
Q/P	●	●	●	●

CECINA (LI)

Antica Cecina

via Cavour, 17
📞 0586 681528.
🕐 Sun.
€€

The setting here is very pleasant with the atmosphere of an old inn. The day's menu depends on the market, especially for fish. Dishes include home-made pasta, fresh local fish, tripe and salt cod cooked in a sweet and sour sauce with onions and potatoes. The desserts are all made on the premises.

CELLAR	●	●		
COMFORT	●	●		
TRADITION	●	●	●	●	●
Q/P	●	●	●	●	●

LARI (PI)

Castero

località Lavaiano
via Galilei, 2
📞 0587 616121.
🕐 Sun evening, Mon.
€€

A must for its meat dishes grilled over charcoal, this pleasant family-run restaurant features typical, simple Tuscan cuisine. The pork, beef (not Chianina), lamb and much else are all choice quality and the ingredients (especially the salumi *) are local.*

CELLAR	●	●	●	
COMFORT	●	●	●	
TRADITION	●	●	●	●
Q/P	●	●	●	●	●

LIVORNO

Antico Moro

via Bartelloni, 59
📞 0586 884659.
🕐 Wed.
€€

The classic local fish dishes – the usual grilled fish and fritto misto *– are on offer here, but there is also steak for dedicated meat-eaters.*

CELLAR	●	●		
COMFORT	●	●		
TRADITION	●	●	●	●
Q/P	●	●	●	

La Barcarola

viale Carducci, 39
📞 0586 402367.
🕐 Sun.
€€

The family who own this restaurant have run it for over 60 years, so they have built up a close relationship with their suppliers. This ensures good quality local fish, which is the mainstay of the menu. Cacciucco is one of the traditional dishes found all year round. There is a good choice of first and second courses, which are exclusively seafood.

CELLAR	●	●	●
COMFORT	●	●	●
TRADITION	●	●	●	●
Q/P	●	●	●

Ciglieri

frazione Ardenza
via Franchini, 38
📞 0586 508194.
🕐 Wed.
€€€€€

This elegant restaurant uses good quality regional ingredients (including fresh vegetables, pigeons and Chianina beef) to produce creative traditional recipes. The bread, pasta and pastry are all home-made.

CELLAR	●	●	●	●
COMFORT	●	●	●	
TRADITION	●	●		
Q/P	●	●		

MARCIANA – ELBA (LI)

Publius   ○

località Poggio
piazza del Castagneto
☎ 0565 99208.
● Mon. ☐ Mar–Nov.
€€

Fine regional cooking and courteous service can be found here. Many of the dishes are based on fresh fish, such as stoccafisso all'elbana, *but there are also meat and game dishes. The restaurant is good value for money and the terrace has a fine sea view.*

CELLAR	●	●	●	
COMFORT	●	●	●	
TRADITION	●	●	●	
Q/P	●	●	●	●

MARCIANA MARINA – ELBA (LI)

Capo Nord

località La Fenicia
☎ 0565 996983.
● Mon. ☐ April–Dec.
€€€€

Elba's classic dishes, such as stock fish with potatoes, are alternated with fresh fish cooked very simply in salt at this seafront restaurant. There are plenty of creative ideas for using the produce from the island and nearby

areas. The desserts, presented in a separate menu, are good. There is an international wine list.

CELLAR	●	●	●	
COMFORT	●	●	●	●
TRADITION	●	●	●	
Q/P	●	●	●	

Rendez Vous – Da Marcello

piazza della Vittoria, 1
☎ 0565 99251/99298.
● Wed. ☐ Mar–Oct.
€€

At this restaurant fish and other seafood are cooked both in simple, tasty dishes and in more sophisticated forms, including potato stuffed with a mixture of polpa di pesce *(filleted fish) and shellfish roasted in a wood-burning oven (along with other kinds of fish).*

CELLAR	●	●	●
COMFORT	●	●	●
TRADITION	●	●	●
Q/P	●	●	●

MONTOPOLI VAL D'ARNO (PI)

Quattro Gigli

piazza Michele, 2
☎ 0571 466878.
● Mon, Sun evening
(10 Jan–31 Mar).
€€

Here flavour is wedded to culture. Many of the traditional dishes are taken from ancient – mostly Renaissance – Florentine recipe books, the fruit of careful historical research. The results are some excellent savoury dishes with fruit as one of the ingredients. More recent tradition is not neglected: there is ribollita, *classic Tuscan meat dishes, and also stock fish and salt cod. In season there are truffles*

and mushrooms from San Miniato. The wine list has a good selection of Tuscan labels. The restaurant has some bedrooms available.

CELLAR	●	●	●	●
COMFORT	●	●	●	●
TRADITION	●	●	●	●
Q/P	●	●	●	●

PISA

Artilafo

via Volturno, 38
☎ 050 27010.
● Sun.
€€€

International cuisine – revisited and revised in some cases – and simple but creative meat and fish courses are on the menu at this tasteful restaurant. There is no printed wine list but the cellar contains about 300 wines from all over Italy.

CELLAR	●	●	●
COMFORT	●	●	●
TRADITION	●		
Q/P	●	●	●

Bruno

via Bianchi, 12
☎ 050 560818.
● Tues, Monday evening.
€€

Enjoy typical Pisan cooking at this rustic family-run restaurant. Dishes include salt cod with leeks, Pisan-style stock fish and seppie in zimino *(cuttlefish soup).*

CELLAR	●	●			
COMFORT	●	●			
TRADITION	●	●	●	●	●
Q/P	●	●			

Cagliostro

via del Castelletto, 26
☎ 050 575413.
● Tues. €€

This highly unusual trattoria *is in an ancient monastery which has been renovated in a modern, airy style and is also used for art exhibitions. The creative seasonal cuisine is based on produce from the land. Traditional Tuscan dishes are not listed on the menu but patrons can order them. The desserts are home-made and the chocolate ones deserve a special mention, especially the steamed chocolate pudding. The wine bar has about 300 Italian wines. There are selections of Italian and foreign cheeses and* salumi *from the Marches.*

CELLAR	●	●	●
COMFORT	●	●	●
TRADITION	●		
Q/P		●	●	●

Osteria dei Cavalieri

via San Frediano, 16
【 050 580858.
● Sun, Saturday lunchtime. €

Interesting Tuscan cuisine offers very good value for money here. Ingredients are fresh, seasonal and mostly local. The cellar has a good selection of Italian wines and the extra virgin olive oil comes from a small producer nearby. The restaurant offers three "tasting menus": fish, meat and vegetarian.

CELLAR	●	●	●	
COMFORT	●	●	●	
TRADITION	●	●	●	●
Q/P	●	●	●	●

PONTEDERA (PI)

La Polveriera

via Marconcini, 54
【 0587 54765.
● Sun.
€€

This restaurant is rich in character and culinary intuition, producing interesting seafood dishes combined with the region's herbs and vegetables.

CELLAR	●		
COMFORT	●	●	●
TRADITION	●		
Q/P		●	●	●

PORTOFERRAIO – ELBA (LI)

La Barca

via Guerrazzi, 60
【 0565 918036.
● Wed. €€

This small restaurant on the seafront offers high quality dishes made with fresh ingredients, all at reasonable prices. The cuisine is mainly seafood, grilled over a wood fire.

CELLAR	●	●		
COMFORT	●	●		
TRADITION	●	●	●	●
Q/P	●	●	●	●

RIO MARINA – ELBA (LI)

La Canocchia

via Palestro, 3
【 0565 962432.
● Mon (except summer).
◻ Mar–Oct. €€

For some years this has been the premier restaurant on Elba, one not to miss. The menu features local recipes plus original ideas based on fresh seafood. There is a broad range of first courses and a good selection of the island's wines.

CELLAR	●	●		
COMFORT	●	●	●	
TRADITION	●	●	●	●
Q/P	●	●	●	●

SAN MINIATO (PI)

Il Convio

località San Maiano
【 0571 408114.
● Wed.
€€

This elegantly rustic restaurant is deep in the countryside. The cuisine is traditional with regional recipes. It specializes in both classic and modern, creative dishes made with the local white truffles. The wine from the owner's estate (Alto Desco) is particularly good.

CELLAR	●	●	●
COMFORT	●	●	●
TRADITION	●	●	●
Q/P		●	●	●

SAN VINCENZO (LI)

Il Bucaniere

viale Marconi
【 0565 705555.
● Tues.
◻ Only in the summer season.
€€

In a wooden cabin on stilts by the sea, Fulvietto Pierangelini, son of the well-known restaurateur Fulvio, who owns the Gambero Rosso (see p184), runs this restaurant. Open only in the evenings, it offers real seafood delicacies. There are one-course meals, antipasti *and first courses, both traditional and creative modern dishes, all using good quality ingredients. The cheese trolley has fine Tuscan cheeses, the desserts are interesting and the wine list (only Tuscan and French) is small but carefully chosen.*

CELLAR	●	●		
COMFORT	●	●	●	
TRADITION	●	●	●	
Q/P	●	●	●	●

Gambero Rosso

piazza della Vittoria,
13
☎ 0565 701021.
◐ Mon, Tues in winter.
€€€€€

*Fulvio Pierangelini is the
owner and chef of this
splendid, unforgettable,
small restaurant – one of
the most famous in Italy –
serving fine food. He has
an unerring instinct for
flavours and scents, and a
quite exceptional ability to
improvise. Everything at
the Gambero Rosso is
perfect: carefully chosen
raw materials from all
over Europe combined
with fresh meat and fish
from his own region. The
dishes are light and full of
flavour, with the cooking
beautifully timed. Tasteful
tables are laid under the
watchful eye of Emanuela,
the* padrona di casa. *The
cellar, which contains an
international range of
wines, is one of the most
outstanding in Italy. Even
the price:quality ratio is
very good if you choose the
"tasting menu".*

CELLAR	●	●	●	●
COMFORT	●	●	●	●
TRADITION	●	●		
Q/P	●	●	●	

STAFFOLI (PI)

Da Beppe

via Livornese, 35/37
☎ 0571 37002.
◐ Mon, Sun evening.
€€€€

*Located in the hills, this
restaurant traditionally
offered a meat-based
menu when the present
owner's father ran it.
Nowadays, fish is*

*favoured on the menu,
but there is still a small
space for the style of the
past. The dishes are based
on local produce, with
ideas from other regions
and countries. There is
a good wine list with an
eye to the whites.*

CELLAR	●	●	●	●
COMFORT	●	●	●	●
TRADITION	●	●		
Q/P	●	●	●	

SUVERETO (LI)

Eno-oliteca Ombrone

piazza dei Giudici, 1
☎ 0565 829336.
◐ Mon. €€€€

*This restaurant is in a
renovated 14th-century
olive mill. Giancarlo Bini
was one of the first – if
not the first – to provide
in his restaurant
(formerly at Grosseto) an
informative list of types
of olive oil and combine
each dish with the right
oil. In his new premises he
has continued along the
same lines, offering a
choice of no fewer than
168 kinds of extra virgin
olive oil from all over Italy.
The cuisine is excellent
and definitely regional.
Note particularly the wild
boar (in the traditional
recipe* alla bracconiera*)
and the game. The
restaurant's* salumi *and
desserts are excellent.*

CELLAR	●	●	●	●
COMFORT	●	●	●	
TRADITION	●	●	●	
Q/P	●	●	●	

TIRRENIA (PI)

Dante e Ivana

via del Tirreno, 207/c
☎ 050 32549.
◐ Sun, Mon lunchtime.
€€€€

*This fish restaurant
specializes in shellfish from
the markets at Viareggio
and Livorno. The dishes,
which reflect the day's
catch, do full justice to
the fish.*

CELLAR	●	●	●	●
COMFORT	●	●	●	
TRADITION	●			
Q/P	●	●	●	

ULIVETO TERME (PI)

Osteria Vecchia Noce

località Noce
☎ 050 788229.
◐ Wed, Tues evening.
€€

*Set in an 18th-century
olive mill in a medieval
town, this restaurant
serves traditional Tuscan
cuisine with a very light
touch. It uses only local
and seasonal produce
and fish brought to the
nearby ports. Everything is
home-made. The* anatra in
dolceforte *(sweet and sour
duck), marinated boar
with polenta, and the
suckling pig are especially
interesting dishes to try.
The wines are Italian –
mainly Tuscan – with the
occasional foreign wine.*

CELLAR	●	●	●	
COMFORT	●	●	●	
TRADITION	●	●	●	●
Q/P	●	●	●	●

VADA (LI)

Il Ducale

piazza Garibaldi, 33
☎ 0586 788600.
◐ Mon. €€€

*Situated in an elegant
19th-century building,
this restaurant serves its
customers traditional
seafood cuisine. Its fish is
supplied almost exclusively
by local fishermen. The*

home-made bottarga *(dried, salted fish roe) uses roe from various kinds of fish.*

CELLAR	●	●	●		
COMFORT	●	●	●		
TRADITION	●	●	●		
Q/P		●	●	●	

VOLTERRA (PI)

Vecchio Mulino

Saline di Volterra
via del Molino
C 0588 44060.
● Mon, Sun evening (winter).
€€

The setting for this delightful restaurant is a renovated old mill. The restaurant's sophisticated cuisine is based on meat (game in autumn and winter), with plenty of fresh vegetables in season, and mushrooms depending on the time of year. The dishes have a regional flavour with some added personal touches. There are some rooms available for people to stay.

CELLAR	●	●	●	
COMFORT	●	●	●	
TRADITION	●	●	●	●
Q/P		●	●	●

CHIANTI AND SIENA

CASTELLINA IN CHIANTI (SI)

Antica Trattoria La Torre

piazza del Comune, 15
C 0577 740236.
● Fri. €€

The tables and chairs at this restaurant are set out in the attractive medieval piazza and the food is cooked on an open spit. The cuisine is typical of

Chianti with ribollita, *home-made pasta,* crostini, *Chianina beef and pigeon, plus a good choice of home-made desserts. The restaurant's cellar stocks a good range of the top Tuscan wines plus a selection of other wines from northern Italy.*

CELLAR	●	●	●		
COMFORT	●	●	●		
TRADITION	●	●	●	●	●
Q/P		●	●	●	●

Pietrafitta

località Pietrafitta
C 0577 741123.
● Thu. €

This hospitable small restaurant with its period furnishings serves a few classic Tuscan dishes, such as local salumi *and* bistecca alla Fiorentina. *Everything is home-made.*

CELLAR	●	●	●		
COMFORT	●	●	●		
TRADITION	●	●	●	●	●
Q/P		●	●	●	

CASTELNUOVO BERARDENGA (SI)

Antonio

via Fiorita, 38
C 0577 355321.
● Mon. In summer daily at lunchtime.
€€€€€

This fine restaurant is celebrated for its excellent seafood dishes. The menu is rewritten each morning, after the dawn purchases at the meat, fruit and vegetable markets. The host, Antonio Farina, has an excellent cellar with prestigious wines from all over the world.

CELLAR	●	●	●	●	●
COMFORT	●	●	●		
TRADITION	●				
Q/P		●	●		

Bottega del 30

località Villa Sesta
via Santa Caterina, 2
C 0577 359226.
● Tues, Wed, lunchtime on weekdays.
€€€€

This small restaurant is set in a 17th-century farmyard above an ancient monastery and is surrounded by vines. Elegant without being too formal, it offers interesting, creative cooking based on old Tuscan recipes. Choose the versatile "tasting menu", which includes some of their specialities.

CELLAR	●	●	●	
COMFORT	●	●	●	
TRADITION	●	●	●	
Q/P		●	●	

Poggio Rosso

località Santa Felice
C 0577 359260.
€€€€€

Set in the farming hamlet of San Felice, where there is also a fascinating historic hotel with well-appointed rooms, this is a stylish restaurant. It serves good, fairly creative, meat-based dishes with special emphasis on the farm's own produce, especially the excellent extra virgin olive oil. The restaurant also serves some seafood dishes.

CELLAR	●	●	●		
COMFORT	●	●	●	●	●
TRADITION	●	●			
Q/P	●				

COLLE DI VAL D'ELSA (SI)

Arnolfo

via XX Settembre, 50
C 0577 920549.
● Tues.
€€€€€

This restaurant is housed in a 500-year-old building in a charming village. There are two menus – one is traditional and the other innovative modern – both featuring excellent, tasty dishes. The service reflects great courtesy and professionalism. The dishes range from fish to local meat, as well as a choice selection of ingredients from other areas of Tuscany. The pastries are not to be missed. The mark-ups on the wine list are very reasonable. There is accommodation available in five bedrooms, which all have a pleasant, relaxed atmosphere.

CELLAR	●	●	●	●	●
COMFORT	●	●	●	●	
TRADITION	●	●			
Q/P	●	●	●		

GAIOLE IN CHIANTI (SI)

Ristorante Badia a Coltibuono

località Badia
a Coltibuono
☎ 0577 749031.
€€

A splendid medieval abbey is the setting for this restaurant, which is run by the Stucchi Prinetti family (their mother, Lorenza de' Medici, is in charge of the kitchen). As a showcase for their wines, the restaurant's owners serve traditional Tuscan dishes, which are sometimes enriched with modern personal touches. Dishes are made with choice ingredients such as Cinta Senese pork and fresh produce either from their own market garden, or supplied by small local growers. The interesting wine list includes fine wines from the family estate together with a selection of other Tuscan and Italian wines.

CELLAR	●	●
COMFORT	●	●	●	●
TRADITION	●	●	●
Q/P	●	●	●

GREVE IN CHIANTI (FI)

Da Padellina

strada in Chianti
corso del Popolo
☎ 055 858388.
● Thu.
€€

This pleasant country trattoria in Chianti serves purely classical cuisine. The ribollita and bistecca alla fiorentina are excellent, while the peposo alla fornacina, an old Impruneta recipe for meat stew, is worth trying. Desserts are home-made and include a traditional zuccotto.

CELLAR	●	●	●
COMFORT	●	●	●
TRADITION	●	●	●	●	●
Q/P	●	●	●

MERCATALE VAL DI PESA (FI)

Il Salotto del Chianti

via Sonnino, 92
☎ 055 8218016. ● Wed, lunchtime on weekdays.
€€€

The fish cuisine of this small stylish restaurant is more Mediterranean than Tuscan. However, for the meat dishes the approach is definitely regional, both in style and ingredients. Fresh vegetables are an essential part of the fish and the meat dishes. The bread and desserts are made on the premises.

CELLAR	●	●	●
COMFORT	●	●	●	●
TRADITION	●	●	●
Q/P	●	●	●

PASSIGNANO (FI)

Osteria di Passignano

badia a Passignano
☎ 055 8071278.
● Sun. €€€

The fish cuisine at this small, stylish restaurant is more Mediterranean than Tuscan, but the meat dishes are definitely regional. The bread and desserts are made in the restaurant's kitchens.

CELLAR	●	●	●
COMFORT	●	●	●	●
TRADITION	●	●	●
Q/P	●	●	●

PANZANO IN CHIANTI (FI)

Il Vescovino

via Ciampolo da Panzano, 9
☎ 055 852464.
● Tues. €€€

A wood-burning oven and a medieval fireplace are two of the attractions of this restaurant. The menu includes updated Tuscan dishes plus recipes from other regions. Fresh fish is served. The bread, pasta and desserts are home-made. There is a wide choice of wines in an ancient cellar which you can visit.

CELLAR	●	●	●
COMFORT	●	●	●	●
TRADITION	●	●	●
Q/P	●	●	●

SAN CASCIANO IN VAL DI PESA (FI)

La Tenda Rossa

località Cerbaia
piazza del Monumento, 9/14
☎ 055 826132.
● Sun, Mon lunchtime.
€€€€€

A busy family team run this smart, but very friendly restaurant, which offers innovative versions of the Tuscan classics as well as new ideas for fish and meat. The starting point is the local market, as reflected in the menu, which is rewritten almost daily. Everything is home-made, including the bread, the service is impeccable, and there is a fine cellar.

CELLAR	●	●	●	●	●
COMFORT	●	●	●	●	●
TRADITION	●	●			
Q/P	●	●			

SIENA

Botteganova

strada di Montevarchi statale, 408, 29
€ 0577 284230.
● Mon. €€€

The Sicilian chef at this smart restaurant knows how to get hold of perfect ingredients. He adapts the local cuisine to produce his own personal version of Mediterranean dishes, with an especially creative approach to seafood. The desserts are skilfully prepared and there is a choice selection of cheeses.

CELLAR	●	●	●	●
COMFORT	●	●	●	
TRADITION	●	●		
Q/P	●	●	●	

Osteria del Fico Mezzo

via dei Termini, 71
€ 0577 222384.
● Sun. €

This cheerful osteria (inn), is as imaginative and informal with its furnishings as it is with the food. Fresh vegetables, salumi, cheeses matured to different degrees of ripeness and excellent house honey are used.

CELLAR	●	●	●
COMFORT	●	●	
TRADITION	●	●	●
Q/P	●	●	●

Guido

vicolo Pier Pettinaio, 7
€ 0577 280042. €€

Tuscan cuisine with some personal touches can be found in this restaurant set in a 15th-century building. The bistecca alla fiorentina and the game merit special mention.

CELLAR	●	●	●
COMFORT	●	●	●
TRADITION	●	●	●
Q/P	●	●	●

Le Logge

via del Porrione, 33
€ 0577 48013.
● Sun, lunchtime on Mon. €€€

Set in the oldest palace in Siena, Palazzo Piccolomini, next to the Logge del Papa, this restaurant is popular with artists. It offers typical Tuscan cuisine (plus some fish dishes) with plenty of traditional recipes and home-made fresh pasta. The wines are mainly regional.

CELLAR	●	●	●
COMFORT	●	●	●
TRADITION	●	●	●
Q/P	●	●	●

Antica Trattoria Papei

piazza del Mercato, 6
€ 0577 280894.
● Mon. €

This is probably the only trattoria in town with a real family atmosphere. The sauces and the pasta are made on the premises: the pappardelle with hare is really special. The dishes

are authentic Sienese cuisine – nothing is frozen or pre-packaged.

CELLAR	●	●	●		
COMFORT	●	●			
TRADITION	●	●	●	●	●
Q/P	●	●	●		

MONTALCINO AND THE SIENESE CRETE

BAGNO VIGNONI (SI)

Antica Osteria del Leone

piazza del Muretto
€ 0577 887300.
● Mon. €

This attractive restaurant is in the centre of this medieval town, which is famous for its hot spa, a pool in the main square. Its four rooms are set in a 14th-century building with exposed beams and a terracotta floor. Home-made pasta such as pici and pappardelle served with a sauce of wild boar, hare or all'aglione (garlic). Other specialities include tripe, guinea fowl with Vin Santo, and mushrooms in season. The desserts are also good.

CELLAR	●	●	●
COMFORT	●	●	●
TRADITION	●	●	●
Q/P	●	●	●

Osteria della Parrata

via del Moretto, 40
€ 0577 887559.
● Wed.
€

A 15th-century barn with a fine panoramic garden is the attractive setting for this restaurant. Grilled food is its speciality. The pecorino cheeses are excellent, as is the lombo bagnato (loin) with balsamic vinegar. Fresh vegetables are widely used in the first courses.

CELLAR	•	•		
COMFORT	•	•		
TRADITION	•	•	•	•
Q/P	•	•	•	•

BUONCONVENTO (SI)

Osteria di Duccio

via Soccini, 76
☎ 0577 807042.
⬤ Wed. €

There is a very welcoming family atmosphere at this restaurant. The food is typical Sienese cuisine with numerous rustic dishes, including crostini and salumi, tagiolini ginestrati (with local chicken and saffron), ravioli of potatoes, ribollita seasoned with oil and onion, pappardelle sulla lepre (only in the open season for hare), faraona in crosta tartufata (guinea fowl in a crust), saddle of rabbit with herbs, purée of chickpeas, patate alla fattoressa (country-style potatoes), porcini specialities (in summer and early autumn), and home-made desserts. The produce is always fresh with ingredients bought in daily. There is house wine or Rosso di Montalcino.

CELLAR	•				
COMFORT	•	•			
TRADITION	•	•	•	•	•
Q/P	•	•	•	•	

CETONA (SI)

Frateria di Padre Eligio

convento di San Francesco
☎ 0578 238015.
⬤ Tues.
€€€€€

Intriguingly situated in a medieval monastery, this restaurant is surrounded by a park housing a community of young people who work in the restaurant and hotel.

The traditional Italian cuisine, with a personal touch, is very good indeed. Most of the ingredients are produced by the community. The menus are hand-painted. Prices are steep, however – think of them as a contribution to this community.

CELLAR	•	•	•	•
COMFORT	•	•	•	•
TRADITION	•	•		
Q/P	•			

CHIUSI (SI)

Zaira

via Arunte, 12
☎ 0578 20260.
⬤ Mon (except summer).
€€

This simple pleasant family-run restaurant in the town centre serves classic local cuisine, which is closely linked to the seasons. It has a fascinating cellar (20,000 bottles) that stretches into Etruscan tunnels hewn out of the rock.

CELLAR	•	•	•	
COMFORT	•	•	•	
TRADITION	•	•	•	•
Q/P	•	•	•	

LUCIGNANO (AR)

Osteria da Totò

piazza del Tribunale, 6
☎ 0575 836763.
⬤ Tues. €

Over the years Lorenzo Totò has become a TV star, appearing on numerous shows and describing his grandparents' recipes, especially the ones with wild herbs. He is also kept busy teaching the secrets of Tuscan cuisine to Japanese pupils. When they are not his guests in Italy, he is off to Japan. His wife and children, Boris and Beatrice, help to run the rustic restaurant, set on an ancient square at the top of the town. The son and daughter follow in the footsteps of their imaginative father, serving up wonderful sauces and soups. The family's extra virgin olive oil is excellent.

CELLAR	•				
COMFORT	•	•			
TRADITION	•	•	•	•	•
Q/P	•	•	•		

MONTALCINO (SI)

Osteria del Vecchio Castello

località Poggio alle Mura
☎ 0577 816026.
⬤ Tues. €€€€

The little convent of the 13th-century Pieve di San Sigismondo housed a restaurant of the same name until March 2000. Now, in its place Susanna Fumi (in the kitchen) and her husband Alfredo Sibaldi (sommelier) have taken over, bringing with them all the history and experience of the Osteria del Vecchio Castello di Roccalbenga which they used to run. Despite the change of location – no longer among the woods at the foot of Monte Amiata but amid the celebrated vines of Montalcino – there are still only 16 covers and the food is as wonderful as ever. The cooking serves only to enhance the excellent regional and seasonal ingredients in harmonious flavour combinations. The wine lists have been increased from two to three: Italian, regional and foreign. Adjacent to the restaurant are a wine store and six large suites.

CELLAR	•	•	•	•	•
COMFORT	•	•	•	•	•
TRADITION	•	•	•	•	
Q/P	•	•	•	•	•

Poggio Antico

località I Poggi
0577 849200.
Mon, Sun evening.
€€€€

Diners have a panoramic view of the countryside at this charming restaurant. The regional cuisine is adapted intelligently, as in the fried vegetables and the gnocchetti di ragù bianco di cinghiale. There are excellent desserts.

CELLAR	•	•	•
COMFORT	•	•	•	•
TRADITION	•	•	
Q/P	•		

Porta al Cassero

Rocca della Fortezza
0577 847196.
Wed. €

A small osteria offering Montalcino cuisine, with classic pinci (or pici) and traditional dishes, from pappa col pomodoro (bread and tomato soup) to a purée of chickpeas and zuppa alla scottiglia di cinghiale (wild boar stew), with the occasional dish from other regions.

CELLAR	•	•			
COMFORT	•	•	•		
TRADITION	•	•	•	•	•
Q/P	•	•	•		

Il Pozzo

località Sant' Angelo in Colle 0577 844015.
Tues. €

Nestling in the hills five minutes from Montalcino, this traditional trattoria serves a select choice of superbly cooked dishes. There is a limited choice of regional wines.

CELLAR	•	•			
COMFORT	•	•			
TRADITION	•	•	•	•	•
Q/P	•	•	•		

Taverna dei Barbi

località Pordenoni
0577 841111.
Tues, Wed evening. €€

This restaurant is next door to the famous Barbi wine store. The décor is rustic yet elegant and the food served is typical Montalcino cuisine.

CELLAR	•		
COMFORT	•	•	•
TRADITION	•	•	•	•
Q/P	•	•	•

MONTEFOLLONICO (SI)

La Chiusa

via della Madonnina, 88
0577 669668.
Tues. €€€€€

Situated in an ancient farmhouse, this is one of the most celebrated restaurants in the region. Dania Masotti presents regional food in a cuisine that is full of character but inspired by tradition. There are charming, but very expensive, rooms too.

CELLAR	•	•	•
COMFORT	•	•	•	•
TRADITION	•	•	•	•
Q/P	•		

MONTEPULCIANO (SI)

Diva e Maceo

via di Gracciano
nel Corso, 90/92
0578 716951.
Tues. €

This simple restaurant is very popular with locals and visitors alike, who enjoy its Tuscan dishes.

These range from classic antipasti to pappardelle al cinghiale, pici all'aglione (considered the best in the area), and grilled or roasted meat. The desserts are home-made.

CELLAR	•	•			
COMFORT	•	•			
TRADITION	•	•	•	•	•
Q/P	•	•	•	•	

La Grotta

località San Biagio, 15
0578 757607.
Wed. €€€

This restaurant, opposite the church of San Biagio, is renowned for its meat, especially the tagliata di Chianina and bistecca alla fiorentina. The rest of the menu offers regional specialities such as antipasti with bruschetta and crostini, home-made pasta and second courses such as duck, stuffed pigeon and rabbit. Everything is delicious. The wine list has some French wines.

CELLAR	•	•	•		
COMFORT	•	•	•	•	
TRADITION	•	•	•	•	•
Q/P	•	•	•		

PIENZA (SI)

Il Prato

via Santa Caterina, 1/3
0578 749924.
Tue. €

Recently taken over by the owners of Silene at Seggiano (see p191), this restaurant is run with the same professionalism. The cuisine and wine list are unchanged. There is a very pleasant garden.

CELLAR	•	•	•		
COMFORT	•	•	•		
TRADITION	•	•	•	•	•
Q/P	•	•	•		

La Taverna di Moranda

frazione Monticchiello
via di Mezzo, 17
【 0578 755050.
● Mon. ©©

*About 10 km (6 miles)
from Pienza, towards
Monte Amiata, you can
find real Tuscan cuisine
at this restaurant. The
pasta is made by hand
and the menu changes
with the seasons. The
antipasti are based on
local salumi; the first
courses are pici served
with simple tomato sauces,
or richer meat sauces;
and the second courses
are meat, including
stuffed pigeon, the house
speciality, and agnello a
scottadito (rabbit with
olives) and steak dishes.*

CELLAR	●	●	●		
COMFORT	●	●	●		
TRADITION	●	●	●	●	●
Q/P	●	●	●		

SINALUNGA (SI)

Locanda dell'Amorosa

località Amorosa
【 0577 679497.
● Mon, Tues lunchtime.
©©©©©

*This is one of the most
important and fascinating
Tuscan restaurants,
situated in a 400-year-old
town. The excellent
cuisine draws on tradition
but is also innovative. The
menu gives a lot of space
to meat dishes but there
is no lack of fish. The
desserts are very good.
The cheeses from the Crete
are noteworthy, as is the
salumi produced by a
local firm. Splendid suites
and rooms in the
medieval town's towers
and walls are available.*

CELLAR	●	●	●	●
COMFORT	●	●	●	●
TRADITION	●	●		
Q/P	●	●		

Osteria delle Grotte

via Matteotti, 33
【 0577 630269.
● Wed. ©©©

*Set in an old lemon grove,
this restaurant has a
fixed-price "tasting menu"
(including Tuscan wine)
with seasonal produce,
meat, game and excellent
hand-made fresh pasta.*

CELLAR	●	●		
COMFORT	●	●		
TRADITION	●	●	●	●
Q/P	●	●	●	

SOVICILLE (SI)

Trattoria Cateni

via dei Pratini, 23
【 0577 342028.
● Wed. ©

*This restaurant has a
panoramic terrace
overlooking Siena. The
arched interior and
antique furniture give it a
traditional feel. The
scottiglia is excellent, as
are the specialities based
on wild boar (pappardelle,
cinghiale alla cacciatora)
and mushrooms (zuppa,
vitella). The pasta and
desserts are home-made.*

CELLAR	●			
COMFORT	●			
TRADITION	●	●	●	●
Q/P	●	●	●	

TREQUANDA (SI)

Locanda del Colle

via Torta, 7
【 0577 662108.
● Wed in the low season.
©

*The dining room of this
restaurant is painted with
floral frescoes, reminiscent
of the old verandas on
Sienese country houses a
century ago. The décor is
Art Nouveau with original*

*period furniture. Here
you can taste simple
dishes, such as picchio-
pacchio, home-made
lunghetti with nana
(muscovy duck), zuppa
Trequanda, Chianina beef
or beef in Brunello wine.
The home-made jams
turn up in excellent tarts.
To sample the food, you
are set a task – a farm
chore, or a guided tasting
of oil or wine.*

CELLAR	●				
COMFORT	●	●	●		
TRADITION	●	●	●	●	●
Q/P	●	●	●	●	

MAREMMA AND MONTE AMIATA

CAPALBIO (GR)

Maria

via Comunale, 3
【 0564 896014.
● Tues. ©©

*Politicians and media
personalities are often
found among the tourists
sampling Maurizio Rossi's
Maremma specialities.
While wild boar dominates
the menu, the tortelli with
truffles, the acquacotta
(soup) and the fried
vegetables are noteworthy.*

CELLAR	●	●	●	
COMFORT	●	●	●	
TRADITION	●	●	●	●
Q/P	●	●	●	

CASTIGLIONE DELLA PESCAIA (GR)

Osteria del Buco

via del Recinto, 11
【 0564 934460.
● Mon. ©

*This restaurant is in an
opening in the ancient
walls of the medieval town.
The cuisine, like the décor,
is pure Maremma. Dishes*

include bruschette *(some with long-forgotten toppings), vegetable and pulse soups, game, and very good fish (including some little-known kinds unusual in a restaurant).*

CELLAR	●	●			
COMFORT	●	●			
TRADITION	●	●	●	●	●
Q/P	●	●	●	●	

GROSSETO

Buca di S. Lorenzo

viale Manetti, 1
[0564 25142.
● Sun. €€

This restaurant serves fish cuisine when local fish is available. At other times it offers traditional Tuscan dishes, including home-made pasta.

CELLAR	●	●	●
COMFORT	●	●	●
TRADITION	●	●	●	●	●
Q/P	●	●	●	

ISOLA DEL GIGLIO (GR)

La Margherita

località Giglio Porto
via Thaon de Revel, 5
[0564 809237. **●** Mon.
○ from Easter–Sept. €

Good home-cooked simple fresh fish dishes are served at this restaurant. Note the delicious first course dish cavatelli *(pasta) with* mazzancolle *(mantis shrimps) and* pecorino.

CELLAR	●	●	
COMFORT	●	●	
TRADITION	●	●	●
Q/P	●	●	●

Trattoria Da Maria ○

località Giglio Castello
[0564 806062.
● Wed. **○** Mar–Dec.
€€

This family restaurant is set in the hills with a delightful view over the Baia di Campese. The restaurant serves a choice of fine fish and meat dishes, including the island's traditional rabbit recipe.

CELLAR	●	●	●
COMFORT	●	●	●
TRADITION	●	●	●
Q/P	●	●	●

Da Santi

località Castello
via Marconi, 20
[0564 806188.
● Mon (except summer).
€€

Here you can enjoy excellent fish cuisine with the type of fish dependent on availability. Classic Tuscan dishes are given the personal touch by skilfully incorporating fresh vegetables.

CELLAR	●	●	
COMFORT	●	●	
TRADITION	●	●	●
Q/P	●	●	●

MASSA MARITTIMA (GR)

Bracali

località Ghirlanda
[0566 902318.
● Tues; Mon evening (except August).
€€€€€

This family-run restaurant offers creative cooking inspired by the regional tradition of light, well balanced meat and fish dishes. The menu includes a masterly, innovative Tuscan lamb recipe consisting of two dishes: one dish is cold, the other, made from leg and ribs of lamb, is served hot. The pastries are also extremely good and well worth sampling.

CELLAR	●	●	●	●	●
COMFORT	●	●	●		
TRADITION	●	●			
Q/P	●	●	●		

MONTEMERANO (GR)

Da Caino Ⓖ

via Canonica, 3
[0564 602817.
● Wed, Thursday midday.
€€€€€

This is one of the most important, up-and-coming restaurants in Italy, renowned for its quality. Although it is off the beaten track and the prices are high, this is one not to miss. It has a small number of covers and a cuisine that mirrors the territory. The salumi *and extra virgin olive oil are from the restaurant's own estate. The desserts and spirits are very good and you can choose from a list of coffees.*

CELLAR	●	●	●	●	●
COMFORT	●	●	●	●	●
TRADITION	●	●	●	●	
Q/P	●	●	●		

SEGGIANO (GR)

Silene ○

località La Pescina Est
[0564 950805.
● Mon.
€

Set in the mountains, this restaurant offers Tuscan home cooking with the emphasis on woodland produce – mushrooms and truffles in season, and wild boar and venison. The meat is mostly grilled over charcoal. The pasta is home-made. There are some rooms available.

CELLAR	●	●	●		
COMFORT	●	●	●		
TRADITION	●	●	●	●	●
Q/P	●	●	●		

Accommodation

Tuscany is probably the region of Italy with the most charming inns and small country hotels offering wonderful hospitality and comfort in settings of great natural beauty. The guide below takes into account, as far as possible, the price:quality ratio, so this means it excludes some of the world's finest and most luxurious hotels – such as Villa San Michele at Fiesole, for example – because the average price of a room goes well beyond the limits set for this guide.

Most of the inns listed here are situated deep in the hills, surrounded by breathtaking countryside. The rooms are furnished with typical Tuscan country furniture and the food on offer is the traditional local cuisine.

Bagni di Lucca (LU)

Locanda Maiola

località Maiola di Sotto
0583 86296.
15–30 Jan, 1–20 Nov.
€

This is a 17th-century Tuscan house, set in the green hills near Lucca, that has been converted to a welcoming family inn. In the kitchen Signora Simonetta makes exquisite dishes reflecting the cuisine of Lucca and Garfagnana, such as her zuppa di farro with vegetables, or the home-made pasta with chickpeas or beans. The five tastefully renovated rooms are furnished with dark wood furniture. The panoramic view is magnificent.

Balbano (LU)

Villa Casanova

via di Casanova, 1600
0583 548429.
FAX 0583 368955.
Annexe ● Nov–Mar.
€€

Nestling in the green hills between Lucca and Pisa, this 18th-century villa offers good value for money. The rooms, some very spacious, have terracotta floors, some fine period furniture and a splendid view over the Valle del Serchio. Next to the villa the Antica Foresteria (annexe), dating back to the 15th century, accommodates guests in smaller rooms, some of

them extremely pleasant. The restaurant, which is open from April to November, serves wholesome home cooking. There is a good swimming pool, which is open to guests from June to September.

Borgo San Lorenzo (FI)

Casa Palmira

località Feriolo, Statale, 302 via Faentina
FAX 055 8409749.
Jan–Feb. €€

A small rural building has been converted into this delightful hotel deep in the green hills between the Mugello and Florence. It has six rooms, each one different, but all furnished in good taste and with objects belonging to the family to give a personal touch. Eat at the nearby restaurant "Il Feriolo", set in a 15th-century monastery, which specializes in good home cooking based on mushrooms and game.

Bucine (AR)

Le Antiche Sere

località Sogna
& FAX 055 998149.
Nov.
€€

A medieval village called Sogna ("dream") is the setting for this fascinating

inn. The owners' idea is to let guests isolate themselves from the outside world and lose themselves in the relaxing atmosphere. The old stables have been converted into the restaurant, which serves an imaginative cuisine with lots of interesting dishes made with fresh produce. The menu changes two or three times a week and there is a good selection of wines. There are four suites with country-style furniture, fireplaces and, above all, no telephone. The hotel has a park, a swimming pool and tennis courts.

Castellina in Chianti (SI)

Belvedere di San Leonino

località San Leonino
0577 740887.
FAX 0577 740924.
15 Nov–15 Mar.
€€€

Set in a tiny rural village, this is a cluster of adjoining houses providing accommodation in 28 rooms, all spacious and pleasantly furnished. There is a lovely garden with a lawn and swimming pool with a great view over the valley. The restaurant serves good, imaginative Tuscan cuisine.

Il Colombaio

via Chiantigiana, 29
& FAX 0577 740444.
all year. €€

You come across this hotel with its inviting name set in a 16th-century farmhouse at the entrance to the village. The rooms, all with 19th-century furniture, have wooden beams and terracotta floors. There is a lovely garden with a swimming pool and a view over the village and valley. Eat at the nearby restaurant "Le Tre Porte", run by the hotelier's son, where real Tuscan food, such as crostini, pasta and ribollita is served.

CASTIGLIONE D'ORCIA (SI)

Cantina Il Borgo

località Rocca d'Orcia
& FAX 0577 887280.
Jan, Feb.
€€

In this little medieval village overlooking the Val d'Orcia, these are three delightful rooms set in one of the fine houses of light-coloured brick. The walls are whitewashed, there are wrought-iron bedsteads and typical Tuscan country furniture. The restaurant offers real local cooking, with exquisite pecorino from Pienza. Do not miss the excursion to the splendid spa, the Bagno Vignoni, which can be visited in the evening when the hot bath in the middle of the piazza exhales vapours reminiscent of a scene from Dante's Inferno.

CERTALDO (FI)

Osteria del Vicario

via Rivellino, 3
& FAX 0571 668228.
Jan. €€

In the Middle Ages this inn was the residence of the vicar of Certaldo Alto. Set in the depths of the Val

d'Elsa, between Siena and Florence, it has 11 rooms, each quite different, very romantic and with fine Tuscan furnishings. The skilled restaurant chef presents a creative cuisine based on beautifully fresh produce – meat, poultry, mushrooms and truffles.

CORTONA (AR)

Relais Il Falconiere

località San Martino
0575 612616.
FAX 0575 612927.
all year.
€€€€€

This splendid 17th-century country house, now converted into a hotel, part of the Relais & Châteaux group, has a stunning hill-top location amid vines and olives facing Cortona. There are 10 rooms, all spacious and filled with period furniture and attractive wall hangings. As well as wooden beams and parquet floors, some rooms have a fireplace. The two suites overlook the garden and swimming pool. The restaurant is renowned for its very fine cuisine, based on genuine local produce.

Locanda del Molino

località Montanare
0575 614192.
FAX 0575 614054.
15 Nov–15 Mar.
€€

Situated a few miles from Cortona, this pleasant, small inn, deep in the countryside, is famed for its authentic cuisine and courteous hospitality. The ground floor restaurant's specialities, like the torte al testo (griddle cakes), reflect Umbrian influence. The rooms on the first floor are all furnished with fine local antiques. There are antique toilets in some of the rooms.

FIESOLE (FI)

Pensione Bencistà

via Benedetto da Maiano, 4
FAX 055 59163.
all year.
€€€€ with half board.

This calls itself a modest pensione but is actually a pleasant villa situated in the hills of Fiesole and, in fact, looks more like a small inn. The living areas are very attractive – there are intimate lounges with fireplaces and there is a small library. The comfortable bedrooms are furnished with period furniture. The restaurant offers good Tuscan cuisine and there is a pleasant garden and terrace with a view over Florence.

FLORENCE

Villa Montartino

via suor Maria Celeste, 19/21
055 223520.
FAX 055 223495.
all year. €€€€€

You can find this corner of paradise just a few miles from Florence on the road from Certosa to Impruneta. Montartino was originally an 11th-century watchtower guarding the valley of the Ema, where goods were brought from Chianti to Florence. The tower was later converted into a charming and graceful mansion. The enormous rooms with four-poster beds and the original terracotta floors contain elegant Tuscan craft furniture. Some rooms have a terrace with splendid views over the surrounding hills. Guests can use the lovely swimming pool. The food is refined but wholesome, using all local produce, including the excellent extra virgin olive oil and

the local red wine –
Chianti. The favourite
Tuscan beef steak dish,
bistecca alla fiorentina,
which a small butcher in
Impruneta supplies to the
villa, is truly wonderful.

GAIOLE IN CHIANTI
(SI)

Relais San Sano

località San Sano
C 0577 746130.
FAX 0577 746156.
● 15 Nov–15 Mar.
€€€

This cluster of stone
farmhouses overlooking
the Chianti hills nestles in
an ancient hamlet. Each
of the rooms has a name
suggesting its character:
for instance, "Il nido" (The
nest) is isolated and
romantic, while "Camera
con vista" (Room with a
view) has a view over the
gently rolling Tuscan hills.
The food served each
evening in the restaurant is
the local cuisine.

LUCCA

Locanda L'Elisa

via Nuova to Pisa
at 5 km
C 0583 379737.
FAX 0583 379019.
□ all year.
€€€€€

This beautiful mauve-
coloured villa was restored
in the early 19th century
by a steward of Princess
Elisa Baiocchi. It has two
rooms and eight suites,
all of them graciously
furnished with 19th-
century mahogany
furniture, four-poster beds
and fine damask fabrics.
The spectacular park has a
swimming pool in it and
a myriad of geraniums,
trees and water-plants.
The veranda-gazebo
housing the restaurant
overlooks the park.

MANCIANO
(GR)

Il Poderino

strada statale Maremmana
at 30 km
C & **FAX** 0564 625031.
● 2 weeks in Jan.
€€

This ancient converted
farmhouse at the gates of
Manciano has 11 spacious,
well-furnished rooms. This
is a very friendly, well-run
hotel with a splendid
panoramic view across to
Monte Argentario. The
restaurant serves Maremma
cuisine with the addition of
some interesting new dishes.

PIENZA
(SI)

Dal Falco

piazza Dante Alighieri, 3
C & **FAX** 0578 748551.
□ all year. €€

Visitors to this attractive
Tuscan town can find
inexpensive family
accommodation at this
small inn situated in the
centre. The restaurant's
cuisine is good; specialities
include excellent pici
all'aglione, hand-made
ravioli, ribollita, and meat
grilled over charcoal. The
simple, comfortable rooms
all have TV and bathrooms
with furnishings in "arte
povera" style.

ORBETELLO
(GR)

Locanda d'Ansedonia

via Aurelia towards
Ansedonia
C 0564 881317.
FAX 0564 881727.
● Feb. €€

This strategically placed
inn has a wonderful view
overlooking the fascinating
lagoon of Orbetello, a few
miles from Argentario and

the Etruscan citadel of
Ansedonia. The 12 rooms
are whitewashed and
furnished in Maremma
style with fine wrought-iron
bedsteads. The restaurant
cuisine is typical of the
area, with Maremma
dishes and seafood – try the
famous acquacotta as well
as excellent Orbetello eel.

PITECCIO
(PT)

Villa Vannini

Villa di Piteccio
C 0573 42031.
FAX 0573 26331.
□ all year.
€€

Surrounded by a pleasant,
quiet garden, this lovely
villa is set just above
Pistoia. Friendly, family
hospitality is extended by
Signora Vannini who
oversees every detail, from
furnishing the rooms to the
home-made produce served
at breakfast and dinner.

RADDA IN CHIANTI
(SI)

Podere Terreno

road to Volpaia,
C & **FAX** 0577 738312.
□ all year.
€€ with half board.

This farm is on the road
to the village of Volpaia,
famous for its Chianti
Classico and olive oil. The
owners, Sylvie Heniez
(who is French) and her
husband Roberto Melosi,
see to every last detail from
furnishing the farmhouse
with genuine rustic
furniture to organizing the
kitchen. The seven rooms
are full of charm and very
relaxing. At mealtimes
everyone eats together
around a single large table
and it is common to hear
two or three languages
spoken by diners from
different continents.

La Locanda

località Montanino
☎ & FAX 0577 738833.
◑ Jan and Feb.
€€€€

This fascinating inn in the splendid Chianti hills was a 17th-century farmhouse. The seven rooms, all quite different, are furnished with handsome country furniture and each has a different colour scheme. They have chests and wardrobes in dark wood, and bedsteads with Viennese woven rush headboards. Particularly interesting is the arched bedroom and a suite with a loggia and a magnificent view. In good weather you can lounge by the pool and nibble pecorino *cheese or* finocchiona (salame).

RADICOFANI (SI)

La Palazzina

località Le Vigne
☎ & FAX 0578 55771.
◑ Nov–Mar.
€€

This holiday farm in the hills of the Alta Valle d'Orcia is in an area rich in spas. The 18th-century Medici villa has bright, spacious rooms, all very tastefully furnished. There is a swimming pool in the garden. The cuisine is based on the revival of ancient Medici recipes and uses the same fresh local produce as in the past. The villa is a good starting point for various sightseeing excursions.

SATURNIA (GR)

La Stellata

località Pian del Bagno
☎ 0564 602978.
FAX 0564 602934.
☐ all year.
€€€

Surrounded by luxuriant vegetation in the Etruscan spa zone, this hotel is the younger brother of the Grand Hotel delle Terme. The beauty of the stone building, the garden and the peace and quiet are incomparable. The pretty rooms are simply furnished. Sample the specialities of the outdoor grill and restaurant, the "Osteria del Bagno".

SIENA

Certosa di Maggiano

strada di Certosa, 82
☎ 0577 288180.
FAX 0577 288189.
☐ all year.
€€€€€

This splendid 16th-century Charterhouse is just outside the centre of Siena. The building is laid out around a courtyard and comprises six rooms and eleven suites, luxuriously and tastefully furnished in a choice of fabrics and colours. In the inner rooms are prized Sienese paintings and antique furniture. The restaurant's cuisine is of a high level, using plenty of fresh ingredients. In summer the tables are laid in the cloister portico. There is a park with a swimming pool and tennis courts.

SINALUNGA (SI)

Locanda della Bandita

località Bettolle
via Bandita, 72
☎ & FAX 0577 624649.
◑ two weeks in Dec.
€€

This small farmhouse in Val di Chiana has just seven rooms, all furnished with wrought-iron beds, country furniture and curtains in shades of blue. The restaurant cuisine is outstanding: it offers local salumi *and speciality meats, Tuscan* crostini, *home-made pasta and excellent Chianina beef steaks. There is a good choice of Tuscan wines.*

SOVANA (GR)

Taverna Etrusca

piazza del Pretorio, 16
☎ 0564 616183.
FAX 0564 614193.
◑ Jan. €

This charming inn is housed in a 13th-century building in this Etruscan village in the Maremma. It has eight air-conditioned rooms with fine dark wooden furnishings and parquet floors. The restaurant, which has a mezzanine and a ceiling with wooden beams, offers typical Maremman dishes like acquacotta, *nettle soup and* pici all'agliata, *as well as modern ideas, such as tomato with marjoram and* ravioli *with* caciotta.

VOLTERRA (PI)

Villa Nencini

borgo Santo Stefano, 55
☎ 0588 86571.
FAX 0588 80601.
☐ all year.
€€

You can find this small rustic-style hotel – a real oasis of peace and quiet – just below Volterra's medieval quarter. The rooms are simple and tastefully furnished; some face the fine swimming pool. Surrounding the hotel is a private park, with trees providing shady spots, and lots of nooks and crannies where you can relax or read a book in peace. The genuine Tuscan cuisine is very reasonably priced and the hotel staff are obliging.

Practical Information

TRAVELLING TO TUSCANY is most easily done by air, but although planes arrive from European airports, there are no direct intercontinental flights, and visitors from outside Europe have to transfer. The nearest intercontinental airports are Milan and Rome. Tuscany's main airport is in Pisa; it receives both domestic and European flights as well as most charter traffic. Florence's airport is smaller and is located slightly north of the city, a short bus ride away from the centre. Almost exclusively, it deals with scheduled flights. Florence is also the main arrival point for the far-reaching European train and coach network, and Pisa has good international rail connections. Once in Tuscany, travel around the region is straightforward by train, coach or car. In the cities, it is best to visit the sights on foot wherever possible.

TRAVELLING BY AIR

Useful Numbers

Alitalia
National Flights
📞 1478 656 41.
International Flights
📞 1478 656 42.
Information
📞 1478 656 43.
W www.alitalia.it

British Airways
📞 1478 122 66.
W www.britishairways.com

Meridiana
📞 055 230 23 14.
W www.meridiana.it

TWA
📞 055 28 46 91.
W www.twa.com

CIT Viaggi
Florence 📞 055 28 41 45.
London 📞 020 8686 0677.
Sydney 📞 (2) 267 12 55.

American Express
Via Dante Alighieri, 22r
Florence 📞 055 509 81.

Airport Information
Florence 📞 055 306 15.
W www.safnet.it
Pisa 📞 050 50 07 07.
W www.pisa-airport.com

Direct flights connect Pisa and Florence to London, Paris and Frankfurt all year round. There are also flights to Florence from Barcelona and Brussels. During the summer months, Pisa can be reached directly from Madrid, Manchester and Glasgow.

There are no direct intercontinental flights to Pisa or Florence, but you can

transfer at Rome or Milan. Alitalia also runs a fast (though expensive) train link between Rome's Fiumicino airport and Florence. You may find it cheaper to get a budget flight to London, Paris or Frankfurt and transfer to another carrier.

Daily scheduled flights to Pisa are operated by British Airways, Ryanair, Alitalia, Air France and Lufthansa from London, Paris, Munich and Frankfurt. During the summer, Viva Air flies from Madrid.

Meridiana operates a daily scheduled flight to Florence from London Gatwick. Sabena flies from Brussels. Austrian Airlines offers flights from London to Florence via Lugano. Excursion fares generally offer the best deal in scheduled flights, but they must be purchased well in advance; at least 14 days in the UK and 21 days in the US.

Pisa Airport

Trains run directly from Pisa's Galileo Galilei airport to Florence's Santa Maria Novella station. To reach the trains, turn left as you leave the airport arrivals hall. Train tickets can be bought from the information kiosk at the airport. The journey to Florence takes an hour and the service runs once an hour, but is less regular or frequent in the early morning and late evening. There is also an infrequent train serving Lucca and Montecatini.

The through train to

Florence stops at Pisa Centrale, and Empoli, where you can change on to the local line for Siena.

The No. 7 bus runs from Pisa airport to the town centre. Buy tickets before you get on the bus from the airport information kiosk. There is also a taxi rank at the front of the airport. Buy some euros before landing, as there are no facilities for changing money in the baggage reclaim hall.

Florence Airport

Florence's Amerigo Vespucci airport, often known as Peretola, is very small. The local SITA bus to the city centre leaves from the front of the airport building. The bus goes to and from the airport every 30 minutes. The bus to the airport leaves from the SITA station at Via di Santa Caterina di Siena, 15r.

Only take a taxi from the official rank. They will charge a supplement for coming from the airport plus another for luggage. There is also an extra charge on Sundays and holidays. Most drivers are honest, but check that the meter is switched on and showing the minimum fare before setting off.

Car Hire

All the major car hire firms have rental offices at both airports. However, it is wise to make hire arrangements well in advance, as it will be cheaper than hiring after you arrive in Italy.

Leaving Pisa airport by car, it is easy to get on to the dual carriageway linking Pisa and Florence.

At Florence airport, it might be easier to take public transport into the city centre and pick up your hire car there.

Airport Car Hire Companies

Avis
Florence Airport (055 31 55 88.
Pisa Airport (050 420 28.
[W] www.avis.com

Hertz
Florence Airport (055 30 73 70.
Pisa Airport (050 432 20.
[W] www.hertz.com

Maggiore
Florence Airport (055 31 12 56.
Pisa Airport (050 425 74.

TRAVELLING BY TRAIN

Travelling across country by train can be a very pleasurable way of getting to and travelling around Tuscany. Italy's state railway (Ferrovie dello Stato, or FS) has a train for every type of journey, from the quaintly, maddeningly slow locali (stopping trains) through various levels of rapid intercity service to the luxurious, superfast Eurostar, which rushes between Italian cities at a speed to match its ticket price. The train network between large cities is very good, but journeys to towns on branch lines may be quicker by coach.

Arriving by Train

Florence and Pisa are the main arrival points for trains from Europe. The Galilei from Paris and the Italia Express from Frankfurt travel direct to Florence. Passengers from London have to change in Paris or Lille.

From Florence, there is also a direct Alitalia train

link with Pisa's Galileo Galilei airport, which can be very useful.

Europe-wide train passes, such as EurRail (US) or InterRail for those under 26 (Europe), are accepted on the FS network. You may have to pay a supplement to travel on fast trains. Always check first before using any private rail lines.

Train Travel in Italy

Trains from all over Italy arrive at and depart from Pisa Centrale and Florence's Santa Maria Novella station, while the Eurostar uses Florence's Rifredi station. If you are planning to travel around, there are passes which allow unlimited travel on the FS network for a determined period of time, such as the Italy Rail Card and the Italy Flexi Rail Card. Available only to non-residents, the cards can be purchased from the station. There is a biglietto chilometrico which allows 20 trips totalling no more than 3,000 km (1,865 miles) for up to five people. This is available from international and Italian CIT offices, and from any travel agent selling train tickets. There are facilities for disabled travellers on some intercity services.

Booking and Reservations

Booking is obligatory on the Eurostar and on some other intercity services, indicated on the timetable by a black R on a white background. The booking office is at the front of Florence station.

Alternatively, you can book on the FS website (www.fs-on-line.com). Users must first register on the site, then follow the instructions on how to book and pay for seats. Tickets booked online can be delivered by courier for an additional charge, or

picked up for free at a self-service ticket machine in stations offering this service, but bring the booking code (PNR) you receive via e-mail after completing the transaction online. Travel agents can book tickets free of charge.

Booking is advisable if you wish to travel at busy times: during the high season or at weekends. Buying your intercity ticket at least five hours before travelling entitles you to a free seat reservation. For a small fee, you can reserve a seat on any train, except local trains.

Booking Agents

CIT Viaggi
Piazza della Stazione, 51r, Florence.
(055 28 41 45.

Palio Viaggi
Piazza Gramsci, Siena.
(0577 28 08 28.

Train Tickets

Always buy a ticket before you travel: if you purchase your ticket on the train, you will be surcharged a percentage of the ticket price. You can upgrade to first class or sleeper by paying the conductor.

If the ticket office is busy, try one of the self-service ticket machines found at most stations. They accept coins, notes and credit cards. The instructions are easy to follow and come in six European languages. If you are travelling no more than 200 km (124 miles), you can buy a short-range ticket (biglietto a fasce chilometriche) from a station newsstand. The name of your station of departure will usually be stamped on the ticket, but if it is not, write it on the back. You must then validate the ticket by stamping it in one of the gold-coloured machines situated at the entrance to most platforms. These machines must also be used to timestamp the return portion of a ticket.

Both the outward and return portions of a return ticket must be used within three days of purchase. Singles are issued in 200-km (124-mile) bands and are valid according to band: for example, a ticket for 200 km (124 miles) lasts for a day, a ticket for 400 km (248 miles) lasts for two days, and so on.

On all intercity trains you will be charged a supplementary fee (supplemento) even if you have an InterRail card. This includes the Eurostar and Eurocity services. The cost depends on how far you are travelling.

TRAVELLING BY COACH

Florence is linked by coach to most major European cities and local companies operate an extensive network of services within Tuscany. Coaches are quicker where there is no direct train link, especially in the countryside. The train is faster for long journeys, but the coach may be cheaper. To plan trips around Tuscany by coach, maps and timetables are available from all the coach companies' offices, which are usually situated near city railway stations.

Arriving by Coach

Santa Maria Novella railway station in Florence is Tuscany's main arrival and departure point for all long-distance coach journeys, and the hub of the extensive local coach network. The Lazzi company runs coach links with major European cities from Florence and sells tickets for Eurolines coaches. Book tickets at their office by Santa Maria Novella station. Express services to Rome are run by Lazzi from Florence and TRA-IN from Siena.

Florence

Florence has four main coach companies. Lazzi serves the region north and west of Florence and SITA the southern and eastern region. The COPIT bus company connects the city with the Abetone/Pistoia region and CAP links Florence to the Mugello area north of the city. All these companies have ticket and information offices a stone's throw from Santa Maria Novella railway station.

Lazzi
Piazza della Stazione.
[C] 055 21 51 55 (all services).
[W] www.lazzi.it

SITA
Via di Santa Caterina da Siena, 15r.
[C] 800 373760 (Tuscany);
055 29 49 55 (national).

COPIT of Pistoia
Piazza San Francesco.
[C] 0573 211 70.

[C]CAP
Largo Fratelli Alinari 9.
[C] 055 21 46 37.
[W] www.capautolinee.it

Siena

Siena's main bus and coach company is TRA-IN, which runs urban, local and regional services. Local services leave from Piazza Antonio Gramsci and regional buses from Piazza San Domenico. There is an information/ticket office in both squares. TRA-IN operates buses to most parts of Tuscany, as well as a direct coach to Rome twice daily.

TRA-IN
Piazza Antonio Gramsci
[C] 0577 20 42 46 (local)
Piazza San Domenico.
[C] 0577 20 42 45 (regional).

Pisa

The city bus company CPT also serves the surrounding area, including the towns

of Volterra, Livorno, San Miniato and Pontedera. Buses leave from Piazza Sant'Antonio. Lazzi runs a service to Viareggio, Lucca and Florence from Pisa, departing from Piazza Vittorio Emanuele II, which has a Lazzi ticket office.

CPT
Piazza Sant'Antonio, 1.
[C] 050 50 55 11.

Lazzi
Piazza Vittorio Emanuele II.
[C] 050 462 88. [W] www.lazzi.it

GETTING AROUND ON FOOT AND BY BUS

Tuscan cities are compact enough to get around reasonably comfortably on foot, and the city buses are relatively cheap, regular and wide-ranging. A single ticket will take you up to 15 km (10 miles) out of town, making the bus ideal for trips from the city centre to outlying areas of Florence, Pisa or Siena. The buses get very hot in the summer and are popular with pickpockets (especially the No. 7 bus), so take care when they're crowded.

Walking

Sightseeing on foot in Tuscan cities is made all the more pleasurable by the fact that there are plenty of squares in which to rest and watch the world go by, or cool churches to pop into when the heat gets too much. Moreover, there are limited-traffic zones in the centre of most towns, which make life slightly easier for pedestrians.

Signs for sights and landmarks are usually quite clear, especially those in Siena. In Florence it is easy to pick out the Duomo and the river and orientate yourself in relation to them. A gentle stroll around the main sights of Florence can take just a couple of hours. The Duomo, Santa Maria

Novella, Ponte Vecchio and the Accademia are all within 10 minutes' walk of each other. The main sights in Pisa are all in the same square. Siena is also compact but hilly, so wear comfortable shoes.

The cities can, however, be unbearably hot in summer. Plan your day so that you are inside for the hottest part. Recuperate Italian-style with a leisurely lunch followed by a siesta. Shopping is more pleasant in the early evening when it is cooler, and the streets start to come alive.

Crossing Roads

Use the sottopassaggio (underpass) wherever possible. The busiest roads also have signals to help you cross: the green avanti sign gives you right of way, in theory, but never expect drivers to recognize this as a matter of course. Seize your opportunity and walk out slowly and confidently, glaring at the traffic and maintaining a determined pace: the traffic should stop, or at least swerve. Take extra care at night: traffic lights are switched to flashing amber and the road crossings become free-for-alls.

City Buses

Florence's city bus company is called ATAF, Pisa's is CPT, and Siena's TRA-IN. All the buses are bright orange. Most lines run until at least 9:30pm, with the most popular running until midnight or 1am in Florence.

In Pisa and Florence, buses run near the main sights. Useful Florentine routes for visitors are the No. 12 and the No. 13 (they make hour-long clockwise/anticlockwise circuits of the city), the No. 7 to Fiesole, and the new "eco-routes" A, B, C and D which are electric or eco-diesel-fuelled minibuses.

Using Local Services

Florence does not have a main terminus, but most buses can be picked up alongside Santa Maria Novella station. In Pisa, most buses stop at the railway station and Piazza Vittorio Emanuele II; in Siena, at Piazza Antonio Gramsci and Piazza San Domenico. There are bus information kiosks at all these points, but they are not always open. Tourist information offices can usually help.

Enter the bus at the front or back and get off through the middle doors. However, when the bus is full, you have to struggle on and off wherever you can.

The four low seats at the front of the bus are meant for the elderly, the disabled and people with children.

Fare dodging is common, but so are inspectors. The fine is at least 50 times the cost of a ticket.

Bus Tickets

Tickets for city buses must be bought before you travel. Buy them from newsstands, bars displaying the bus company sign (ATAF, APT, TRA-IN), tobacconists, or at the bus termini. If you are likely to make a few trips, buy several tickets at once; they become valid when you timestamp them in the machine in the bus. There are also ticket vending machines in the streets, which take any coins and low-value notes.

Ticket prices and validity vary from town to town. You can usually buy a ticket valid for one, two or sometimes four hours' unlimited travel. The time limit starts when you stamp your ticket on the first bus. You can also buy daily passes, or a tesserino consisting of one or four tickets, each valid for a number of rides. A tesserino is slightly cheaper than the same number of single tickets. You just

stamp it as and when needed until you have made the permitted number of trips.

Long-Term Passes

If staying for a long time in one town, a monthly pass for unlimited travel is a good idea. You will need an identity card with your photograph. These are available for a small charge from the ATAF Ufficio Abbonamenti located in Piazza della Stazione. In Siena, photocards are available from the TRA-IN office in Piazza San Domenico. Monthly passes can be bought wherever bus tickets are on sale.

In Florence, the best bus ticket for visitors is the plurigiornale, from the ATAF office, newsstands, bars and tobacconists. These are valid for two, three or seven days. The ATAF also sells a ticket called an abbonamento plurigiornaliero, valid for between 2–25 days. These are non-transferable.

You can also buy a carta arancio, valid for seven days on trains and bus lines within the province of Florence. You can buy it from any train, coach or bus company ticket office.

Useful Addresses

ATAF
Ufficio Informazioni & Abbonamenti, Piazza della Stazione, Florence.
W www.ataf.net

CPT
Ufficio Informazioni, Piazza Sant'Antonio, 1, Pisa.
C 050 505 511 W www.cpt.pisa.it

EUROLINES
UK C 01582 404511.
W www.eurolines.co.uk

Taxis in Tuscany

Official taxis are white in Tuscan cities, with a "Taxi" sign on the roof. Only take taxis at official ranks, not offers from touts at the stations. There are supplements for baggage, for rides between 10pm and 7am, on Sundays and on public holidays, and for journeys to and from the airport. If you phone for a taxi, the meter starts to run from the moment you book the taxi; by the time it arrives there could already be several euros clocked up. Generally, taxis are costly. Taxi drivers are usually honest, but make sure you know what any supplements are for. Italians give very small tips or nothing at all, but 10 per cent is expected from visitors.

In Florence, there are ranks at Via Pellicceria, Piazza di Santa Maria Novella and Piazza di San Marco.

In Siena, taxis can be found in Piazza Matteotti and Piazza della Stazione, and in Pisa at the Piazza del Duomo, Piazza Garibaldi and Piazza della Stazione.

Booking Numbers

Florence Radiotaxi
055 47 98 or 055 42 42 or 055 43 90.

Siena Radiotaxi
0577 492 22.

Pisa Radiotaxi
050 54 16 00.

MOTORING IN TUSCANY

A driving tour of Tuscan vineyards makes a great holiday, if you are prepared for high fuel costs and erratic Italian driving. If you are staying in Siena or Florence, with no plans to travel around, there is little point in having a car: both are small enough to walk around and parking is difficult and expensive. If staying in the countryside and visiting towns by car, it is best to park on the outskirts and walk or take a bus into the centre.

Arriving by Car

Drivers from Britain need a Green Card for insurance purposes and the vehicle's registration document. EU nationals who intend to stay for more than six months and do not have the standard pink licence will need an Italian translation of their licence, available from most motoring organizations and Italian tourist offices.

The ACI (Automobile Club d'Italia) provides excellent maps and invaluable help. It will tow anyone free, and offers free repairs to members of affiliated associations, such as the AA or RAC in Britain, ADAC in Germany, the AIT in France, the RACE in Spain and ANWB in Holland. SOS columns on motorways allow instant, round-the-clock access to the emergency services.

Car Hire

Car hire in Italy is expensive and, ideally, should be organized through a tour operator before leaving for Tuscany. Cars can be pre-booked through any hire firm with branches in Italy. If you hire a car when in Tuscany, a local firm such as Maggiore may be cheaper. Book well in advance, especially for weekend outings.

To hire a car you must be over 21, and have held a licence for at least a year. Visitors from outside the EU need an international licence. Make sure the hire package includes collision damage waiver, breakdown service and insurance against theft.

Bike and Moped Hire

A day spent cycling out in the countryside can be a healthy and relaxing pastime, and a moped or scooter makes lighter and swifter work of the Tuscan hills. Bicycles can be hired

for around 3 euros per hour; moped prices start at about 25 euros per day. Helmets are mandatory on mopeds. Bicycles can also be hired from the main paying parking areas of Florence for a cheaper price.

Rules of the Road

Drive on the right and, generally, give way to the right. Seat belts are compulsory in the front and back, and children should be properly restrained. You must also carry a warning triangle in case of breakdown.

In town centres, the speed limit is 50 km/h (30 mph); on ordinary roads 90 km/h (55 mph); and on motorways 110 km/h (70 mph) for cars up to 1099cc, and 130 km/h (80 mph) for more powerful cars. Penalties for speeding include spot fines and licence points, and there are strict drink-driving laws as elsewhere in the EU.

Driving in Town

City centres are usually fraught with one-way systems, limited-traffic zones and erratic drivers, and are only recommended to the confident driver. In Lucca, Siena and San Gimignano, only residents and taxis may drive inside the city walls. Visitors may go in to unload at their hotel but must then park outside the walls.

Pisa has limited-traffic zones around the Arno, and the rule for tourists unloading also applies in Florence, with its zona traffico limitato or zona blu, which covers most of the centre. There is a pedestrian zone around the Duomo, although pedestrians here should be prepared, nevertheless, to step aside for taxis, mopeds and bicycles. The latter two often do not comply with traffic-light instructions.

Parking

Official parking areas are marked by blue lines, usually with meters or an attendant nearby. There are two large underground car parks in Florence: at Santa Maria Novella station, open daily 6:30am until 1am; and on the northeast side of Piazza della Libertà. The disco orario *system allows free parking for a fixed period, mainly outside city centres. Set the disc to your time of arrival and you then usually have one or two hours* (un'ora *or* due ore). *Hire cars have discs, and petrol stations sell them.*

If you park illegally, your car could be towed away. In Tuscany, one day a week is set aside for street cleaning, when parking is forbidden. This is indicated by signs saying zona rimozione *with the day and time. Beware of residents-only parking areas, marked* riservato ai residenti.

If your car is towed away, phone the Vigili, *the municipal police, to find out where it has been taken.*

Driving in the Countryside

Driving on the quiet Tuscan country roads can be a pleasure. However, distances can be deceptive. What may look like a short trip on the map could actually take much longer because of winding roads. Some back roads may not be surfaced, so beware of punctures. You may also find driving at night disorientating as roads and signs are generally poorly lit.

Tolls and Petrol

Tolls operate on motorways, but there are some free dual carriageways. Tollbooths take cash or pre-paid magnetic "swipe" cards called Viacards, *available from tobacconists and ACI. Motorway service stations occur at irregular intervals,*

and there are fewer petrol stations in the countryside than the cities. Hardly any outside the cities take credit cards. Many close at noon and reopen about 3:30pm until 7:30pm; few open on Sundays. Many in the countryside close in August.

At petrol stations with self-service pumps, put notes or credit cards in the machine. Lead-free petrol is senza piombo.

City Car Hire

Avis
Borgo Ognissanti, 128r, Florence.
[055 21 36 29.
c/o de Martino Autonoleggi,
Via Simone Martini, 36, Siena.
[0577 27 03 05. W
www.avis.com

Hertz
Via Maso Finiguerra, 33r, Florence.
[055 239 82 05.
W www.hertz.com

Maggiore
Via Maso Finiguerra, 31r, Florence.
[055 21 02 38.

Cycle and Moped Hire

Ciclo Posse
Pienza.
[0578 71 63 92.
W www.cicloposse.com

Motorent
Via San Zanobi, 9r, Florence.

DF Bike
Via Massetani, 54, Siena.
[0577 27 19 05.

DF Moto
Via dei Gazzani, 16, Siena.
[0577 28 83 87.

Breakdown

Automobile Club d'Italia
Viale G. Amendola, 36, Florence.
Via Cisanello, 168, Pisa.
[050 95 01 11.
Viale Vittorio Veneto, 47, Siena.
[0577 490 01.

Emergencies [116.

Towing Away

Vigili (Municipal Police)
Florence [055 30 82 49.
Pisa [050 91 03 78.

Siena [0577 29 25 58.

24-Hour Petrol Stations, Florence

AGIP
Viale dei Mille.
[055 58 70 91.
Via Senese.
[055 204 97 85.

FOOD AND DRINK IN TUSCANY

A Typical Tuscan Meal

The traditional Tuscan meal begins with antipasti, *such as* crostini *or* bruschetta *and a plate of cured meats* (salumi), *followed by the first course* (primo) *which is often pasta with a meat sauce, or a hearty soup. The* secondo, *the main course, is usually a meat dish such as* bistecca fiorentina, *poultry or fish. Many restaurants serve a "tasting menu"* (degustazione guidata) *serving three or four smaller portions together. Tuscan desserts* (dolce) *include the traditional* biscotti *or* cantucci *(see p34) and many home-made* (fatti a casa) *cake-like desserts. (Note: at the time this guide was published there was a temporary ban on* bistecca fiorentina *and all beef on the bone in Italy.)*

Visiting Estates

Wine-makers welcome visitors and it is usually quite easy to arrange a visit to an estate. They vary considerably, but many offer tours and wine tastings and sell produce. They are commercial enterprises: estate owners cannot spend all day chatting to visitors, so it is best to telephone to make an appointment. Agriturismi *(farm and vineyard estate holidays) are becoming increasing popular and there is a wide choice of farm houses, apartments and rooms in villas to rent, but be sure to book well in advance.*

General Index

A

Acquacotta con i funghi 162
Agliana (PT) 66
Agnello al testo 63
Agnello in fricassea 123
Agnello toscano 160
Albinia (GR) 164
Alice 57
Amanita caesarea 64
Amanita ovoidea 163
Amanita vaginata 110
Amberjack 14
Anchovy 57
Anghiari (AR) 172
Anguilla 161
Ansonica Costa
   dell'Argentario 157
Arbutus honey 135
Arbutus unedo 139
Arcidosso (GR) 164
Arezzo 23, 38, 172
Arista 105
Arista di maiale arrosto 163
Artichokes 85
Arsella nero 15
Asciano (PI) 88
Asciano (SI) 140
Asparagus acutifolius 139
Asparagus, wild 139
Autumn porcini 16

B

Baccalà alla fiorentina 42
Baccalà in dolceforte 87
Baccalà in zimino 90
Badia Tedalda (AR) 38, 172
Bagni di Lucca (LU) 192
Bagno Vignone (SI) 187
Balbano (LU) 192
Barberino in Val d'Elsa (FI)
   112
Barco Reale di Carmignano
   25
Bavettine sul pesce 92
Beccaccia 59
Berlingozzi 63
Berlingozzo 66
Bianco dell'Empolese 26
Bianco di Pitigliano 156
Bianco Pisano di San Torpé
   81
Bianco Vergine
   Valdichiana 26,
Bianchetto 18
Bibbona (LI) 88, 180
Bilberry 65
Biroldo 63
Bistecca alla fiorentina 32
Bistecca (chop) 32
Bivigliano (FI) 38
Black cabbage 108
Blackberries 37
Blackbird 58
Black-eyed beans 83
Black morel 86

Black porcini 17
Black truffle 19, 63
Blood sausage 29, 109
Boletus aereus 17
Boletus duriusculus 138
Boletus edulis 16
Boletus lepidus 87
Boletus luteus 36
Boletus pinicola 16
Boletus reticulatus 16
Bolgheri 80
Bolgheri (LI) 88
Bolgheri Sassicaia 81
Borage 87
Borgo a Mozzano (LU) 66
Borago officinalis 87
Borgo San Lorenzo (FI) 172,
   192
Branzino 57
Brigidini 63
Brunello di Montalcino
   128
Buccellato 60
Bucine (AR) 192
Buglione 167
Buonconvento (SI) 140, 188
Buristo 29, 137
Buristo di Cinta 104
Butcher's broom 111

C

Cacciucco alla livornese 81
Cacciucco alla viareggina 73
Calamaretti 14
Calamint 37
Calamintha nepeta 37
Calamaro 14
Calci (PI) 89
Caldaro 164
Calenzano (FI) 39
Camaiore (LU) 66, 177
Camaldoli (AR) 39
Campiglia Marittima (LI) 89
Camporgiano (LU) 67
Candia dei Colli Apuani 52
Cannellini di Sorana 61
Canocchia 56
Cantharellus cibarius 138
Cantucci 107
Cantucci all'anice 35
Cantucci di Montalcino 134
Capalbio (GR) 190
Capannori (LU) 51, 67, 177
Capers 87
Capocollo 29
Capoliveri-Elba (LI) 89, 180
Cappa gallina (clam) 55
Capparis spinosa 87
Capraia a Limite (FI) 39
Caprese Michelangelo (AR)
   173
Capriolo 159
Carciofi 85
Carciofino sott'olio 85
Carmignano 25

Carmignano (PO) 39, 173
Carne in galera 119
Carrara 68, 177
Casciana cauliflower 85
Castagnaccio 43
Castagnolo 163
Castagneto Carducci (LI) 89,
   181
Casteldelpiano (GR) 164
Castelfranco di Sopra (AR)
   173
Castellina in Chianti (SI)
   112, 185, 192
Castellina Marittima (PI) 90
Castelnuovo Berardenga (SI)
   114, 185
Castiglioncello (LI) 90
Castiglione della Pescaia
   (GR) 164, 190
Castiglione d'Orcia (SI) 193
Castiglion Fiorentino (AR) 40
Cauliflower 85
Cavallucci 106
Cavo – Elba (LI) 90
Cavolfiore 85
Cavolo nero 108
Cavolo sulle fette 144
Cecina (LI) 181
Cefalo 161
Certaldo (FI) 193
Cetona (SI) 188
Chiusi (SI) 140, 188
Colle Val d'Elsa (SI) 114, 185
Cortona (AR) 23, 40, 173,
   193
Crespina (PI) 90
Cutigliano (PT) 178
Cée alla livornese 93
Cée alla pisana 83
Chanterelle 138
Cherries 63
Chestnut flour 34, 61
Chestnut honey 134
Chestnuts 34
Chestnuts, dried 61
Chianina beef 32
Chianti 99, 100, 131
Chianti Classico 101
Chianti Colli Aretini 26
Chianti Colli Fiorentini 24
Chianti Colli Senesi 101,
   131
Chianti Colline Pisane 81
Chianti Montalbano 25
Chianti Rùfina 24
Chickpea polenta 84
Chine of pork, from Cinta
   Senese pigs 105
Chiocciole alla nepitella 37
Chops, of wild boar 158
Ciavardello 163
Cibreo 46
Cicalo 56
Cicciole 162
Cieche o cée 83

Cimballo 36
Cinghiale 158
Cinghiale al vino bianco 102
Cinghiale in agrodolce 140
Cinta prosciutto 104
Cinta Senese 104
Cioncia 53
Cipolle in forno 133
Clams 15, 55
Clitocybe geotropa 36
Coccora 64
Coccora in insalata 64
Cockles 55
Coda di rospo 78
Colle di Val d'Elsa 185
Colli dell'Etruria Centrale
    26, 53, 82, 103, 131
Colli di Luni 52
Colline Lucchesi 53
Collo ripieno 142
Colombaccio 59
Colombina 64
Common sow thistle 139
Coot 59
Coppa 29
Coppiette 161
Corata di cinghiale 157
Correggiolo, cultivar of
    olive tree 13
Costolette di cinghiale 158
Crabs 56
Crayfish 56
Crithmum maritimum 162
Crostini alla toscana 44
Crostini con i cimbali 36
Cuttlefish 79

D
Dentex 57
Dog rose 111
Donoratico (LI) 90
Dormiente 36
Dried pasta 84
Dried porcini 17

E
Eel 161
Elba Aleatico 82
Elba Ansonica 82
Elba Ansonica Passito 82
Elba Bianco 82
Elba Rosato 82
Elba Rosso 82
Elba Rosso Riserva 82
Elvers 83
Empoli (FI) 174

F
Fagiano 58
Fagioli al fiasco 40
Fagioli all'uccelletto 114
Fagioli dell'occhio 83
Fallow deer 159
Farinata 84
Fiesole (FI) 173, 193
Filetto della Lunigiana 60
Finocchiona 28, 109, 137
Fiorone 16

Fivizzano (MS) 68
Florence 22, 40, 174, 193
Foiano della Chiana (AR) 43
Folaga 59
Folaga alla Puccini 59
Follonica (GR) 165
Forte dei Marmi (LU) 178
Fosdinovo (MS) 69
Fragolini 55
Frantoio, cultivar of olive
    tree 13
Frittata finta 151
Fucecchio (FI) 175
Fungagnello 162
Funghi con la nepitella 138

G
Gallinella 54
Gaiole in Chianti (SI) 115,
    186, 194
Garfagnana spelt 62
Gemma d'abeto 35
Germano 58
Ghizzano (PI) 91
Gilthead bream 54, 161
Girello (topside) 33
Gobbi 84
Gobbi in gratella 84
Gran farro 68
Grappa 109
Grappa aromatic 63
Greve in Chianti (FI) 116, 186
Grey mullet 161
Grey tricholoma
    mushroom 111
Grifi 104
Grifola 64
Grisette 110
Grongo 78
Grosseto 165, 191
Guanciale 28

H
Hake 79
Hare 159
Helvella monachella 86
Hippophae rhamnoides 65
Hygrophorus limacinus
    110
Hydrophorus marzuolos
    36
Hygrophorus penarius 138
Hygrophorus russula 162

I
Isola del Giglio (GR) 166,
    191

J
John Dory 57

L
Lactarius sanguifluus 86
Lactuca serriola 139
Lamporecchio (PT) 69
Lampredotto e trippa in
    zimino 41
Lardaiolo rosso 162

Lardo 29
Lardo from Colonnata 63
Lari (PI) 181
Lasagne bastarde 60
Lastra a Signa (FI) 175
Laudemio olive oil 31
Leccino, cultivar of
    olive tree 13
Lepiota procera 138
Lesser boletus 138
Lesso rifatto 145
Licciana Nardi (MS) 69
Lido di Camaiore (LU) 69
Livorno 91, 181
Lobster 56
Lombo (salted chine of
    pork) 137
Lucca 51, 69, 178, 194
Lucignano (AR) 140, 188
Lyophyllum fumosum 162
Lyophyllum georgii 64

M
Mackerel 55
Magliano in Toscana (GR)
    166
Maiale ubriaco 25
Mallard 58
Manciano (GR) 166, 194
Man-on-horseback
    mushroom 110
Mantis shrimp 56
Marciana (LI) 92, 182
Marciana Marina – Elba (LI)
    182
Maremmana, cultivar of
    olive tree 13
Marina di Campo-Elba (LI)
    92
Marmellata di rosa canina
    111
Marradi (FI) 175
Maruzzelle (sea snails) 55
Marzola 18
Marzolino 108, 133
Massa 71
Massa Marittima (GR) 154,
    191
Mazzancolla 15
Mercatale Valdarno (AR) 118
Mercatale Val di Pesa (FI)
    118, 186
Merlo 58
Merluzzo 79
Milk-cap mushroom 86
Ministra di ceci 65
Minestrone di farro 62
Mirtillo nero 65
Misto di scoglio 15
Mixed sea fish 15
Monkfish 78
Monsummano Terme (PT)
    71
Montalcino (SI) 141, 188
Montecarlo 53
Montecarlo (LU) 71
Montecatini Val di Cecina
    (PI) 92

Montecucco 157
Montefollonico (SI) 145, 189
Montemerano (GR) 167, 191
Montemurlo (PO) 44
Montenero d'Orcia (GR) 167
Montepescali (GR) 167
Montepulciano (SI) 126, 146, 189
Monteroni d'Arbia (SI) 78, 148
Montescudaio 80
Montescudaio (PI) 92
Montespertoli (FI) 118
Montignoso (MS) 72, 178
Montopoli Val d'Arno (PI) 182
Mora di rova 37
Moraiolo, cultivar of olive tree 13
Morchella conica 86
Morchella esculenta 86
Morellino di Scansano 156
Mormora 54
Morselletti 137
Mortadella 137
Moscadello di Montalcino 128
Moscardini (squid) 55
Murlo (SI) 148
Mussels 55
Mutton 35

N
Nasello 79
Necci con la ricotta 61
Nepitella 37
Noce 33
Novello di Montalcino 129

O
Oil from the Colli Aretini 31
Oil from the Colli Fiorentini 30
Oil from the Colli Senesi 136
Oil from the hills of Pisa 84
Oil from the Maremma Grossetana 160
Oil from the Maremma Livornese 83
Oil of Chianti 109
Oil of Lucca 61
Oil of Monte Albano 31
Oil of Pratomagno 30
Oil of Rùfina 30
Olivello spinoso 65
Ololo bianco 163
Ombrina 55
Orata 54
Orbetello (GR) 168, 194
Ossi di morto 136

P
Paganico (GR) 168
Pagro 15
Palazzuolo sul Senio (FI) 44, 175

Palombo 78
Pane con i Santi 107
Pane di Altopascio 60
Pane sciocco 35
Panforte 113
Panforte di Siena 106
Pan pepato 106
Panzanella 38
Panzano in Chianti (FI) 119, 186
Pappa col pomodoro 112
Pappardelle sulla lepre 122
Parasol mushroom 138
Parrina Bianco 157
Parrina Rosso 157
Partridge 59
Pasta secca 84
Pasta secca all'uovo 84
Pattona al testo 67
Pecorino 35, 109
Pecorino, fresh 133
Pecorino from Garfagnana 62
Pecorino in oil 133
Pecorino of Pienza 132
Pecorino, mature 132
Pecorino, semi-mature 132
Penne in salsa d'erbette di primavera 139
Pepolino 37
Pesce ragno 56
Pesce spada 14
Pescia (PT) 178
Pesto toscano 108
Pheasant 58
Picchiante 95
Picchio pacchio 143
Pici 108
Pici con l'anatra muta 129
Pieducci (pig's trotters) 28
Pienza (SI) 126, 148, 189, 194
Pietrasanta (LU) 179
Pieve a Nievole (PT) 72
Pieve al Bagnoro (AR) 44
Pimpinella 37
Pinarolo 36
Pinci 137
Pine nuts 87
Pinus pinea 87
Pintail (duck) 59
Piovra 54
Pisa 76, 92, 182
Pistoia 51, 72, 179
Piteccio (PT) 194
Pitigliano (GR) 155, 168
Pleurotus eryngii e ferulae 162
Pochard 59
Podenzana (MS) 179
Poggibonsi (SI) 120
Pollastrella al dragoncello 136
Pollo alla cacciatora 169
Pollo alla diavola 115
Pollo con le olive 116

Polpa di cinghiale 158
Polpo di scoglio 54
Polyporus frondosus 64
Polzo 33
Pomino 26
Pontassieve (FI) 44
Ponte a Moriano (LU) 179
Pontedera (PI) 93, 183
Pontremoli (MS) 72
Porcini d'autunno 16
Porcini d'estate 16
Porcini del freddo 16
Porcini in oil 17
Porcini, dried 17
Porcini nero 17
Porcupine 159
Porgy 15
Portentoso 36
Portoferraio-Elba (LI) 93, 183
Prato 45, 176
Prato biscuits 34
Pratovecchio (AR) 176
Procchio (LI) 94
Prosciutto di cinghiale 159
Prosciutto di Cinta 104
Prugnolo (mushroom) 64
Prunus spinosa 111
Puttanaio 31

Q
Quail 59

R
Radda in Chianti (SI) 120, 194
Radicofani (SI) 149, 195
Ramerino 163
Raviggiolo 133
Razza 78
Red mullet 79
Reggello (FI) 46
Ribollita 117
Ricciarelli 107, 120, 137
Ricciola seriola dumerili 14
Ricotta 35, 133
Ricottine della Lunigiana 62
Rigatino 27, 137
Rigatino di Cinta 105
Rio Marina-Elba (LI) 183
Rivolti con ricotta 150
Rock octopus 54
Roe deer 159
Rombo 57
Rosa canina 111
Rosemary 163
Rosmarinus officinalis 163
Rosso di Montalcino 129
Rosso di Montepulciano 131
Rosso di Sovana 157
Rubus species 37
Rùfina (FI) 46
Ruscus aculeatus 111
Russula cyanoxantha 64
Rustic Christmas cake 106, 107

S
Saddled bream 57
Saddle fungus 86
Saffron 137
Salame di Cinghiale 159
Salame di Cinta 105
Salame of wild boar 159
Salsicce 158
Salivoli di Piombino (LI) 94
Salsiccia 29
Samphire 162
San Casciano Val di Pesa
    (FI) 121, 186
San Gimignano (SI) 98, 121
San Gimignano Rosato 102
San Giovanni alla Vena (PI)
    94
Sanguisorba minor 37
San Miniato (PI) 76, 183
San Quirico d'Orcia (SI) 149
Sansepolcro (AR) 23, 47, 176
Santoreggia 65
San Vincenzo (LI) 183
Sarago 79
Sardina 15
Sarteano 149
Satureja montana 65
Saturnia (GR) 169, 195
Sausage 29, 109
Sausages, wild boar 158
Sbriciolona 28
Scad 55
Scallops 55
Scaloppine ai porcini 52
Scampi 56
Scampo 56
Scandicci (FI) 47
Scansano (GR) 169
Scaveccio 161
Schiacciata con l'uva 107
Schiacciata di Pasqua 107,
    137
Schiaccioni 35
Scorfano 79
Scorpion fish 79
Scorzone 19
Scottiglia 166
Sea bass 57, 161
Sea buckthorn 65
Sea snails 55
Seppia 79
Seppie in zimino 89
Sgombro 55
Shark, smooth-hound 78
Shoulder of Cinta pork 105
Siena 98, 122, 187, 195
Sinalunga (SI) 149, 190, 195
Sloes 111
Snipe 59
Sole 55
Sonchus oleraceus 139
Soppressata 29
Soppressata di Cinta 105
Sorano (GR) 169
Sorbus torminalis 163
Sovana (GR) 154, 195
Sovicille (SI) 190
Sow thistle 139

Spaghetti all'ammiraglia 168
Spall 105
Sparnocchia 15
Spicchio di petto 33
Spinach 85
Spinaci 85
Squid 14
Staffoli (PI) 184
Stracotto alla fiorentina 39
Strawberry tree 139
Striglia di scoglio 79
Striped bream 54
Sugared almonds 63
Sugarello 55
Sugo di chiocciole 148
Sugo di pecora 35
Sulla clover honey 134
Summer black truffle 19
Summer boletus 87
Summer porcini 16
Sunflower honey 134
Suro 55
Suvereto (LI) 94, 184
Swordfish 14

T
Table olives 63, 160
Tagliatelle ai funghi 110
Tartufo bianco pregiato 18
Tartufo d'inverno 19
Tartufo nero pregiato 19
Tavernelle Val di Pesa (FI)
    123
Teal 59
Telline alla livornese 91
Terontola (AR) 47
Terranuova Bracciolini (AR)
    177
Testaroli 61
Thrush 58
Thyme 65
Thymus communis 65
Thymus serpyllum 37
Timo 65
Tirrenia (PI) 184
Tonno del Chianti 109
Tordelli lucchesi 69
Tordo 58
Torrone 107
Torta di Cecco 107
Torta di erbe 71
Torta di Montalcino 137
Torta di pepe 60
Torta natalizia rustica 106
Totani ripieni 165
Totano 55
Tracin 56
Trequanda (SI) 150, 190
Tresana (MS) 73
Tricholoma acerbum 163
Tricholoma columbetta 110
Tricholoma equestre 110
Tricholoma portentosum 36
Tricholoma terreum 111
Triglie alla livornese 94
Trippa alla fiorentina 47
Trippa alla livornese 94
Trippa con le spugnole 86

Trote 62
Trout 62
Truffle, March 18
Tuber aestivum 19
Tuber borchii 18
Tuber brumale 19
Tuber macrosporum 18
Tuber magnatum 18
Tuber melanosporum 19
Tuber mesentericum 19
Turbot 57
Turtle dove 59
Tuscan lamb 160

U
Uliveto Terme (PI) 184
Uzzano (PT) 179

V
Vaccinium myrtillus 65
Vada (LI) 184
Val d'Arbia 131
Valdarno cockerel 35
Venus clam 55
Vernaccia di
    San Gimignano 102
Vernaccia Riserva 102
Viareggio (LU) 73, 180
Villafranca di Lunigiana (MS)
    73
Vinegar 109
Vin Santo 100, 103
Vin Santo del Chianti 103
Vin Santo di
    Montepulciano 130
Vino Nobile di
    Montepulciano 131
Volterra (PI) 77, 95, 185, 195
Vongole verace 15

W
Weever 56
White bream 79
White truffle 18, 63, 109
White wax cap 138
Widgeon 59
Wild asparagus 139
Wild boar 158
Wild lettuce 139
Wild thyme 37
Winter black truffle 19, 63
Winter savory 65
Woodcock 59
Woodland honey 134
Wood pigeon 59

Y
Yellow morel 86

Z
Zolfini beans 34
Zuccotto 34
Zuppa di ceci 151
Zuppa di fagioli
    con i pieducci 28
Zuppa di lenticchie con
    fagiano 147
Zuppa frantoiana 70

Acknowledgments

DORLING KINDERSLEY would like to thank the following associations and people whose contributions and assistance have made the preparation of this book possible.

Donatella Cinelli Colombini, president of Movimento Turismo del Vino; Sylvie Heiniz, agriturismo Podere Terreno alla Volpaia; Flavio Zaramella, president of Oil Masters Corporation; journalists Stefano Tesi (Firenze) and Marzia Tempestini (Prato); Sauro Brunicardi, Ristorante La Mora; Romano Franceschini, Ristorante Romano; Fulvio Pierangelini, Ristorante Gambero Rosso; Lorenzo Totò, Osteria Da Totò, Lucignano; Ristorante La Torre del Mangia, Milano; Loris Bocconi, fishmarket wholesaler in Milan; Sandro Carelli, SAMA, Milan; Azienda agricola Belsedere, Trequanda; Hubert Ciacci, Montalcino; Pa.Ri.V., Sinalunga; Silvana Cugusi, Montepulciano; butchers shops: Franco Scarpelli in Lucignano, Cecchini in Panzano in Chianti, Falorni in Greve in Chianti, Porciatti in Radda in Chianti, Chini in Gaiole in Chianti, Pollo San Marco in Arezzo; Moris Farms, Massa Marittima; Fattoria di Celaja di Crespina; Aziende agricole Danei (Giglio), Acquabona and La Chiusa (Elba).

PICTURE CREDITS
Guido Stecchi (mushrooms, herbs and fruits, typical products, farms), Paolo Liverani (herbs and fruits), Giuseppe Masciadri (pp 71, 85, 169); many pictures come from Image Bank, APT of Versilia, Livorno and Arcipelago toscano, and from Comune di Montespertoli (Florence).

penguin.co.uk/vintage